HAND TROLLER

HAND TROLLER

By Mike McConnell

Writers Club Press

San Jose New York Lincoln Shanghai

HAND TROLLER

Writers Club Press
an imprint of iUniverse, Inc.

For information address:
iUniverse, Inc.
5220 S. 16th St., Suite 200
Lincoln, NE 68512
www.iuniverse.com

Front and back cover photoes by Mim McConnell; www.tongass.com

ISBN: 0-595-21426-6

Printed in the United States of America

This Book is dedicated to my wife Mim. Without her support and encouragement this project would never have been possible

Contents

CHAPTER 1 1

CHAPTER 2 7

CHAPTER 3 15

CHAPTER 4 21

CHAPTER 5 29

CHAPTER 6 41

CHAPTER 7 49

CHAPTER 8 57

CHAPTER 9 67

CHAPTER 10 75

CHAPTER 11 85

CHAPTER 12 93

CHAPTER 13 101

CHAPTER 14 111

CHAPTER 15 119

CHAPTER 16 129

CHAPTER 17 139

CHAPTER 18 149

CHAPTER 19 165

CHAPTER 20 175

CHAPTER 21 185

CHAPTER 22 197

CHAPTER 23 207

CHAPTER 24 219

CHAPTER 25 229

CHAPTER 26 239

Afterword 245

Glossary.. 247

1

The old, Gray Marine engine hums its monotonous tune in my ear as we plow down Sumner Strait. I look over at Dick's boat a few hundred yards off my port side. Her bow wave turns the mirror-calm surface of the water into a series of metallic green, black, and blue humps that roll smoothly astern. My gaze shifts forward to the red bell buoy a mile or so ahead. It marks the last rock pile before the turn west toward Cape Decision and Chatham Strait. I look longingly at the cape and my brain calculates the miles still to run. "Let's see: one to the can, eight to Decision Pass, then twenty-five to Port Alexander. Thirty-four miles to go. Six miles per hour. Six into thirty-five is a little over five. Let's say six hours to go. Its eleven-thirty now; we'll be tied to the dock in P.A. by five-thirty.

I look over at Dick—he's not there! I lean out the window and look back. The Spray is a half-mile behind and looks dead in the water. I back the throttle down to an idle and take the microphone for the CB radio off its hook.

" Dick, what's up?"

No answer. I put the wheel hard over, and when the bow points at the Spray I throttle back up to running speed. While steaming toward the other boat I see white smoke pouring out of the wheelhouse windows. I throttle back as I pass down his port side, and as the back deck becomes visible I turn the boat around to come alongside.

Dick's pilothouse is completely full of white smoke, which is streaming out of the doors and windows. As I approach, he staggers out the door with a fire extinguisher in his hands. I reverse hard to stop alongside, step aboard the Spray with a line, and tie it loosely to his mid-cleat.

"What the hell happened? Is the fire out? You okay?" I yell excitedly.

"The roof was on fire around the exhaust stack, but I think it's out now," Dick answers, laying the fire extinguisher on the hatch cover and dusting himself off. The extinguisher is a dry-chemical type full of gritty, white powder, which covers Dick from head to toe. He takes off his glasses, which have protected his eyes from the powder; he looks like a raccoon. I chuckle and turn to look in the door. The powder has settled and the smoke mostly cleared. What a mess! Every surface in the boat has a layer of the white, chemical on it. Dick's bunk is in the pilothouse; it's also covered with the dust. Down below—stove, table, food—everything is white. I look back at Dick; he's poking at the charred wood around the exhaust pipe with a fish knife.

" Looks like it's out," he says, tossing the knife on the binnacle.

"You can't start the engine till we clean up this mess; maybe I better tow you back to Louise Cove. What started the fire, anyway?" I ask.

"I think the engine is out of time. It has a rattle in it that has been getting worse all day; sounds like a pre-ignition knock. I was about to give you a shout on the radio and suggest we anchor for a while to have a look at her when I smelled smoke," he answers.

"I think it's calm enough to stay alongside instead of towing you; that way you won't have to steer and you can clean up the mess," I say, stepping back out on deck.

Dick follows me out the door. We shove a few fenders between the boats to protect the wood and then add a couple more lines, bow and stern. I climb back aboard the Nomad and put her in gear. As the boats begin to move, I slowly open up the throttle and turn the wheel until the bows point toward Louise Cove, a small bay on the east side of Kuiu Island.

So much for making Port Alexander today. I can see Dick with a vacuum cleaner in his hands moving around in his wheelhouse. I don't envy him the task of cleaning up the extinguisher powder. I had a fire under my oil stove last winter; it took hours to vacuum it up. The chemical powder gets into every corner in the whole boat and is miserable to get rid of. He's lucky he has the 12-volt vacuum cleaner aboard.

As we grind slowly toward the anchorage, my thoughts drift back over the miles we've run. We are two and a half days out of Ketchikan on our way to Port Alexander for the 1980 salmon-trolling season. I had fished out of P.A. in '76 and '77 and had wanted to go back.

Dick is an old "dock rat" that I met in Ketchikan during the spring of 1975 while I was buying my boat. He lived aboard his handtroller, which was tied up across the float from the Nomad. He was a crusty, old curmudgeon, always good for a cup of coffee and an hour or two of good yarns. Whenever I was in town I always made it a point to visit with him, and we had become good friends over the years.

During the course of our conversations the subject of P.A. and the good King salmon fishing had come up often. Every year we had decided we would go there, but one thing or another kept us from doing so. This year, as spring approached, there was nothing hanging us up. So here we are on our way. We left Ketchikan on May 1st and ran to Salmon Bay in the northeast corner of Prince of Wales Island. The next day we ran to Louise Cove on Kuiu Island. The weather had been calm and the trip was uneventful—so far. We got a late start the third morning and were only a few miles from the anchorage when the fire changed our plans.

I stretch, rub my aching neck, and check on the old-timer. He's standing on deck smoking a cigarette and gazing off into the distance. He looks over at me, grins, and shakes his head. It's one of those rare, fine, spring days that make you excited to be alive. The sky is a blue dome overhead; its lower edge jagged where it meets the snow-capped mountains. The Spruce, Cedar, and Hemlock-clad slopes tumble into the shimmering water. Reflections of the sky and mountains are a mixture of blue, green, silver, and black on the mirror-like surface.

I pull back on the throttle as we pass through the narrow entrance of the cove, and Dick moves to his foredeck to lower the anchor. When I find just the right spot I shift into reverse and as the boats slowly come to a stop Dick shoves the big Forfjord anchor off the bow. As the chain rattles out through the roller, I keep backing down to lay it out on the bottom. When Dick is satisfied with the scope, he sets the brake on the winch. The anchor digs into the mud bottom and in a few yards the boats stop moving.

"Looks like she set," he yells over the engine noise.

I nod and shift into neutral. I let the engine idle for a while to cool down and then kill the ignition.

Blessed silence....

You have to have spent a day trapped in an enclosed space with an engine running at 1800 r.p.m. to really appreciate what I mean by "blessed silence." The noise and vibration wear on your nerves and exhaust you more than a day of hard, physical labor. The feeling of relief when you finally shut down at the end of the day must be similar to what one of those Indian Fakirs feel when they get up off a bed of nails. Indeed, it's as fine a form of self-abuse as you might enjoy any-where.

We stand on the deck of the Spray for a few moments enjoying the silence and the beauty of our surroundings. Louise Cove is a small, round bay a few miles north of Cape Decision, on south Kuiu Island. Low-timbered hills and a steep, rocky shoreline surrounds it, except on the west side, which has a small creek running out of a low pass. Sand, gravel, and silt deposited by the stream have formed a tidal flat where it runs into the bay. The tide is out and along the water's edge I can see clams squirting in the late- afternoon sun. Looking east, out the nar-row entrance and across Sumner Strait, you can see Calder Peak, one of the highest mountains on Prince of Wales Island.

"We better quit gawkin' around and see what's wrong with the machine," Dick says. I look at him with a rueful grin and we head below.

Inside, Dick removes the engine covers and gets a trouble light out of a locker in the galley. He plugs the light into a cigarette lighter receptacle and turns it on. He hands me the light. I shine it on the injector pump while he examines the drive coupling which controls the timing. Sure enough, it has slipped. The key that holds it in place has sheared and broken the keyway wall in the shaft. I won't go into details, but we spent the rest of the day jury-rigging a new key and re-timing the engine. Obviously a new coupling and shaft will be in order when we get to P.A.

"I'll cook supper," Dick offers, wiping the engine grease off his hands on a paper towel.

I grunt noncommittally. His cooking is pretty basic. Tonight we have Dick's favorite: "Alpo and Eggs"; a true gourmet delight. The recipe is as follows:

"1 can roast beef hash, chopped up in a cast iron skillet, with a few eggs cracked over it.

Cook till eggs are set.

Serve with Wonder Bread (white sandwich).

Dessert: a couple of cups of instant coffee and a cigarette."

I skip the cigarette in favor of half-a-roll of Tums.

We trade yarns till about nine, then hit the bunks. The night passes. I dream about driving the boat on dry land while lassoing halibut with a rope that keeps tangling around my feet. The nightmare is probably caused by breathing toxic intestinal gas all night brought on by dinner at "Dick's Fine Foods."

2

I awaken at six-thirty A.M. Ravens are squawking in the trees ashore and the chef is coughing his guts out next door. I hold my breath till he gets control. In my mind's eye I see him pop a couple of Primatine tablets in his mouth and wash them down with coffee. It's incredible the extent of recreational abuse the human body can take and still function. Dick is 63 years old and was an alcoholic for many years. He has kicked the booze, but the cigarettes are killing him. I shake my head and climb over onto the Spray.

"Sounds like the TB ward at the veterans hospital over here," I growl as I climb down into the foc'sle.

"Coffee's on," Dick says, shoving the instant coffee across the table. I spoon some into a mug and fill the cup with hot water from the kettle simmering on the oil stove. I sit down at the table and stir my coffee.

" Looks like a good traveling day. You get the weather yet?" I ask.

" High pressure is going to hold, winds in lower Chatham: light and variable," Dick answers.

"All right! Looks like we'll make it today if the machinery holds together. You want breakfast or should we just get going?" I ask.

"Ah, hell, let's take off…sooner I'm tied to the boards in P.A., the better," he says.

"Okay; I'll go fire up the noise-maker," I say tossing down the dregs of my coffee and putting the mug in the sink.

I climb back aboard the Nomad, check the oil, crack the throttle, pull out the choke, then hit the starter. The little four-banger coughs to reluctant life, runs rough for a few minutes till the carburetor warms up, then settles into a steady hum. I hear Dick's old Ford diesel grind to life. It belches out a cloud of half-burnt fuel, still a little bit out of time. After we let the engines warm up for a while, Dick hauls up the anchor and I untie from the Spray and back away. When I'm clear, I put the gearshift into forward and point her toward the harbor entrance.

Sumner Strait is glassy, flat calm, not a ripple on it. The sun is well up in the east and its shimmering rays turn the water into liquid gold. After clearing the rockpiles along the shore, we head south toward the bellbuoy that marks the turning point. It's a beautiful morning and the water to the west reflects the green hills of Kuiu Island. The surface is covered with hundreds of gulls feeding along the kelp beds and rock ledges that line the shore between Louise Cove and Point St. Albans. The tide is still ebbing, which gives us a boost down the strait, and we soon round the buoy on St. Albans Reef, then turn west toward Cape Decision.

The hours pass slowly. My mind sorts through memories of the past or speculates about the season to come. I think of the small fishing town of Port Alexander and the interesting folks who live there. As the Fairway Islands pass to port I flash back four years to another trip from Ketchikan.

My ex-wife and our year-old son had wintered at Happy Harbor that year. We were house-sitting for "Boots" McAlester, who was down south having a cancerous lung removed. We had gotten a letter from a friend who had gone to P.A. a year earlier. Ray encouraged us to come to P.A. because the Bureau of Land Management was giving away parcels of land, the fishing was good, and there was a fish-buyer in the summer. We could stay with Ray and his family until we found a place of our own. It sounded good to us, so we saved up fuel money and headed out on April 1st with everything we owned crammed in the boat. Another friend, Rick, went with us because his girl friend was living at Ray's place.

We left Happy Harbor on a calm, spring day with a good forecast. At that time the boat only had a tiny pilothouse and no sleeping quarters. We took a small backpacking tent and a large sheet of Visqueen for shelter. Our plan was to camp ashore at night. The trip would only take two or three days, depending on weather.

We got a late start that morning, so we decided to anchor in Windfall Harbor on the east side of Kasaan Peninsula. I should have known better. The small bay has a local reputation of being a blowhole, but I was young and dumb and thought I could second-guess the weather.

We arrived at Windfall about an hour before dark, paddled ashore with our camping gear, and then set up for the night. It was clear and calm, so we didn't make a very elaborate camp, just put up the tent for Jane and I and the baby. Rick rolled his sleeping bag out by the fire. We cooked a simple supper, enjoyed the sunset and fire for a while, then turned in for a few hours of sleep.

Sometime later I awoke to the sound of wind in the trees. I got up and stirred the fire to life. Rick crawled out of his sleeping bag.

"Where the hell did this come from?" he asked, hunkering down across from me and lighting a cigarette with a glowing stick from the fire.

"Damned if I know. Sounds like we're not going anywhere in the morning. Never can believe the dang weatherman," I answered, giving the fire a poke.

Even as we talked the wind was increasing. Great, roaring williwaws were rumbling off the mountain to the west and the first big raindrops were hissing into the fire. I went back to the tent. It was too dark and windy to go check the boat, so I figured I might as well try to sleep. As I settled into the tent Jane asked, "Is the boat okay?"

"I hope so; it's a long walk to Kasaan from here, and we don't have much food ashore," I replied, as I tried to find a spot for my hips that didn't have a lump in it.

The wind was getting worse and the rain was hammering down on the tent. I had tied a small rainfly over the roof but the wind was so strong that the flimsy plastic began to shred. It wasn't long before the rain was leaking through. The hollow we were laying in was filling with water and I could feel it soaking up through my sleeping bag. Jane was laying on her back with Luke on her chest; luckily he was asleep. There was nothing to do but lay there and suffer.

My mind kept turning to the boat. I had had a difficult time getting the anchor to set and so didn't have much hope that she would survive. Everything we owned in the world was hanging on that tiny anchor and I expected to find her on the beach in the morning. If she went ashore on a smooth beach we could probably re-float her; but if the wind blew her out into the surf (which I could hear crashing on the rocky shore near the entrance) she wouldn't last long.

The night seemed to go on forever as we lay there in the water worrying about the boat and trying to keep Luke dry. Luckily he slept through the night without making a sound. Eventually the first gray, watery light of dawn began to filter through the sodden roof of the tent. I could hear Rick moving around outside. As I eased out of the tent as quietly as I could, the wind cut through my wet clothes like a knife. Cold as it was in the tent, it was worse outside. I could see Rick a few yards away lashing poles together to make a shelter big enough for all of us.

I walked out on the beach to look for the boat. Miraculously, it was still right where we had left her. What a relief! No one had any idea where we were and it was several miles up over the mountains to the nearest people. I knew we could wait out the weather for a few days, but loosing the boat would have been a real disaster for us. Not only was it our ticket out of here, but it contained all our belongings and was our only means of making a living. Unfortunately though, our skiff was gone. From where I stood most of the shoreline was visible, but the small rowboat was nowhere to be seen.

I turned and went back into the woods to help Rick with the shelter. I knew the baby would be awake soon, and Jane would need to get up out of the puddle she was laying in. Luke had slept all night while the rest of us suffered, so he would be ready to rock and roll anytime now.

Rick had a pole frame lashed together and we soon had the Visqueen pulled over it and tied securely. There was no hope of getting a fire going; everything in the world was soaked. We had a two-burner Coleman stove and about two gallons of Blazo, so we set the stove up on some flat rocks and then fired up both burners. Rick put two more stones on the flames to radiate heat and soon humid warmth permeated the shelter.

"Looks like the boat made it," Jane said, as she pulled back the flap and entered the shelter. .

"Yeah, but the skiff is gone," I replied, warming my wet back by the stove.

"Did you look out in the entrance? The wind was blowing that way and the tide has been ebbing for a while," Rick said, as he warmed his hands.

"No, I was afraid to. The surf coming in off the strait has been crashing on that beach all night. If that's where it wound up, all we'll find is a few boards," I answered.

"Maybe we should go look for it now. It's daylight enough to see and if we can find it we might be able to repair it enough to get out to the boat."

"Yeah; if not, we might be able to round up enough small logs to make a raft," I said.

Rick and I left the warmth of the shelter and walked through the dripping woods to the outer beach. We found the skiff right away; it lay on a gravel beach. The planks were pulled away from the transom and there was a fist-sized hole in the bow. The bottom was full of gravel, seaweed, and driftwood and she looked pretty forlorn.

"Let's clean her out and drag her around to the point where we had the fire last night; maybe we can patch the holes," I said, as I began scooping gravel out with my hands. Rick pitched in. When we had the rocks and kelp cleaned out we carried the small boat around the point and laid it on the gravel beach by the drowned fire. As we looked her over Rick said, "There's a few nails in the camp box; I'll go get them and the hatchet. Maybe we can nail the transom back on."

"We can probably wrap Visqueen around the whole boat to keep the water out. It only has to get me out to the big boat once. I can pull the Nomad right up to the beach here so we can load up when the weather breaks," I said.

As we headed back toward the shelter to get the things we needed to repair the skiff, I noticed that the wind and rain had let up. Maybe by afternoon the swells would calm down enough so we could leave. Jane had a pot of coffee on the Coleman when we entered the welcome warmth of the shelter; my stomach growled at the smell of it.

"I'm going to make some oatmeal with raisins; do you guys want some?"

We both nodded affirmatively as we savored the warmth of the shelter. We soon had our hands wrapped around mugs of hot coffee. Luke gurgled from the backpack, oblivious to our misery.

"I think that when the weather breaks we better fall back to Happy Harbor for a few days and regroup. We'll never get the sleeping bags dried out here and we're going to be too tired to travel," I said, sipping my coffee.

They both agreed. When we finished eating, Rick and I went out to work on the skiff. The wind had died considerably and shifted to the west; a sign that the front had passed and the storm was about over. There were a few patches of blue sky showing through the clouds and the rain had stopped.

We collected some Spruce pitch that was bleeding from log wounds on the trees along the beach by the harbor entrance. I whittled a putty knife out of a thin piece of Cedar, so I could smear the pitch in the open cracks and seal the seams. When I had the open seams packed full of the sticky stuff, Rick nailed the planks back to the transom with eight-penny nails. When that was finished we wrapped Visqueen around the whole boat and held it in place by nailing strips of wood to the upper plank. When the boat was covered we cut off the excess and stood back to admire our handy work. It looked pretty crude, but we had done our best with what we had to work with. There was nothing left to do but launch her and see if our repairs were successful.

We picked the little boat up carefully and carried it out till the water was almost at the top of our boots before setting her gently in the water. I climbed in and paddled out to the Nomad with a board that Rick had beachcomed; the oars, of course, were nowhere to be found. The plastic must have had a lot of small holes in it because the skiff leaked like a sieve, but I made it to the boat without sinking and climbed aboard. She seemed to have survived the storm without damage; a miracle indeed. Some of the gusts must have been eighty-knots or more, with a steady forty to fifty-knot wind in-between them.

The boat had a four-cylinder, Universal, gas engine that was mostly worn out and sometimes cranky to start. It fired right up, however, and I soon had the anchor up. I idled slowly toward the sandy beach in front of the camp. The boat only drew two feet of water, so when the forefoot touched the sand I shut the engine down and stepped ashore with a line. Rick took the rope up the beach and tied it to a tree limb. The tide was coming in for about four more hours, so she would lie there safely. I used some gas and motor oil to get the fire going again, and after a while I realized that a few parts of my clothes were actually getting dry. Things were looking up.

As the morning progressed the weather gradually improved. By mid-afternoon the swells in Clarence Strait had become manageable for our small boat. We loaded our wet belongings into the Nomad, cleaned up the campsite, and headed back to Happy Harbor. Our next attempt in early May was successful; Jane and Luke flew to P.A. while Rick and I had an uneventful trip in the boat.

We were lucky to have fared as well as we did. If we had lost the Nomad we probably would never have gone to Port Alexander. Too bad you can't always rely on luck; stories like this don't always have a happy ending.

3

I am startled out of my reverie by a deep, groaning sound; it seems to come from the engine. I look down at the motor humming contentedly beside me and then glance out all the windows. Dick is a few hundred yards off my port side, and we are abeam the lighthouse that marks Cape Decision. Everything seems to be okay. Suddenly the noise comes again.

"BUUUUUUUUUUUWWWWWWWAAAAAAAAA."

What the...? I look at the motor again but nothing seems to be wrong with it. "BUUUUUUUUUUUWWWWWWW-WAAAAAAAAA."

I look out the starboard window at the lighthouse again.

"BUUUUUUUUUUUWWWWWWWAAAAAAAAA."

"Dummy—it's the foghorn at the lighthouse! Stop daydreaming and pay attention," I mutter, grinning at myself.

Cape Decision Pass is an opening between the south end of Kuiu Island on the north and Coronation Island to the south. As you transit the pass heading west into lower Chatham Strait, the Spanish Islands and Coronation Island are to your left and Cape Decision is on the right.

The area around the cape is totally exposed to the open ocean. It's shallow and has strong, tidal currents that can produce spectacular tide rips. The pass also marks the jump-off point for the crossing of Chatham Strait to Baranof Island. There are twenty-five miles of open water to Port Alexander and all are exposed to the North Pacific Ocean. It is a dangerous crossing and not to be taken lightly. The crossing to Port Alexander is a four-hour run for Dick and I in our small boats. Today the wind gods smile us upon us; it's flat calm.

Baranof Island is a row of jagged, snow-capped peaks to the NW, and as we round the cape I point the bow at No Name Mountain. This small mountain stands just south of town and will be the steering mark for P.A. I look over at Dick to see if he has made the turn...

"Damn!"

A mile south of us a Coast Guard cutter is steaming full-bore right at us. I grab the CB mike and holler at Dick, "Better dig out your driver's license, Cap, here comes the Gestapo."

"Ah, crap! That's all we need," Dick replies.

"Looks like they're going to board us. Let's stay on course and make them work for it." Dick clicks his transmit button a couple of times in reply.

The cutter is making about twenty-five knots, so in a few minutes they have stopped ahead of us and are lowering a big Zodiac skiff into the water. I throttle back and say to Dick, "We might as well stop and get this over with so we can be on our way across."

Dick clicks the mike button a couple of times to let me know he heard and agrees. I see his boat slow down and soon the Zodiac approaches the Spray, stopping alongside. As usual there are about six men in the boarding party, armed to the teeth. I see several assault rifles, a shotgun or two, and all have sidearms. I find the armaments not only ridiculous but insulting as well. They must think we might go berserk any minute and attack them. My mind drifts as I wait for them to finish with Dick.

Suddenly the old, black troller shudders. False panels fall away and the boat unfolds out of itself until it's ten times its original size. As its three hundred-foot bulk looms over the tiny, ninety-foot cutter, giant guns rise up out of the decks, and with a blinding flash and a thunderous roar of cannon fire the super-troller rakes the cutter from stem to stern with sausage-size, explosive bullets. But in the nick of time the well-armed and heroic boarding party leaps aboard the Spray from the Zodiac. With machine guns blazing they mow down "Dick-The-Perp"- Scourge of the Inland Sea, and as hundreds of machine-gun bullets slam into his chest, his decrepit body is thrown across the wheelhouse to land in a smoking heap on the cartridge-covered deck. The cutter is saved and another menace to "amerika" passes into oblivion.

But wait…two streaks of white bubbles race toward the crippled cutter. In the confusion of the firefight they forgot about the evil Nomad lurking nearby—she has fired two deadly torpedoes from the cover of the smoke. They strike the white vessel at the waterline, amidships, and explode with a horrendous blast. When the smoke clears, the Coast Guard ship is sinking. The boarding party leaps back into their Zodiac with a shout of outrage and heads for their stricken ship.

On the bridge of the Spray a claw-like hand pulls a lever on the binnacle, the huge, pirate ship folds back into herself and then slips away into the pall of heavy smoke from the burning cutter. As the little, innocent-looking handtrollers rendezvous on the other side of the oily, black cloud, Dick-the-Perp steps out on deck. With a toothless grin he strips off the bullet-riddled, Kevlar vest that has saved him from a fate worse than fishing.

As the two desperadoes disappear into the west the skipper of the cutter crawls out of the oily water into the crowded Zodiac. He shakes a stained fist and shouts across the distance, "I'LL BE BACK!" As his words echo across the water a hand emerges from each wheelhouse window, middle fingers raised in salute.

I click back to reality as the boarding party approaches.

"Permission to come aboard, skipper?" the officer in charge shouts.

A ridiculous question considering the fact that they will arrest me if I say no; I motion them aboard. Hands grab my rail and three men climb into the boat. I notice they have .45 automatics in belt holsters with the hammers cocked. There is a leather strap under the hammers, but it burns me up anyway. I consider it rude and ungentlemanly to enter another man's home with a loaded and cocked firearm. I tell them so. The officer in charge politely informs me that the Commandant of the Coast Guard has mandated that all boarding parties will be armed. He says that he agrees, that it is probably unnecessary, but he must follow orders.

I ask what the purpose of the boarding is. He tells me they are on a training patrol and the boarding is routine (whatever that means). I tell him politely that I wish they would conduct their training somewhere other than the middle of Chatham Strait. He shrugs and asks to see my papers. I produce my State ID and Coast Guard registration.

While he inspects my papers, the Zodiac cruises slowly around my boat, twenty yards out. The other three stormtroopers clutch their weapons in white-knuckled hands, trying to look menacing. Somehow it doesn't come off very convincingly. There is something laughable about a twenty-year old, baby-faced kid who shaves his peach-fuzz chin once a week, holding a machine gun. Actually, I don't think it's funny at all. When a government treats every citizen like a potential criminal, and then teaches impression-able, young men that simple fishermen trying to make a living are dangerous to society, the people of that country are in trouble.

They soon satisfy themselves that I'm operating legally and prepare to leave. The skiff comes alongside.

"Do you have any comments about how the boarding was conducted, other than the guns?" the boarding officer asks as the others clamber into the Zodiac.

"I appreciate your politeness, but you have cost us over an hour of running time. I wouldn't mind so much if we were in a safer area, but making a crossing like this in these little boats…an hour could make the difference between life or death to us. You know how fast sea conditions can change out here," I reply.

"I'll mention that to the skipper and write it up in my report," he said as he boarded his boat and pulled away.

In spite of my complaining, I respect the men who operate the boats and aircraft and the heroic searches and rescues they perform. I just wish the government wouldn't use them for fish-cops to police our own fisheries. It creates hard feelings toward them that is, for the most part, unmerited.

I put the boat in gear and turn on course for P.A. Dick is idling alongside and soon I see a puff of smoke come out his stack as he throttles up. The weather stays calm and the hours pass slowly.

Long-distance running at six miles-per-hour can be a fine form of torture; the hours either crawl by at a snail's pace and you are aware of the slow passage of each minute, or they can pass unnoticed as your mind wanders off into some daydream. The closer to your destination you get, the slower time flows. You gaze longingly at the spot you are heading for, trying to determine if it is getting any closer. Today I feel like a bug crawling across some vast and endless desert. My brain has used up all of its fantasies and is tired of either future tripping or rooting around in the past. I look at the clock every five minutes and squirm around in my seat. My neck hurts, it's too hot, and I'm about five cups over my coffee quota.

The miles finally give in to the persistent racket of the little engine; the red can that marks the entrance of Port Alexander's harbor finally hoves into view. I yank the mike out of its holder and push the transmit button. "Well partner, it looks like we might make it yet!"

"I'm ready; my butt's so flat from riding this seat that the cheeks feel like they got corners," he comes back.

"There's a set of range markers inside the entrance. Favor the can on your starboard side and stay on the range till you clear the gut. Then you can head straight for the dock; it's just past the red building on pilings," I say.

"Okay. I'm going to stop outside the entrance to get the tie-up lines on and the fenders out," he says. I click the mike button a couple of times and throttle back to an idle. I pull the shift lever into neutral and step outside to rig my lines and bumpers also. When everything is ship-shape and ready for the dock, I go back into the house and wait for Dick to finish.

"You go in first; I'll follow you," he says over the radio when he gets back into the wheelhouse. I give the mike a couple of clicks, then shift into forward and head for the buoy. As the range markers appear, I let the boat drift to port. When the upper marker is perfectly aligned over the lower one, I hold her steady on course until I am clear of the narrow entrance. We made it!

4

The old, cold storage buildings are a welcome sight as we idle toward the dock, but I notice several changes. The store building and the warehouse next to it have been painted beige with brown trim and the roofs are clad with new, brown, steel roofing. The fish-house on the pier has also been painted. The whole buying-station seems to be vibrating with a buzz of activity. When I left P.A. in the spring of 1977 Pelican Cold Storage Co. had just purchased the business from Dick Gore, who was retiring to Washington State. Apparently the whole place was being refurbished.

The state dock is also teaming with action. We idle slowly around the airplane float that is attached to the north end of the main dock. As we pull alongside the dock several people come to grab a line and help us tie up. I recognize a face as I step off the boat with the centerline and tie it to the bullrail.

"I thought this boat looked familiar," Steve Garnick says, as I finish tying the boat to the dock. "I figured you would be back some day. It looks like you made some changes to the boat," he adds.

"Yeah, I needed a place to sleep aboard. It took most of last summer to put the new house on her, but fishing wasn't that great in Clarence Strait, anyway," I reply.

In '77, before I had left P.A., Steve, two other men, and I had taken the Nomad to Port Malmsbury on Kuiu Island for a spring Black bear hunt.

"What you been doing since I left, Steve?" I ask.

"I finally gave in and bought a boat; swore I would never fish but couldn't stand it. I bought the Sad-Eyed Lady from Bruce Tenney last spring."

"All right! Are Fred and Rick still around?" I ask. They were the other two who went on the bear hunt.

"Fred still has the Willow and Rick is fishing his skiff. Fred's house burned down last winter, so things haven't been too good with him," he answers.

"That's too bad; nobody needs that kind of luck. I better turn off the machine before it swallows its tongue and chokes to death," I joke. "It's good to see you again, Steve."

"Yeah, I better get back to work. See you around," he says, as he walks off up the dock. I go over to the Spray; Dick is standing on deck, looking around at the town.

"You want a tour of beautiful, downtown P.A.?" I ask Dick as I walk up to him.

"Sure; I need to stretch the kinks out after four days at sea," he answers, climbing off the boat. We saunter toward the ramp that goes up onto the pier. I see a couple of familiar faces as we pass between the boats tied to either side of the float. Some people give us a pleasant "Howdy" or "How ya doin'" as we pass and others only offer a non-committal grunt or pretend we don't exist. Fishermen are a varied lot; some are friendly and out-going, always ready for a few yarns or a discussion about fishing, the weather, politics, etc. Others see every stranger as a threat to their lifestyle. We are all sorts of misfits and dropouts who can't, or won't, make it in the so-called "normal" world. We've come here from many, different backgrounds looking for freedom and adventure.

Dick and I stop and chat with several other people that I recognize and then climb the ramp to the pier. As we walk toward the shore I realize just how many changes have happened to the old, cold storage plant. I see several new buildings, new fuel tanks, and people working everywhere. There is a feeling of energy and excitement in the air that is contagious.

The harbor at Port Alexander is a small lagoon with a narrow entrance to the south. The main part of the town is strung out along the east side of the bay and is called "Tract A." On the west side of the harbor, or "Tract B," there are several new houses along the beach that have been built in the last five years or so. Others, in various stages of construction, are scattered throughout the woods above the beach out of sight from the harbor. In the early-seventies the Bureau of Land Management gave away parcels of land in Tract B on a first-come, first-serve basis. To get the title you only had to pay the survey costs and build a habitable, sixteen by twenty-foot house on the lot. These lots are all claimed now and new houses are springing up everywhere.

At the head of the pier on the Tract A side an eight-foot wide boardwalk runs east for a few hundred feet, then turns left to pass between bushes that overhang the walkway on both sides. We walk along slowly, savoring the emerald green of the salmonberry bushes and the buzz of bumblebees on the pink blossoms. The patches of cool shade under the towering Spruce and Hemlock trees are a welcome relief from the warm, spring sun.

The walkway leads north for about a quarter-mile and there is an occasional house along either side. About halfway along the walk is an old building with shiplap siding and many-paned windows that serves as city hall, library, and community center. This old building was discovered hidden in the berry bushes during the rebirth of the town in the late-fifties.

Next to Bear Hall, as it is now called, is a new school building that has been built during the years I was away. It is finished with oiled, wood siding, but looks too modern alongside the older building. We wander on slowly, enjoying being ashore and soon come out of the trees at the head of another ramp that leads down onto the back dock. We stand for a while gazing at the rugged mountains northwest of town, their snow- capped peaks shimmering in the midday sun.

The back float is also humming with activity. There is a small troller high and dry on the tide grid, getting its bottom scrubbed in preparation for new copper paint. On other boats people are painting, doing minor repairs, or getting ready for the first day of the season that opens in less than two weeks.

"What do you think of P.A., partner?" I ask, as we turn and head back down the boardwalk.

"Nice place; I wouldn't mind living here. Maybe I'll sell the boat in a couple of years and buy a lot to build a shack on," Dick answers.

"Yeah, I've been thinking of moving back. It would be nice to not have to make that run from Ketchikan twice a year, and I like the idea of having a buyer this close to the grounds…do more fishing and less running that way. Maybe next year I'll get rid of the float house and bring all my junk out with me; live on the boat, or house-sit, or something."

"Sounds like a plan to me," Dick says, lighting a cigarette.

When we get back to the south end of the boardwalk we decide to take a tour of the cold storage plant. As we walk through the hubbub of activity, I realize that the town is booming and the sleepy, little village I remembered from a few years ago is gone forever. I'm not sure I like it.

We walk down the new boardwalk to the store. When we enter a big, red-haired man sticks out his hand and says," Hi, I'm John Hughes; I'm the plant manager. You guys be fishing here this year?"

We shake hands and introduce ourselves.

"Yep, that's the plan," Dick says.

"Good, glad to hear it. If there's anything you guys need let me know. We've got showers and laundry machines going in at the back of the warehouse; there's fuel at the dock and the ice machines are about ready to go. If you're going to fish halibut, I need your bait order as soon as possible so it can come down on the packer from Pelican," John says with enthusiasm.

"That won't be necessary. We might try to troll up a few, but we're not going to run any longline gear," I answer.

"Okay, sounds good. Best of luck to you and if there's anything I can do let me know," he replies.

We look the store over. It seems well stocked with all the essentials, like Dick's favorite source of nutrition: roast beef hash, or "Alpo", as he calls it. Dick buys a pack of cigarettes and I replenish my snoose supply. As we stand on the boardwalk outside the store a big, black, packing-boat comes slowly through the entrance and heads for the fish house. John Hughes comes out the door behind us and hurries toward the pier, gathering up people as he goes to help with the unloading. The Superior is deck-loaded with lumber and other supplies needed to get the plant ready for opening-day.

We walk slowly back to the front dock; the day is winding down. The people who don't live on their boats are heading home for dinner. As we make our way around the piles of gear and other stuff on the float Dick says, "Better come over for supper; I've got everything for goulash."

My gut does a snap roll; it least it isn't Alpo and eggs again.

"Okay," I say, "if you promise not to put canned peas in it."

He chuckles and says, "You got no class at all kid...don' t know what's good...don't appreciate good gourmet cooking when ya find it."

"Ain't no gourmet cooking I ever seen what called for canned peas," I grumble. "You'd starve to death in a week if you ever lost your damn can opener, ya old bilge rat," I add.

"You young punks got no respect for your elders at all. It takes years of training and experience to attain my level of culinary excellence."

"You mean years of living off slumgullion stew made on a hot plate in some flea-bag hotel in Ketchikan while you're waiting for your next rockin' chair check to appear in your mail box at the Foc'sle Bar, don't ya?" I offer.

Dick chuckles. We both enjoy these exchanges of insults now and then. It's like an art form and every once in a while a good series of them will come out spontaneously.

"Come on over in half an hour or so. I'll put the grub on right away; won't take long to boil the macaroni and fry the burger. You can open the peas while I throw the rest of it together," he says with a grin as we climb aboard our boats.

As I tidy up the mess left over from four days of traveling, I think about Dick and what a good friend he has become. He is about as unpretentious a person as you could find anywhere. He earned his living for years driving logging trucks around SE Alaska in the summers, then drank up his savings in the winter in Ketchikan. A few years before I met him he decided one day to quit drinking, and so just quit. Period. He bought an old wood cabin cruiser in '75 and rebuilt it himself, including installing a new diesel engine. He fished that boat till '79 when he sold it and bought the Spray. The Spray was an old Navy hull from WW II and was mostly a floating wreck. Dick borrowed a few hundred bucks from another friend and got her in fair working order over the winter. We had put a new mast, rigging, and trolling poles on the boat this spring, in March, and had her mostly ready to fish by the end of April.

Here is the kind of guy Dick is: in March, I had mumbled something about not having enough money for fuel to get to P.A.. It turned out I had enough, but when I got to town in late April to fuel up for the trip, he had saved money out of his social security checks so we would both have enough fuel to make the trip. Friends like that are rare.

I finish my chores, grab a loaf of bread, and head for the Spray. The grub is ready, so we dish up and wolf it down without much conversation. The goulash isn't bad or maybe I'm just hungry. No peas. We clean up the dishes and each brew a cup of instant coffee to settle our dinner while we discuss the events of the day. Dick fires up a smoke and I take a big dip of snoose. Sometimes life ain't so bad...

While we're sitting there enjoying our coffee, out on the deserted dock a big otter slithers onto the airplane float and shakes the water out of his fir. He looks around carefully for his archenemy, "Willie Bruiser." Bruiser is a medium-sized, black mutt with a giant-sized chip on his shoulder. In his mind the dock belongs to him and otters aren't welcome. Apparently Willie is asleep or somewhere else because his usual bellow of rage when the otters crawl out on the float isn't forthcoming. The otter, figuring this is his chance, waddles off down the float hoping to luck into a free meal. He checks each boat in turn as he proceeds down the dock, and when he gets to the Spray he climbs onto the back deck and sticks his head in the door.

As Dick and I sit spacing-out over our coffee we feel the boat rock like someone has come aboard. We look up at the door just as the otter slides over the combing into the wheelhouse. He stops about four feet from me and we look each other in the eye. He turns and hops up onto Dick's bunk.

"HEY, YOU STINKIN' SON OF A BITCH, GET THE HELL OUT OF MY GODDAMN BED!" Dick shouts, leaping to his feet and knocking over his coffee.

There is a loud thump as the otter's feet hit the deck He's out the door and over the side in an instant.

SPLASH.

I crack up laughing as Dick lunges for the door.

"STAY THE HELL OFF MY BOAT, TOO, OR I'LL. HAVE YOUR DAMN HIDE!" He shouts after the otter that is long gone by now.

From over on the beach I hear Willie Bruiser let out a bellow. Dick comes below and mops up coffee.

"Cheeky bastard. Don't mind them coming aboard, but they ain't welcome in my bed. Damn critter might decide to take a crap there or something." He wrings the dish sponge out in the sink.

"You ain't got no appreciation for wildlife at all. Why that poor dumb critter was probably tired and needed a nap, or else he got a whiff of that greasy old fart sack of yours and thought he'd freshen it up a bit for you," I say, still laughing.

Willie is on the dock now patrolling up and down, stopping here and there to peer down the cracks between the planks and occasionally letting out a series of annoying barks. The otter is long gone.

Dick finishes cleaning up the mess and stirs up another cup of "mud."

"My damn bed probably smells like dead fish now. I can't believe that thing came right in here and hopped up on my bunk like he owned the place," Dick says, flicking his lighter on the end of a cigarette with a shaky hand. "I'll shoot that sucker if he comes in here again."

"I'm getting the heck out of here; this place is dangerous," I say as I get up and rinse out my cup. "I'll see you in the morning."

"Don't rush off; I think it's safe now," Dick says, grinning.

"Oh, I'm worn out; I'm going to hit the rack. I'll see you in the morning."

"Okay; come on over for coffee."

"Yeah; see you then," I say as I climb off onto the dock. I amble over to my boat, crawl into the foc'sle, and crash. It's been a long day.

5

I am naked, sneaking down a long hallway, looking for a bathroom. I gotta pee real bad and there must be a toilet here somewhere. God, I hope nobody opens one of these doors. What the hell happened to my clothes, anyway?

I'm standing at the end of a row of toilets that disappear into the distance. I go to the first one—it's full to the brim! I look at the second one; it's full, too. I walk down the row of commodes, but they're all full. I'm desperate and look to see if anyone is watching, then try to pee in one of the toilets; but I can't seem to get her started...I hear voices—oh, no-o-o, what do I do now? I got no clothes and they'll think I plugged all these toilets!

Gradually I realize I'm on the boat and the voices I hear are out on the dock. I look at my watch; it's six-thirty A.M. I swing my feet onto the cold deck and grab my socks off the line over the oil stove. The socks are stiff, so I give them a vigorous rub and yank them on my feet and shove my feet into my rubber boots. Ducking into the wheelhouse, I look out at the day. The top of No Name Mountain is hidden in a heavy, gray mist and small, white clouds race past the dark, green slopes. There is the feel of coming rain and wind in the chill morning air.

I shrug into my old, gray, halibut jacket and pull the snoose can out of the pocket. I tap the lid with my forefinger, open the small, round container, take a pinch of the noxious, brown powder, pack my lower lip, and replace the lid. I shudder as the drug takes hold. As usual, my brain suggests that it might be a good idea if we dispensed with this foul habit before our lower lip rots off. "Maybe when this box is gone," I mutter to myself, shoving the container back in my pocket. "Besides, my image requires it." I step out onto the dock.

Coming down the dock toward me is a short feller with a bushy, red beard and long, blond hair hanging out from under a greasy, black, Greek, fisherman's hat. His halibut jacket is unbuttoned, even in the chill morning air.

"Hey-y-y," he says, as he walks up to me with his rolling gait, "I wondered when you'd be back."

"Hi, Jim. I didn't see the ole' Mecca Maru at either dock; figured you were in Juneau or Little Port Walter. How ya been, anyway?" I ask, as we shake hands.

"Great man, this is my boat now," he says, pointing at the nice horseshoe-sterned, boat named Juanita H. that is tied up behind me.

" All right; looks like a dandy. Where is the old Mecca?" I ask.

" Sold her to a guy in Juneau. Last I heard she was dying on the mud flats in Gastineau Channel. She was pretty well shot, so it isn't much loss. What's up with you, anyway?" he asks.

"Jane and I split up a couple of years ago; she's down in Portland. Last year I put the new house on the boat and a new motor in. The fishing season was kind of a dud, so I went core-drilling in August for a couple of months and then wintered in Kasaan Bay at Happy Harbor," I answer.

"It's good to see you again; I've been wondering what happened to you guys. Well, I better get to work; stop by the house later and have a drink," he says, climbing aboard his boat.

"It's good to see you, too, Jim; I'll see you later. I'm going to mooch a cup of "panther piss" from my running partner and then get to work too," I say, heading up the dock in the direction of Dick's boat.

"Water's hot," Dick says from the pilothouse door and then disappears inside. I climb down into the galley, stir up a cup of instant paint remover and sit down at the table.

"Well, Cap, what's the thought for the day? Looks like the otters didn't get ya," I say.

"How about hot cakes first, then we better order the parts for my engine. Don't have much time to get it fixed before the opening."

"You have a parts book for this thing?" I ask.

"Yeah, I'll dig it out after we eat," he says, getting up and putting the skillet on the stove.

The Krusteze dough gods are soon cooking and before long I'm sopping syrup off a paper plate with a couple of ten-inchers. When we finish eating, Dick gets out the engine manuals and we figure out which parts he needs. He writes down the part numbers on a scrap of cardboard torn off the end of a cigarette carton. We down the dregs of our coffee and head outside.

While we were having breakfast it has started raining and the wind has come up from the south. Overhead, heavy gray clouds flow swiftly by and seagulls are soaring effortlessly in the steady stream of moist air. There is not much action on the dock this morning. The wind and rain have put an end to the painting and repair work; only inside chores are the order of the day until the storm passes.

At the phone booth Dick calls in his parts order. While he is on the phone I look down the boardwalk and marvel at the change. The dappled sunlight of yesterday is gone, replaced with wet green. The sodden, salmonberry leaves drip forlornly on the wooden walkway. When Dick is finished with his call we head back to the boats. It's raining harder now and the wind has increased.

"I might have to have a nap; sure as hell can't do much of anything else on a day like this," Dick says, as we walk down the ramp.

"Pretty ugly, all right; it'll keep the barnacles on your back from drying out, though," I reply.

"Wouldn't want that to happen, that's for sure. What are you going to do?" he asks.

"I'm going to tie up some king leaders, then I'll probably take a snooze, too. I had a pretty restless night; spent hours trying to find a place to take a leak, but all the toilets were full. Must be your cookin'," I answer.

Dick laughs and says "I'll see you after a while. You can fix your own damn lunch; then maybe you'll appreciate good cookin'."

I step aboard my boat and go inside. It's cozy in the wheelhouse and the warmth from the little "Gypsy" oil stove is welcome after the cold and wet of the outside. I take off my sodden jacket and hang it by the stove. I turn on the radio and tune in C.B.C. from Prince Rupert, Canada, the only decent radio station available.

While Peter Zosky rambles away on some obscure topic, I get out my tackle box and hang a roll of one hundred-pound test leader on a line overhead. I pull four fathoms of the clear nylon line off the reel, measuring with my outstretched arms, then clip the piece off with a toenail clipper. I lay the clipper on the dash and pick up a swivel with a snap attached. I pass the end of the leader through the eye of the swivel, then wrap the end around the standing part four times. Now I bend the end back and pass it through the loop above the swivel, then I pull on the leader with one hand and the snap with the other, taking out most of the slack. Next I wet the loose knot with saliva to lubricate it, then hook the eye of the snap on a fishhook with the point broken off that is screwed to the binnacle.

To finish the process, I pull the knot tight with both hands, un-hook it, and snip off the short tail of leader that sticks out of the knot. I find the other end of the line and repeat the procedure. When the snap swivels are tied on both ends, I wrap the completed leader on an empty line spool, strip off another four-fathom hank of line, and repeat the process.

As the morning passes I tie about twenty-five main leaders. I'll need ten to start fishing the first day and the rest are spares. They wear out pretty fast if the fish are biting and the extras allow me to replace dam-aged ones quickly.

I take a break about noon and fry up an egg sandwich for lunch. When I'm finished, I brew a cup of coffee and take a dip of snoose. It's still raining hard outside and the dock looks deserted. "Might as well get some tail leaders tied up, too," I think to myself, as I dig out a pack-age of dark, olive-green "hoochies" and tear open the plastic bag.

There are six of the plastic squid in the bag and I tie each of them on a twenty-eight inch piece of ninety-pound test line with a figure eight loop on one end and a number-seven Mustad salmon hook on the other. As each lure is finished, I file the point of the hook until it is sticky-sharp and coil the leader in a re-sealable storage bag. When the green ones are all tied I do a package of blue and then a package of purple. I'll tie more colors later, but these are the basic ones and will get me started on opening-day.

My hands have tied so many leaders over the years that I hardly have to think about what I'm doing. As the hours pass I half-listen to the radio and think about fishing. The leader tying is the beginning of a process of "psyching myself up" for the season. It's time to put everything else out of my mind and concentrate on fishing. King salmon are very particular about how the gear is presented and it requires diligence and persistence to catch them. I am lucky because my mentor was one of the best King fishermen who ever wet a line. As I tie up the hoochie leaders I remember the invaluable lessons he taught me one spring a couple of years ago.

I first met Bob Lewis at Happy Harbor in the early-seventies. I was living in a small float house attached to Dave Salee's logging camp and was working for Dave occasionally. But mostly I was just hanging out, eating the king's deer and trying to avoid work if possible. Bob fished the bay regularly and liked to tie up at Boots McAllister's dock for the night when he was in the area. I had spoken with him a couple of times, but thought he was kind of a smart-ass. Bob is an extremely intelligent man and has little time for "b.s." I was young, cocky, and full of myself, so we didn't have much in common.

In '75, after Jane and I were married, we were living at Boot's place taking care of her animals while she recovered from surgery in the lower 48. That was the year we bought the Nomad and I was longlining for halibut around Kasaan Bay. One evening Bob and I were tied stern-to-stern at the dock. He was puttering around in his cockpit putting his gear away for the night, and my deckhand, Steve, and I were struggling to gut about ten large halibut that we had just caught

Steve and I were grunting, cussing, and trying to hang an eighty-pound fish up by the tail to gut it like a hog. There's nothing stupider than a dead halibut, and if you don't know how to handle them they can be a real bitch to clean. We were blood and slime from head-to-foot and not making much progress.

"For God's sake, let me show you guys how to dress a halibut!" Bob said, walking up behind us.

I let go the line we were using to lift the fish and tried to wipe the gnats off my forehead with a slimy sleeve. "Okay," I said, grinning stupidly.

Bob climbed aboard, grabbed the fish by the gill plate, and threw it up on the hatch-cover with ease. My jaw hit the deck! It looked like the fish had flown the three feet up by itself. Bob picked up the "Old Hickory" butcher knife off the hatch-cover and tested the edge with his thumb.

"I see you've got the right knife, but I can't tell which side is supposed to be the sharp side; you have a file?" I produced one. He looked at it and looked at me with a raised eyebrow, then worked on the knife.

"You're knife has got to be sharp, otherwise you will work yourself to death on the first ten fish. On a real halibut boat you have to be able to dress as much as one thousand pounds an hour so you can keep up with the roller. You have to know how to handle the fish and keep your knife sharp or you won't last through the first haul." He flipped the fish over on it's back, pulled the gill plate open with his thumb, then made a series of rapid cuts. Before I could figure out what he was doing, the guts and gills flew over the side in one piece. He gave the fish a couple of scrapes along the spine with the scraper and the job was done.

I was stunned. It was taking Steve and I about ten minutes to clean a fish that size; Bob had just done it in about thirty seconds! He flipped another fish on the hatch and made the cuts slowly, explaining each move to me as he executed them. After he had done a couple more my mind started to grasp the process. He put two small fish up and we went through the moves together. My hands learned the technique and by the time the fish were all dressed I was doing it by myself with little coaching. I was still clumsy and slow but I had the basics down.

"Thanks, Bob, I really appreciate you showing us how to do this; we weren't making much progress on our own," I said, as he stepped back onto the dock. I didn't realize it then, but this simple sharing of knowledge was to benefit me greatly in the future. I worked many years as a deckhand during the halibut derbies of the late-eighties and early-nineties when speed at cleaning fish was the difference between having a job or not.

I guess my willingness to learn from him made Bob inclined to share his trolling expertise with me a couple of years later. I had switched from longlining to handtrolling and was working the same "drags" in Kasaan Bay that he fished. There was a kind of etiquette among trollers in those days, a set of unspoken rules that worked to everybody's benefit. Unfortunately, some of the new people that were entering the fishery were unwilling to follow these rules, so the old-timers weren't very interested in helping us out. I went out of my way to be polite to Bob on the fishing grounds, always giving him room when he had the right-of-way, and not crowding up behind him when we were both going the same direction.

I thought I was doing pretty good; I was catching ten or twelve fish a day with about a fifteen-pound average weight. One night I was tied up behind the Lady Mae, stern to stern. Bob and I were both working in our cockpits finishing putting the gear away for the night and cleaning up.

"How's it going; you getting them?" he asked.

"Oh, not too bad; got ten today," I replied, smugly.

"Ten! What are you doing wrong? Come here, let me show you something," he said with a mischievous grin. I climbed onto the float, walked over, and stepped aboard the Lady Mae. Bob climbed out of his pit and opened the hatch cover. Laying down in the hold was a pile of huge kings; it looked like there were about twenty-five or more fish, most over twenty-five pounds and some much larger.

"That's just the evening bite; I caught forty-eight for the day. Yesterday I got fifty-three and a couple were over fifty pounds," he said. I was bewildered; I thought I was doing good, but obviously something was wrong.

"Let's go back to the pit; I'll show you what I'm running," he said, heading aft. I probably learned more about King salmon fishing in the next hour than I would have discovered on my own in the next ten years. Bob had been trolling for twenty-five years and was a thinking man. He kept detailed logs that contained information on weather, tides, depths, speed, colors of lures, and patterns of presentation that other fishermen would have killed to get their hands on. He was meticulous with his gear, washing everything with soap and water every few hours to remove his scent, and each arrangement of lures was based upon years of experimenting to find out what worked and what didn't.

After showing me the gear and explaining how to use it, he said, "Tomorrow, be on the drag at 4:30 A.M. so you don't miss the tide-change. You can follow me a couple of boat-lengths back; do exactly as I do. If I turn, you turn; if I speed up or slow down, you do the same. If I change gear, I'll hold up what I'm changing to so you can see it. When the fish quit biting we'll move over to Daisy Island and fish that drag through the evening tide-change. There has been a good afternoon bite there the last few days." I agreed to follow his lead, thanked him politely, and went back to my boat to tie gear like he had shown me.

When I had the boat ready for the next day, I turned in for the night and was on the drag at first light. Bob left the harbor just ahead of me. When he slowed down and put out his gear, I did the same. As we turned into the first hole on the drag I saw Bob hauling in a line. The leaders were unsnapped from the wire as they broke the surface, then coiled swiftly in the gear tray behind the cockpit. It was an education to see him work—like watching a dance: unsnap, coil down, unsnap, coil down—all the while steering the boat precisely through the intricate turns necessary to follow the bottom contours. Each time the boat turned he would adjust the throttle slightly to keep the lures moving at the speed necessary to trick the fish into biting.

Before too long I saw him shut the gerdy off and grab a gaff hook. He reached down, unsnapped the leader from the trolling line, then clipped it to a wire beside the cockpit combing. He pulled in the leader, hand over hand, piling it on deck behind the pit. He reached down with the gaff, whacked the fish smartly on the head, hooked it with the gaff hook, and flipped it smoothly aboard. After unhooking the fish he coiled the leader and then ran the line up to the next spread. This leader also had a nice fish on it and he soon had that one aboard, too.

Suddenly, I realized that both of *my* poles were bouncing furiously. The fish were fighting so vigorously it felt like they were going to tear the poles off the boat. I dove through the door into the pit and reeled in the starboard line. As I cranked I could feel the fish fighting back. He was yanking so hard that I had to stop cranking and give back line several times before I got to the leader with the fish on it. He was on the very bottom spoon and as the snap broke the surface the big King leaped completely out of the water behind the boat. He shook his head from side to side, trying to get rid of the green, plastic, plug that was hanging out of the corner of his mouth.

I grabbed my gaff and pulled him over to the boat. Every time I tried to get him within reach of the gaff hook he would shake his head and strip the leader back out of my hands. When the fish would come to the end of the slack the twenty-pound lead cannonball on the end of the trolling wire would come clear out of the water.

I was having trouble keeping the boat on the drag while I fought him and I thought I was going to loose him for sure, but he was well hooked and soon began to tire. Somehow, I managed to steer the boat and fight the fish at the same time and gradually worked the big fish up to the boat. When he was swimming quietly alongside the cockpit, I pulled his head out of the water and conked him between the eyes with the gaff handle. The fish rolled on his side and stopped fighting, so I turned the gaff over in my hand and sunk the hook into the head, pulled on the leader with my right hand, lifted the gaff handle with my left, and flopped him into the cockpit.

As I worked the big Mustad salmon hook out of his jaw, my heart was pounding with excitement. I marveled at how beautiful he was—shimmering, blue, green, gold, and purple, laying there bleeding on my deck. I stood there looking at him, feeling sadness for taking his life, but the rattle of the other pole soon reminded me that there was a fish on that line, too.

I put the line I had up back down as fast as I could, then cranked up the other one. There was another nice big fish on the flasher and green hoochie, second spread up from the bottom, and after a similar struggle I soon had that one aboard, too. As we turned around for another pass down the drag the first pole was shaking again, and by the time we turned for the third pass I had six nice fish aboard. Before I knew it, the morning had passed, the tide had changed, and the fish had stopped biting. Bob pulled his gear aboard and headed for the harbor to take a nap, have some lunch, and ice the morning catch. I made a couple more passes while I put my fish in the hold and ate a sandwich. There were eleven fish aboard with an average weight of around twenty pounds. I'd never caught that many fish in one day before—and it was only noon!

I trolled across the bay to Daisy Island and waited for the afternoon bite to start. As the hours passed, I scratched out a couple more fish, then around 3:00 P.M. I saw the Lady Mae steaming toward me. As he cruised by, Bob came out on deck and raised his hands questioningly. I signaled fifteen by flashing fingers and pointed to the port pole, which was shaking vigorously. Bob grinned and went back into the wheelhouse. When he was far enough ahead of me, he turned onto the drag and slowed down to trolling speed. Soon he was in the cockpit snapping on leaders as the lines went down. I was too busy with my own work to watch him.

The fish finally stopped biting about 7:00 P.M. I was exhausted, so I pulled the gear aboard and headed for the dock. I had caught twenty-one fish and was elated. That was double my best day ever and the average size was twenty-percent larger than usual. At the dock, I was grinning from ear-to-ear like an idiot. Bob just smiled; he didn't say how many he had caught and I didn't ask.

The sound of Dick banging around on his back deck brings me back to the present. The rain has let up and my hands have finished the last of the tail leaders. I open the door and holler over at Dick. "What's all the racket over there? How the heck do you expect me to sleep with you rattling around? Sounds like you're dragging chain out of a well-casing or something."

"About time you got up; you're gonna sleep your life away. Before you know it you'll be an old fart like me and won't remember how you got that way," he yells back.

"Sleep—my rosy-red behind! I got all my leaders tied up while you've been lounging in the rack like some debutante."

Dick snorts and says, "Better come have a cup and try to wake up. Sounds like you've been having one of your potty dreams again."

I put my gear-tying tools away and head over to the Spray. We stir up a cup of coffee and chat for a while. Dick has cooked a pot of ham hocks and beans for dinner. They aren't too bad and I eat two bowls.

"Looks like you 'll. be looking for a crapper all night again, the way you're packing away them beans," Dick says, as I mop the last of the juice out of my bowl with a slice of bread.

I wonder out loud why beans are always referred to as "them beans" when proper English would demand that they be referred to as "those beans". He gives me a blank look and fires up a cigarette.

After supper we take a short walk on the boardwalk, then turn in early. The wind has switched to the SW and there are some clear patches in the sky. Looking forward to better weather tomorrow, I settle into my bunk with a paperback novel, satisfied with the day's accomplishments. It's not long before my eyelids grow heavy with sleep and I turn out the light to dream of big King salmon.

6

The dawn breaks clear and calm. I wake up early, energized by the prospects of a beautiful spring day. Often in May, we are blessed with special mornings like this one. The sunrise is early this far north in late spring, about 4:30 A.M., and when I get up the sun is already above the trees. I stir up a cup of coffee and go out on the dock. The sky is a wonderful Robin's egg blue and the golden morning light paints the steep mountain slopes to the west various shades of green and yellow. I sit on the bullrail sipping my coffee, enjoying the warmth of the sun on my back and the spectacular view.

"'What did you dream about last night?" Dick asks as he sits down beside me, coffee in one hand and cigarette in the other.

"Morning, Cap, pretty nice day shaping up, huh?"

"Yeah, quite an improvement over yesterday," he answers. "I might have to get out a paint brush later."

I look at him with a raised eyebrow. "You feeling okay? That sounds pretty ambitious to me."

"I've got a couple of leaks in the foredeck; think I'll smear some Silver Seal on it. I'm tired of getting dripped on. What you got planned?" he asks.

"I think I'll change oil in the little machine, then maybe polish some spoons. After that, who knows; maybe nothing."

"Sloth is a sin, ya know," he says, giving me a pontifical raised eyebrow.

"I'll be able to keep you company in hell, Cap." We chuckle. Dick throws the dregs of his coffee in the bay and stands up.

"How about bacon and eggs, hash browns and toast?" he asks with a twinkle in his eye.

"Okay! I'm going to start the engine and let her warm up while we eat," I say, getting up, too. "See you in a few minutes."

I go aboard the Nomad, fire up the Gray, then wait while the carburetor warms up. When the motor is finally purring contentedly, I head for the Spray. Dick has breakfast almost ready, and when the toast is done we eat.

"Well, Partner, I'm going to put this coffee buzz to work," I say, stuffing my paper plate in the trash bag, then rinsing out my cup and hanging it on a hook over the sink.

"Yeah, me too," Dick says."If I don't get moving, I'll have to take a nap."

I head home to deal with my oil change. The dock has come alive while we've eating. Skiffs are running up and down the harbor, and down the dock I can see several people working on gear or standing around talking. It promises to be a busy day.

Aboard the boat, I get out the things I will need to perform the onerous task of getting the dirty oil out of the engine. The drain plug in the oil sump is inaccessible, so the oil must be sucked out through the dipstick hole. I take the oily, brass hand-pump out of the plastic bag full of rags, where it lives, and shove the small suction tube down the narrow hole into the oil pan. When I feel it hit bottom, I position the pump-outlet over a small bucket and pump slowly.

Oil is a demon-possessed substance; it has an uncanny ability to get all over everything no matter how careful you are to not spill any. The first squirt, of course, overshoots the bucket, splatters onto the deck boards and up the side of the fuel tank. I mutter obscenities under my breath, adjust the pump at a different angle, and try again. By the third stroke my nose itches unbearably. I try to ignore it but I feel a sneeze coming on. Rubbing my nose on the sleeve of my wool coat only makes it worse, so I finally give in. Laying the pump on the bucket, I tear a paper towel off the roll and blow my nose vigorously.

Somehow, I manage to bump the bucket with my foot and knock the pump off into the bilge under the engine. As it disappears into the bilge monster's lair, it sprays a stream of oil on the motor, the engine timber, and the leg of my pants. Of course, I haven't pumped the bilge yet today, so the pump disappears under water. On top of everything else, as I grope in the now oily water under the engine, my snoose can falls out of my shirt pocket and lands in the bucket of oil—where else? @#$%^&*!!! I rescue my chew and wipe it off as best I can with a paper towel, then make another try for the pump. I have better luck this time, but it drips more oil and water on the engine, the deck, and me before I get it wiped off and the tube back into the dipstick hole.

The rest of the oil change goes fairly smoothly, and eventually I get the old oil out, the new in, and the mess cleaned up. I hate machines. Ought to be a law against anything with more than one moving part. I indulge in a brief fantasy about the original handtrollers who fished out of rowboats: simple, cheap to operate, and no oily, cantankerous machines to contend with. Just a nice camp on the beach, and the packer picking up the fish every couple of days. But then, there is the rain and wind and sleeping in a tent on the hard ground...well, maybe I'll put up with the machine for a while yet. Best thing about the old days is that we only have to remember the good parts.

Looking outside, the beauty of the day soon draws me out on the dock with my spoon bucket and the Brasso can. The warm spring sun soon cooks the grumpiness out of my brain and I begin to feel better. I can mark one more chore off the list of things I must get done before the opening.

As I sit on the bullrail, polishing the big brass and copper spoons, I can see Dick brushing paint on his deck.

"Looks like you're workin' too hard over there, skipper," I holler at him.

"What was all the cussin' I heard issuing out of that vessel a while ago? There was so much blue smoke coming out the door, I almost came over with a fire extinguisher to put out the fire," he yells back.

"The pump almost whipped me, but I managed to wrestle it into submission and get the job done. You know how I love machinery."

"I'd of come over and given you a hand, but I was afraid you might hit me with a wrench or something, so I decided to mind my own business."

"It was probably a wise choice, considerin' the way the oil was flyin' around there for a while. Might have got your environment polluted or somethin'."

"Wouldn't want that, might kill the moss on my back, and I'd freeze next winter."

I hear voices down the dock, and looking that way, I see three familiar faces headed our way. It's Steve, Rick, and Fred—the three guys who had gone hunting with me at Port Malmsbury a few years ago—and another fellow I don't recognize. I stand up and greetings are exchanged all round. Steve introduces me to the stranger who turns out to be his brother Keith. Dick walks over and I introduce him to everyone.

"I hear you had some bad luck last winter, Fred," I say.

"Yeah, burned the cabin down, lost everything: food, clothes, rifles, hides; it was a total loss," he answers.

"Man, that's too bad," I reply. "What happened, anyway?"

"I filled the barrel stove with wood, then left the house. I must have forgotten to close the draft. I guess the fire got too hot and the logs behind the stove caught fire. When I got home it was already too late; I couldn't even get in to save any of my stuff. By the time they got there with a fire pump, and ran a hose all the way up from the beach, about all we could do was keep the trees behind the house from catching fire."

"Boy, that's too bad. You got everything you need? I've got a spare rifle you can have," I offer.

"I'm pretty well covered. Steve gave me a gun, and other people chipped in with clothes, food, and things. I'm okay."

"How you doin', Rick?" I ask.

"Hey, great, man! It's good to see you again. Karen had the baby, Zach, and she's pregnant again. We're living over at Conclusion Bay, in the old herring reduction plant. Come over and check it out sometime," he answers with his usual enthusiasm.

"Yeah, okay; I was over there a few years ago, when the Webs and Greenstreets were living there. Nice place, but cold in the winter," I say.

We reminisce a while longer, then they wander off up the dock. Dick and I decide to go to the store and pick up a few things; my Copenhagen tastes like motor oil, and we need meat and bread for dinner. As we walk up the dock, we hear a great bellow of guttural laughter coming from a little, white house on the beach.

"BUWAGHAW HAW HAW HAW!"

"What the hell is that?" Dick says.

Suddenly, an ape-like form falls out the door of the house with a crash. A short, gray-haired man, with an ax handle in his hand, shouts as he comes out the door after the other man, who is laying on the ground looking up at him."...AND DON'T COME BACK, MISTER, OR I'LL BLACK THE OTHER EYE!"

"I had forgotten about those guys," I say, as we watch the drama unfold. "The one on the ground is "Dirty Dick" Whitham and the other is Tully Knutsen. Dirty Dick is probably one of the most obnoxious drunks that ever licked the dregs out of a homebrew crock."

"They've been drunk for three days," "Little-Jim" Hendricks says from the cockpit of the Juanita H., where he is overhauling halibut gear. "Tully had a case of whiskey sent out from town, and Dick sniffed it out."

"I remember when I was here a few years ago, Tully got a case of whiskey in on the mail-plane one day. Mike Frantz and Dirty Dick met the plane to pick up Mike's groceries, and when they discovered that Tully had a case of booze on the plane, they decided to deliver it to him. They loaded Mike's grub and the whiskey in the skiff, then went over to the beach in front of Tully's house and disappeared inside with the booze. A week later the boat was still laying on the beach in front of Tully's house with the groceries still in it, or what was left of them. The ravens and crows had had a field day; there was paper and plastic strewn up and down the beach, and the stuff that was left was covered with bird crap," I say.

Jim laughs and says, "I remember that one; Pat Frantz had been trying to find Mike the whole time. She was calling every house in town, day and night, on the old crank phones, driving everyone nuts."

"Why the heck didn't she just come down and get him?" Dick asks.

"She only had one oar in the water most of the time, never went outside, and didn't like anybody stopping by the house," Jim answers.

"I think that one ended up in a fight, too, with Tully whackin' Dick with an ax handle," I say.

"They always end up fighting, but nobody ever seems to get hurt," Jim says, shaking his head.

The altercation has moved back inside, so we drift on up the dock toward the store. As we turn off the main boardwalk onto the cold storage property, we see several men gathered around an old D4 cat. Gore had left it behind when he sold out to Pelican. I recognize Steve and Keith Garnick and Dave Gifford. Dave is up to his elbows in the tractor's innards.

"What's happening?" I ask as we walk up to them.

"They're getting rid of all the junk around here. They were going to cut this tractor up with a torch and haul the pieces out and sink them, but I think I can get it started. The plant manager said I could have it if I can get it out of here. I put in clean oil, flushed out the fuel in the lines, and put in fresh fuel. If I can get the starting motor to run, I know the diesel will go," Dave says, wiping his hands on a rag, and then wrapping the starting rope around the flywheel of the starting motor and giving it a yank. It fires, but doesn't start. Dave gives it a squirt of starting fluid and tries again. POW! BANG! CLUNK! SNORT!

"She almost went that time," Steve says. Dave wraps the rope around the notched groove in the flywheel again, then gives it another hard spin. POPPOPPOPPOPPOP! It takes off this time, and settles into a rough idle. We all grin at each other like a bunch of idiots. Dave revs up the starting motor a couple of times, then pulls the clutch in to spin the diesel. The little starting motor growls with the sudden load, and the diesel turns over slowly, belching white smoke out the stack. Suddenly, the diesel roars into life. Dave adjusts the throttle to an idle, and shuts off the gas to the starting motor. As the engine warms up, it smoothes out and settles into a steady rumble.

After looking the engine over for leaks, Dave climbs up into the seat. He pulls the friction handle on the blade winch, and the rusty pulleys squeal in protest as the blade jerks up off the ground. He looks at us with a wild grin, puts the gearshift into low, and pulls in the clutch. The little Cat lurches forward at a walking pace, its sprockets and track idlers squawking and squealing as the little machine lurches forward.

The muffler has rusted away at the manifold, and the exhaust bellows a base note to the cacophony of racket from the tracks. Dave tries a few turns and raises the blade up and down a couple of times; everything seems to work. As the old Caterpillar clanks around the cold storage lot, all of us tag along like a bunch of street urchins following the king's carriage through the streets of London. He walks the tractor back to its parking spot and shuts it down. We all chuckle with delight.

A crowd of cold storage workers have gathered around. John Hughes walks up to Dave and says, "If you want a day's work tomorrow, I've got some things that Cat could do around the yard here." Dave agrees to come by the next day, and as the crowd breaks up, Dick and I head for the store.

Dinner that night is fried chicken with mashed potatoes, and when we have finished stuffing ourselves, we go out to sit on the bullrail with our coffee. The sun is low in the west and the shadows glow with a deep lavender hue. As the air cools in the alpine meadows, it flows down the valleys, bringing with it the wonderful, sweet, pungent, smell of heather. The Varied thrushes sing their evening song from the tree tops, and everything is right with the world, at least our part of it.

"Well, I'm for the rack," Dick says, getting up as the sun disappears behind the mountains.

"Me, too; see you in the morning," I say, and head for home. It's been a full day, and I don't have to read many pages of my paperback before my eyelids grow heavy. I turn off the light and head for dreamland.

7

The days pass quickly as May 15th approaches. The Halibut and King salmon openings are on the same day this year, and most boats will be fishing the seventy-two hour halibut derby. I look forward to the season with growing excitement. My boat is as ready as I can make it, all the gear is tied and polished, and the engine tuned to perfection. Dick and I sit chatting with several other people in the morning sun while we wait by the airplane float for the mail-plane to land. Dick's parts should be on the plane today, and if they are, we plan to spend the day installing them in his engine. The season opens at midnight, tomorrow night; so we are anxious to get the old Ford running properly, in time for opening-day.

As we wait, my friend Rick, who is the postmaster in P.A., saunters by with a bucket to wash the otter poop off the airplane float. I think they crap there just to annoy Rick. My imagination presents me with an image of the otters hiding somewhere, cracking up with laughter, while they watch him perform his mail-day ritual. As soon as the plane leaves and the airplane float is deserted again, they will be back to make another deposit. The dogs love to roll in it, to perfume themselves for their masters, and can't understand why humans don't seem to appreciate the finer things in life.

"Here it comes," someone shouts, pointing to the NW. We all look and sure enough, we see the tiny, black dot above the saw-tooth ridge on the horizon. Mail-day is always exciting in the small rural communities of SE Alaska. For most, it is the only contact with the outside world, other than a few phones and radios. The arrival of the mail-plane is always good for a morning of socializing, even in bad weather.

The red and white Dehaviland Beaver banks through the gut that leads to the back harbor, then levels out and settles smoothly into the water. The pilot taxis slowly to the float and kills the engine at the last minute. As the plane coasts toward the dock, he climbs down onto the pontoon, grabs the tie up line, and steps off the still-moving plane. You can tell he has performed this maneuver many times, and as the plane passes the middle of the float, he expertly drops a loop over the big metal cleat that is bolted to the edge of the dock. The plane snubs to a stop, and the pilot throws another couple of turns around the cleat, to hold the plane in position while the freight and mail is unloaded.

"Hey, Ken, how you doin'," Rick says, as the pilot straightens up from tying the line on the cleat. "Looks like a nice day for flying," he adds.

"Yeah, it's beautiful; I saw five mountain goats above Gut Bay, on the way down."

"Wow, far out," Rick says as Ken opens the cargo door and ties it to the wing strut.

The old Beaver is packed full of boxes and green mailbags. Ken pulls them out of the plane, one at a time, and hands them to Rick, who passes them on down the line of eager, willing hands. The mail is stacked in one place, and the freight in another. As it accumulates, people who are expecting something examine each package in hopes that their item has arrived. Dick's box appears in the freight pile and we head back to the Spray to install the parts. As we begin to work, we hear the plane's starter whine, then the engine explodes into life. The plane taxis down the harbor and turns around. The big, Pratt and Whitney, radial engine howls to full-throttle and the Beaver screams past the dock. As the floats break free of the water, the pilot throttles back and the racket slowly fades into the distance.

"That's so loud, it hurts," Dick says, as the noise slowly becomes bearable.

By the time the plane is gone, we have the engine-cover off and the tools out. We must remove the front gear-housing to replace the damaged shaft that drives the injector pump. I won't go in to details, but it is a dirty, frustrating, time-consuming task, and no way to spend a nice, spring day. But it must be done, so we just do it.

By late afternoon, we have the engine back together. It starts reluctantly and runs rough, so we go through the timing procedure several more times until it finally starts easily and runs smoothly. This is not an easy task, as one of us must try to peer through a tiny hole in the bell housing to align the timing marks. This hole is only visible by propping a small mirror in the bilge and shining a flashlight on it. I have to hang upside down in order to see the mirror and call out instructions to Dick, who then turns the engine a little at a time with a big pipe wrench. It takes several tries and much cussing, but mind finally prevails over matter, and we have the marks aligned.

With the machine at last running properly, we clean up the mess and put the tools away. Dick heats water for washing, and after we have scrubbed off the oil and grease, he whips up a pan of Alpo and eggs for supper.

"Well, Cap, that nasty chore is done," I say as we eat.

"Thank God, I'm about done in. I sure appreciate your help. I couldn't have managed it alone," Dick replies between bites.

"Not a problem…you'd have done the same for me," I answer.

We finish eating, then take our coffee outside to enjoy the late-afternoon sun. As we sit marveling at the beauty of this magical place, we see a white boat idling slowly out of the gut that leads to the back harbor.

"Who's that?" Dick asks, taking a drag on his cigarette.

"Looks like the Tyke II, Dirty Dick's boat. The party must be over." Unfortunately, I was wrong. The boat stops in the middle of the harbor, and as it sits there, we can hear the radio blasting out of the deck speakers. After sitting still for a few minutes, it starts moving again. It turns toward the dock and slowly approaches at right angles to the float. There is a crew baiting halibut gear on the back deck of a boat tied to the outside of the dock. The Tyke II idles right up to them and stops inches away.

"Knock it off, Dick!" the skipper yells over the sound of KTKN radio blasting from Dick's deck speakers.

"BUUHAWWHAWWHAWW!" We hear his guttural, drunken laughter over the racket of the radio.

"Move off, Dick!" the man on the other boat yells, throwing a herring that splatters off the windshield of the Tyke II. The old, white boat backs slowly away, then moves on down the dock. He finds another boat where people are working and noses up to them also. We are too far away to make out the words that are exchanged, but they don't sound too friendly, either.

"What a jerk," Dick says flipping his cigarette butt in the water and finishing his coffee. Down the dock we hear more shouting, followed by Whitham's brutish, drunken, laughter over the racket of the blaring radio.

"Jane and I lived right across the back harbor from him, when we were here a few years ago. One night around 11:30, after we had gone to bed, we heard an altercation over on the other side of the bay. There was a bunch of arguing, then Dirty Dick singing "Allouette" at the top of his voice, more shouting, then a couple of gunshots. Over the next few hours there was more singing, punctuated with gun shots and shouting. We lay there through the whole night, expecting a bullet to come flying through the house any time. I heard the next day that he fired a couple of shots into the bed beside his wife."

"Why doesn't somebody call the State Troopers, and have them come pick him up?" Dick asks.

"They have, but the cops just sober him up for a few days, then turn him loose, and he comes right back," I answer.

"He better not come nosing around my boat like that, or I'll throw something worse than a herring at him," Dick grumps. "I'm going to bed; see you in the morning. Come over for coffee when you get up," Dick says, as he heads home.

"Yeah, okay; goodnight Partner."

I get up and stroll down the dock and back before I turn in. The Tyke II is tied to the dock at the foot of the ramp, with the speakers still going full volume on the back deck. I go to bed and read for a while, then turn the light out and try to go to sleep. The racket down the dock is too much, and as I lay there trying to tune out the noise, I recall the first time I laid eyes on Dirty Dick…

Jane, Luke, and I had been in P.A. about two days, and we were staying with the Pillen family in an apartment over the warehouse, on the cold storage property. Sharon offered to watch Luke for a while one evening, if we wanted to take a walk. Jane was ready for a break, so we took Sharon up on her offer. We hadn't been all the way to the other end of the boardwalk yet, so we decided to walk to the back float for a look around. It was a pleasant, summer evening, and we were enjoying our walk. Just before we reached the end of the boardwalk, we passed a small house on the right-hand side. There was obviously a party going on, and we could see through the windows that the place was packed with people. As we walked by, the door opened and a voice yelled, "Hey, come on in and have a beer!" We looked and saw a bald man with a gray beard, motioning us over. We looked at each other and Jane said, "What the heck, why not." So we walked up the path to the house.

"Hi, I'm Tom Perrigo, who the hell are you?" the man in the door said with a twinkle in his eye. We introduced ourselves and followed him into the house. It was stifling hot in the narrow kitchen, and so crowded we could hardly close the door behind us.

"Hey, Marvel, pass a couple of beers over; these people are dry!" Tom shouted over the babble in the room. Two tall, plastic glasses filled with foamy beer appeared and we each took one.

"Homebrew," Tom said, with obvious pride. "Marvel and I make it all the time. Drink up." I tasted the frothy, yellow liquid. It tasted like dish soap, and I really had to try hard not to make a sour face.

"Good," I lied, not wanting to hurt his feelings. I didn't much care for beer anyway, and this had to be the worst I had ever tasted. Tom was asking us what our plans were, and when we told him we were looking for property, he immediately launched into a sales pitch, trying to sell us his house. As Tom talked, the door behind me suddenly slammed open, I saw Jane's eyes open wide with shock. I turned and looked toward the door. Standing there was what had to be a Neanderthal throwback of some kind. It let out a bellow of whisky-breath laughter that would have blown me off my feet if there had been room to fall down.

As I stood there in shock, Tom shoved between Jane and I, shouting,   "GETOUTOFMYHOUSEYOUDRUNKIN'SONOFA-BITCH!"

He shoved the figure over backward, and yanked the door shut with a crash. I stood there, dumbfounded. Most of my beer was on my shirt, and Tom was muttering obscenities under his breath as he turned around to face the now-silent crowd.

"That was Dirty Dick Whitham, and he's not welcome in my house," Tom said, without further explanation.

After choking down another one of Tom's soapy homebrews, we slipped out the door and went home.

"God, that beer was awful," Jane said as we walked back up the boardwalk.

"Has a pretty good kick to it, though," I replied, feeling the alcohol coursing through my system.

"Dirty Dick sounds like an interesting character. I wonder what Tom is mad at him about," Jane said as we neared home. We found out later that they were both on the city council and had some difference of opinion about city business.

…I finally give up trying to sleep. The racket from the Tyke II is driving me crazy and I'm getting fed-up. I get up and pull my clothes back on. I take a pair of wire cutters out of the tool box and go outside. It's almost dark as I walk up the dock toward the racket at the foot of the ramp. I step up on the bullrail and look in the window of the Tyke II. Whitham is passed-out on the bunk in the wheelhouse. I step carefully on deck and snip the wires leading to the deck speakers, which are bolted to the back of the cabin. There is instant silence, and stepping back off the boat I hot foot it toward the Nomad. As I hurry down the dock, I hear someone fumbling around on the Tyke II and then a bellow of rage, "!@#$%^&*()_+." The words are slurred with alcohol and unintelligible, but it's not too hard to figure out that the old drunk has discovered the cut wires. The other Dick is standing in his pilothouse door when I get back to our end of the dock.

"What did you do? Sounds like he's fit to be tied." Dick asks.

"I cut about a foot out of the speaker wires," I reply.

Dick chuckles as we stand listening to the commotion down the dock. In a few minutes the speakers crackle and hiss back to life with the volume turned up even higher. A door crashes open somewhere down that direction, and a mighty voice shouts over the noise, "SHUT THAT DAMN RADIO OFF, DICK, BEFORE I SHOVE IT WHERE THE SUN DON'T SHINE. I MEAN IT, SHUT IT OFF NOW!"

The radio clicks off. There is more grumbling and banging around for a time and then sweet silence.

"Maybe we can finally get some sleep," Dick says, disappearing into his wheelhouse. I crawl in my bunk and sleep undisturbed till morning.

8

The dawn breaks clear and warm. I awaken late to the sound of action on the dock. I lay in the rack for a few minutes listening to the sound of voices and outboard motors. This is the last day before the season kicks off and I can feel the tension in the air. I worry that I have forgotten some critical task, or that the fish won't be there, or that I won't be able to catch them if they are. Finally I shake off the anxiety and get up. Dick is already puttering in his cockpit, so I stir up a cup of turpenhydrate # three and pack my lip with snoose. Fortified for the day I go out into the cockpit and look over at Dick.

"Morning. Pretty ambitious for this early in the day, aren't ya Cap?" I ask.

"'Bout time you got up. The day is half over and you ain't turned a wheel yet," Dick retorts.

"I figure this is the last morning for a while that I can do it without guilt, so what the heck."

"Yeah, well, you young whippersnappers need your rest. I suppose you'll be out there before it's light enough to see the marks on yer trollin' wire."

"Oh, I thought I'd wait till the froth settles at the red can. I'll probably go out about nine, put in a couple of hours, and then come in for a nap," I joke, climbing on to the dock and perching on the bullrail.

"Wonder what kind of shape old Whitham is in this morning?" Dick asks, hanging another brass spoon in the aluminum bucket tied behind his cockpit.

"At least he finally turned off that damn radio," I reply. Dick chuckles, squeezing the eye of a # 9 blued hook over the ring on another new Superior King spoon, then hangs it in the bucket. It's the last one in the box, so he pours a bottle of Hydrotone in the bucket and fills it up

with water. Emmersing the spoons in the mixture keeps them from tar-
nishing in the salt air.

"Looks like you're goin' in for heavy metal this year, Partner," I
remark.

"I suppose you're going to drag herring, eh," Dick says.

"Works for me, Cap; you ought to try it."

"If I have to use a dead fish to catch 'em I'm gonna stop fishin'," he
says with disgust. We've had this conversation before, and I realize I'm
wasting my breath trying to convince him to use bait. His mind is
made up and that's that. Our conversation reminds me that I still have
to go to the store to buy my bait and ice for tomorrow.

"I'm going to putt over to the fish house and get iced up before the
rush starts," I say, finishing my coffee and going back aboard the
Nomad.

"I'll be right behind you," Dick says, climbing out of his cockpit
and heading for the wheelhouse.

I start the engine and while it's warming up I open the icebox
behind the pilothouse. It contains various articles that have accumulated over the winter. After the stuff is stowed elsewhere, I turn on the
deckhose and scrub out the hold with soap and bleach, to kill any bac-
teria that might be lurking there. When the fish box is ready, I untie
the lines and back away from the dock. Idling slowly toward the fish
house, I size up the position of the ice shute, and decide to put the starboard side of the boat against the pilings. I go past the last piling then
turn hard to port, and as the boat comes alongside the two pilings
under the shute, I shift to reverse and add enough throttle to stop the
forward motion. There is a light breeze coming out from under the
dock, and if I'm not quick enough, it will push the boat away from the
pilings. Stepping quickly out the door, I grab the center tie-up line,
and throw it around the piling as fast as I can, and lay it off on the
cleat. I congratulate myself for a perfect landing, thankful for not
embarrassing myself in front of the audience up on the dock.

"How much ice do you need?" the man looking down from above asks.

"About 500lbs., and ten packages of bait," I call back.

"Okay; it will take me a minute to shovel it into the auger. When you're full let the extra go overboard. I'll get your bait after we get you iced up."

"Sounds good to me," I say, pulling the twelve-inch, black, rubber hose into the boat, and pointing the end into the hold. Suddenly I hear the auger motor come on. There is a grinding hum coming from the hose, and soon the snow-like, chipped ice starts pouring down the hose. The flow of ice increases until I can hardly keep the hose pointed into the fish box, and in a few moments the box is full. I force the end of the hose over the side, and the last of the ice pours into the water. I smooth the ice out in the hold, lay the ice blankets over it, and close the lid.

"Here's your bait," I hear the iceman call from above me. Looking up, I see him lowering a bucket on a line. When it comes within reach I grab it, and take out the trays of herring. There is also a clipboard in the bucket with the bill for the bait clamped to it. I sign the ticket and return it to the bucket. The cost of the bait will be deducted from my first paycheck.

"Good fishin'," the iceman says, as he pulls up the bucket.

"Okay, thanks," I reply, untying from the piling and shoving off. As I pull ahead to the fuel float, the Spray lands under the ice shute behind me.

"What do you need," the fuel man asks as I tie up.

"Regular gas," I answer, unscrewing the cap to the starboard fuel tank. He hands me the hose, and I insert the nozzle into the filler pipe, then squeeze the handle. When the starboard tank is full, I drag the heavy hose around to the port side, and fill the other tank. The tanks hold thirty gallons each, enough to fish for about a week. When I'm finished, I hand the hose back to the man, and he piles the slack on the dock. He fills out a charge slip for me to sign; the cost of the fuel will also be deducted from my first paycheck.

"Okay," he says, taking the clipboard back from me. "Hope you have good fishing tomorrow."

"Thanks, I hope so too," I reply, as I push the boat away from the dock. I shift into gear and head back to the dock. "I'm really ready now," I think to myself, as I idle back to my tie-up spot at the main dock. When the boat is tied up securely, I look up and see Dick coming around the airplane float. He turns to come alongside the dock, and as his bow goes by, I grab the bowline off his foredeck. When the boat stops, I throw a clove hitch around the bullrail, and top it off with a half-hitch.

"Well, Cap, we got that nasty chore done. Did you take on fuel?" I ask as Dick finishes tying up the stern line.

"No, I dipped the tanks this morning and I've got a couple hundred gallons left. That will last me two or three weeks, the way I fish."

"One advantage of taking all those naps is it saves fuel, and the machinery don't wear out so fast."

"Saves wear and tear on the skipper too," he says with a grin. "Must be coffee time; I'll buy."

We mix up a cup and Dick gets out a loaf of bread and the peanut butter. We enjoy a bachelor's lunch, and follow it with a nicotine fix and another cup of Taster's Choice.

"Where are you going to start out in the morning?" Dick asks, lighting up a smoke.

"Well…I guess I'll go up to Conclusion; there's a pretty good "cookie jar" there that shouldn't be too full of halibut gear. If there's nothing there, I'll probably come back down this way, give Breakfast Rock a rub, and then try Poor Man's Bay after that. Should be something in one of those holes," I answer.

"I'll tag along till I learn the drags, I guess. How deep will you start out?" he asks, sipping his coffee.

"Port Conclusion is a twenty fathom drag. I'll probably put out eighteen to start with and see what happens. I'll start out with a Superior on the bottom of one line, with a flasher and a green, baited hoochie two fathoms above it, then another spoon four fathoms above that. On the other line, I'll use a green plug on the bottom, with a flasher and baited hoochie above it, and then another green plug. If it's a clear day, I'll probably switch to blue hoochies and darker plugs. As the sun comes up, the color of the sky changes. The Herring and Needlefish that the Kings are feeding on change color with the light, so you need to adjust your lure colors to match. Kings are pretty particular," I answer.

"Sounds too complicated to me; think I'll just stick to my spoons. If they don't bite on those, I won't have to clean so many fish.

"Why the hell don't you hire yourself a deckhand; then you can sit in the wheelhouse all day and let him do all the work," I ask, finishing my coffee.

"Maybe I will…might ask that Garnick kid, Keith, if he comes around," Dick says, as I get up to leave.

"I'm going to take a walk up the boardwalk…be too busy for the next few days," I say, climbing up to the wheelhouse and stepping out on deck.

"Hang on, I'll go with you; if I stay here, I might tip over in the bunk. Don't want to take a nap today, so I can go to bed early. I suppose you'll want to leave before daylight in the morning."

"Yeah, we better fire up about 3:30. It's a half-hour run up there, and I want to have the gear in the water as it's getting light. We probably should run up tonight and anchor up. We could sleep in a little later in the morning, and are less likely to have to put up with Dirty Dick's radio up there," I answer.

"Sounds like a plan to me. We can run up before supper, then eat after we get the hook down."

"Okay," I say, as we start up the dock.

As we walk up the ramp to the pier, there is a young couple at the top with a wheelbarrow full of halibut gear, waiting for us to clear the ramp before starting down the steep incline with the heavy load. There is a beautiful Golden Retriever, wagging her tail and grinning at us as we approach the top. When I get to the dog she puts her front feet up on my chest and tries to lick my face.

"Sashun, get down," the woman scolds the dog. "Sorry, we're trying to break her of that habit, but she gets excited and forgets sometimes. Did you guys just get in?"

"No, we've been here for about a week and a half. I lived out here in '76 and'77," I say, introducing Dick and myself. "How long have you been here?"

"I'm Jean and this is Marty. We bought Cleaver's house last summer. We lived in Juneau before that."

"All right! Do you guys fish?" I ask.

"Yeah, we fish out of our 16-foot Lund. We're going to do the halibut opening first, and then handtroll after that. Will you be fishing halibut?" Marty asks

"No, we're just here for trolling. I used to fish halibut but haven't for several years now," I answer.

"We better get busy; we have to haul some more stuff down this afternoon. See you guys later," Jean says.

"Okay, nice meeting you," I say, as we head on up the ramp.

"Seem like nice people," Dick says.

"Yeah, they sure do," I reply, as we saunter up the main boardwalk, enjoying the summer afternoon.

After our walk and a stop at the store, we get back to the boats about 4:00 o'clock. We stow the grub and fire up the engines. After they have warmed up, we untie and head for the harbor entrance. We soon round the red buoy, and turn left into Chatham Strait. We throttle up to running speed and in a few minutes, when Crow Island has passed astern, we turn north and head for Port Conclusion. The water is calm as glass and reflects the timbered hills perfectly.

Port Alexander is a narrow inlet in the south side of a low peninsula that juts out into Chatham Strait. Port Conclusion is the next inlet up the strait, north of town. The peninsula forms the south shore of the large open bay. The sawtooth ridge visible from town is the north side of Conclusion. We soon round the small tree-clad island that marks the entrance of the bay, and follow the shoreline back south about a mile, to Calm Cove. Calm Cove is a beautiful, tiny anchorage that is open to the northwest. It is a good anchorage in calm weather, but can be uncomfortable in northerly winds. There is a nice, sandy, crescent beach in the back, and Dick drops his anchor in five fathoms, just off the beach. When he has the hook set I tie alongside, and we shut the engines off. This is one of my favorite places in the world, and as the last echoes of our motors fade into the distance, we stand on our decks and savor the tranquil beauty that surrounds us. The water of Conclusion Bay is utterly flat calm. There is not a breath of wind to mar its glassy surface. Out in the middle distance, a pair of Humpback Whales puff their misty breath into the still air, and in a few seconds the sound reaches us.

"HUFFF (inhale)…HUFF (inhale)…" As they sound, the black and white tails wave for a moment above the glassy surface, and then disappear. All that is left is a rapidly vanishing cloud of mist, shimmering in the late-afternoon sunlight.

"Quite a spot," Dick says.

"Boy, I didn't realize how much racket there is in town," I say, marveling at the silence. Dick goes below and puts the macaroni on to boil for goulash. *"Hope I've got enough Tums,"* I think to myself, grinning. While Dick cooks, I lay out the gear I'll use in the morning; snapping the new leaders to the plugs and flashers, and arranging them in order on the gear tray, bolted to the back of the boat. The bottom lure must be on the top of the pile, and there is an art to getting them to coil just right, so they will go out without tangling. It will barely be light enough to see when I start fishing in the morning, so everything must be perfect. When the spreads are laid out to my satisfaction, I take several packages of herring out of the ice, so they will be thawed out enough to use in the morning. I inspect the bait closely for the first time, and realize that it is old and freezer burned, probably left over from last year. This is a bummer; the bait works best if it is fresh, and this is obviously not. The small herring are brown around the heads, and they look like they have been thawed and refrozen. Bad bait costs me money and the cold storage too; their profit is dependent on the number of fish we catch. They're bending over to pick up pennies, and dollar bills are falling out of their pockets!

"Quit making love to those dead fish and come eat, before I throw it to the sand fleas," Dick hollers out his door.

"Okay, I'll be right there," I answer, putting the bait under the gear tray, so the mink or otters don't steal it in the night.

"They sure saw me coming on that bait; it looks like it was half rotten before they froze it. Probably some they had left last year," I say, as I sit down to eat.

We dig in and enjoy our supper without comment. The goulash isn't bad, even if it does have peas in it, and I eat two helpings. When we finish and the mess is cleaned up, we take our coffee out on deck to savor the sunset, which is turning the hills to the west a golden purple color. It is so still we can hear the whales huffing out in the strait, and the Varied Thrushes are singing their night song in the Spruce trees ashore.

"Tomorrow is the big day, Dick," I say, sipping my coffee.

"Yeah, it's time to do it and stop talkin' about it."

"Looks promising along the drag; lots of birds and seals, and I saw several patches of feed on the surface on the way in. In the morning, we can start putting the gear out as soon as we leave the harbor. The bottom slopes right off to twenty fathoms just beyond the kelp," I reply.

"Okay; I'll wait till you are a ways up the drag, then put my gear in and follow you. Are there any eye openers along here?" he asks.

"No, it's a pretty easy drag. Along the cliffs it drops right off to twenty fathoms and then slopes to thirty. If it shallows up just turn out and you'll be okay. You want to rub it as close as you can up by the island; that pocket between the island and the point is the spot. When the tide is flooding, the fish lay in that hole, watching for feed to wash through the gut."

"I'll stay out some for the first pass and watch you; don't want to loose a lead on the first pass of the first day of the season," Dick says.

"Whatever turns your crank, Cap. It's nine o'clock; I'm going to hit the hay. See you about four," I say, as I climb over onto the Nomad.

"Goodnight."

I set the cursed alarm clock for 3:30 and crawl into the sleeping bag. I read for a while but my eyelids soon grow heavy. I put the light out and try to go to sleep, but my mind won't turn off. I lay awake most of the night tossing and turning, unable to stop worrying about tomorrow. Finally around midnight, I fall into a deep sleep.

9

The rude clatter of the alarm clock startles me out of some vague uneasy dream. It is sitting on the binnacle, in the wheelhouse, so I have to get all the way out of bed to turn it off. If I leave it within reach of the bunk, I will turn it off and go back to sleep. I stagger drunkenly to the main cabin and mash down on the button that stops the annoying racket. I stand looking out the windows while my brain tries to make the transition to wakefulness. It's like a kind of jet lag but I finally realize that I am conscious and that it is getting light outside.

I pull out the dipstick to check the oil…it's full so I shove the rod back in the hole, then start the engine. While it's warming up, I put on my clothes and mix a cup of instant coffee with water from the teakettle that has been simmering on the back of the stove all night. As I take the first sip, Dick's old Ford diesel grinds over a few times, then rumbles to life. I put the coffee cup on the oil stove so it will stay warm, then go out to untie from the Spray. When the lines are loose I push the boats apart, then lower the trolling pole on the starboard side. By the time it is down and locked, the boats have drifted far enough apart to lower the other pole. When both poles are down and secured, I check the tag lines to make sure they are not tangled, then slip the stabilizers over the side. I give everything one last look, then go in and put the transmission into forward.

As the boat moves slowly out of the small cove I sip more coffee, then turn on the fathometer and the CB radio. I'm wide-awake now, excited and anxious to get the gear in the water. The birds are already feeding and it just plain looks fishy. As the bottom drops off to fifteen fathoms, I put the half-finished coffee back on the stove, and step out into the cockpit to set the gear.

The first thing over the side is the twenty-pound lead ball that is tied to a swivel, which is spliced onto the end of the one-sixth inch, stainless steel, trolling cable. I take the brass and copper spoon that is snapped to the first leader, out of the bucket and throw it into the water behind the boat. When the four fathoms of nylon leader are stretched out behind, I remove the snap from the short wire on the gear tray and snap it on the trolling wire, right above the cannonball.

Now I release the brake on the gerdy and lower the line until the two-fathom marks come off the reel. The next spread is a flasher, so I open a package of herring and remove one of the small silver fish, grumbling to myself about the age of the bait. I lay the Herring on a scrap of plywood between the gear trays, then cut the belly off with the bait knife. When it's trimmed just right, I hook the stainless steel #7 hook up through its back, then slide the hollow, plastic squid over its head. When I have it adjusted to look as realistic as possible, I flip the flasher and hoochie over into the water behind the boat. When the leader is trailing along behind with no kinks or knots, I snap it on the wire between the brass markers, two fathoms above the cannonball.

And so it goes, alternating spoons and flashers until I get to the eighteen-fathom marker, where I clip on the tag line. The tag line is tied to the outer end of the trolling pole, which is a twenty-foot long Cedar pole, hinged to the side of the boat amidships, and guyed fore and aft. The pole hangs from the mast and angles out from the boat at about forty-five degrees while fishing.

As I let out the line after attaching the tagline, it swings away from the boat until it is towing aft of the outer end of the pole. When the port line is towing to my satisfaction, I repeat the process on the starboard side. The whole routine takes about fifteen minutes, and when I am finished I step back into the wheelhouse.

I sit behind the wheel, enjoying my coffee, with one eye on the depth sounder and the other on the shoreline. The trick is to dangle the lures along the bottom contour, turning in and out of all the nooks and crannies, so that the array of lures resembles a school of feed. I'm soon at the north end of the drag, and turn into the pocket where the tidal current is pouring through the narrow gap, between the small island and the point. When the bottom comes up, I turn out sharply, sweeping the starboard line in and out of the hole.

Suddenly the pole bounces up and down violently. I turn the boat back onto the drag, then the other pole bounces. I get the boat heading parallel to the north side of the island, and go out to the cockpit to crank up the fish.

As I run through the gear, I find two nice fish on the starboard line and one on the port side. I manage to get all three fish aboard without too much trouble, and when the lines are back down I turn around to head back down the drag. Dick is in the pocket when we meet, so I stay well out to give him room. After we have passed, I turn in and work the drag back to the south end. I troll down to the anchorage cove, then turn back north without another hit.

As I work the pocket again, nothing happens, but along the north side of the island both poles take off again. The fish have moved, which is common during a bite. I turn the boat around and go out to run through the gear. This time there are two fish on the starboard side and nothing on the port line. One of the spoons has its hook turned and jammed at the swivel. There has been a fish on it but he has managed to shake the hook. The other line seems to be fishing better, so I change from plugs to brass and copper spoons, so both lines are the same.

As soon I am clear of Dick, who's on his second pass, I turn back north without going all the way down to the south end. I troll through the pocket, then out around the island. Along the north shore of the island both poles bounce, but the port side is shaking so violently that the whole boat is rocking. I check the depth sounder to see if the leads are on the bottom…I'm in twenty fathoms so it must be fish!

I point the boat out into deeper water, then go out to crank up the lines. The port line is dragging back and winged out to the side. My heart pounds! It must me a big one to pull back that hard. As the line comes in, I can feel the fish shaking his head from side to side, trying to throw the hook. When he is really fighting hard, I give back line to deny him a solid purchase to pull against. As each spread breaks the surface, I try to coil it in the gear tray while the fish is resting. Slowly the line comes up, and the leaders come off one by one.

As the flasher above the last spoon breaks the surface, I unsnap it carefully, then pull it in slowly so it doesn't spook the fish, which is only twelve feet below it. When the flasher is aboard, I look around and adjust my course a bit to miss a kelp wad ahead of the boat, then slowly crank in the last two fathoms of line. Suddenly the line pulls way back and the huge fish leaps clear out of the water. The cannon ball lifts above the surface for a moment, then sinks as the fish heads for the bottom. I give back line until I feel him stop pulling. Suddenly the wire takes off forward and out as the fish charges ahead, then runs out perpendicular to the boat, and then goes slack. "Damn, I've lost him!" I think. I crank the gerdy slowly until I see the leader just under the surface. I reach down into the water with the gaff hook and snag the leader. As I pull up on it, carefully, I can feel the weight of the fish still on the line! My heart pounds with excitement again. I take the leader in my hands and pull the fish slowly toward me. I can see the big Superior spoon fluttering in the sunlight, just beneath the surface, and trailing docilely along behind is the fish.

He is so dark down the back that he is almost invisible and he looks enormous. This is the tricky part. As the head comes alongside, I must pull it out of the water and whack him smartly right between the eyes. It must be done quickly and smoothly, or the fish will spook and make another wild run. I get my feet set, then make sure the leader is free to run out if I miss-gaff. I grip the leader between the gaff handle and the fingers of my right hand then slide my hand down toward the fish. Now I grip the leader with my left hand, about two feet from the spoon. I raise the gaff with the hook up, and when it feels right, I pull up on the leader with my left hand. The instant the head clears the water, before the fish has a chance to react, I bring the gaff down as hard as I can. BONK!!! It hits him just right; he rolls over on his side, stunned. I turn the hook down and sink it into the gill plate. As the hook penetrates to the handle, I straighten my back, pulling on the leader with my left hand and the gaff handle with my right, and slide the fish over into the boat. I conk him again, to make sure he is dead, then unhook the spoon from his jaw.

I stand there for a few moments, trembling as the adrenaline metabolizes out of my system. The fish is beautiful; blue-green down the back, purple and gold down the side, and silver-bellied. As usual, I feel a touch of sadness for killing him, but it soon passes. The fish looks to be about forty pounds, maybe forty-five, and is worth almost one hundred dollars. He is the sixth fish of the morning, all of them over twenty pounds. The season is off to a pretty good start!

I look around. I'm out in the strait quite a distance from the drag, so I point the boat back toward the island, then put the port line back down. When I'm finished, I run the starboard line, but there is nothing on it; the fish that rattled the pole has escaped. As soon as the lines are squared away, I gut the sixth fish and put them in the icebox.

As I troll slowly back toward the drag, I mix up a fresh cup of mud and call Dick on the radio.

"Ahoy there, Partner, are you in 'em?"

"Oh, yeah, throwin' them over both shoulders. I got two so far," he answers with a note of disgust.

"I have a handful, I guess; not very many but the size is good."

"What are you getting them on…bait, I suppose?" he asks.

"Yeah, and copper and brass," I reply.

We pass each other at the island and Dick comes out on deck as he goes by. He points at his port pole, which is bouncing up and down, and grins at me as he heads for the pit. My inside pole takes off a moment later and I go out to run the line. It's another twenty-pounder, and by the time I have him aboard the other pole is shaking.

The morning passes quickly, and when the tide-changes at noon the bite fizzles out. The halibut opening starts at noon and there are several boats setting gear in Conclusion Bay.

By mid-afternoon the boredom has set in and I look longingly at the anchorage, thinking of a nap. I dismiss the idea and have another cup of coffee instead. Dick and I chat on the radio for a while, till we run out of things to talk about. I keep working the drag thoroughly, knowing that the fish will start biting again eventually; I want to be ready for them. I have eleven nice fish aboard, and if I can catch a few more this evening, it would shape up into a profitable day.

About four o'clock, a small, white, fiberglass boat comes steaming around the island. It slows down alongside me as I run through the gear, freshening up the bait and cleaning the kelp off the wires. Her name is Celedo, and as she matches speed on my starboard side, a giant of a man emerges from a hatch in the wheelhouse roof.

"Hi," he shouts across the few yards that separate us. "Do you mind if we make a halibut set in here?"

"No," I shout back. "If you stay out in fifty fathoms or so you won't bother us. I made that set a few years ago and loaded up."

"Okay, thanks. How are you guys doing, any Kings around?" he asks.

"We got a few this morning, but it's been dead since tide-change," I answer.

"Well, I hope they start biting for you again. Thanks for the info, we'll probably see you at the dock," he says.

I wave and go in the house as he throttles up and charges toward the head of the bay.

"What was that all about?" Dick asks over the radio.

"He wanted to know if he could make a halibut set here without getting in our way. I told him to stay out in fifty fathoms, there's a pretty good halibut set out there. He should pull a few hundred pounds out of it. Seemed to be a decent chap," I answer.

"Nice of him to ask, anyway. You catch anything lately?"

"Nope, haven't had anything but a couple of shakers since the tide-changed. I saved one for supper, I'm about ready for a bit of salmon; been a long winter," I say.

"Sounds good. Let me know when you're ready give it up for the day, I'll put some spuds on to boil," he says back.

"I'm going to stick it out till tide-change; I got a hunch those fish are still here and will bite again on the flood."

"Okay, that's what I was thinking, too. Let's see…it's about five, something should happen pretty soon," Dick says.

I turn into the cookie jar behind the island, and when the outside line stops on the inside of the turn coming out, the pole bounces vigorously up and down. I let the boat continue out into deeper water, then straighten out parallel with the north side of the island.

"All right, Cap, ya talked one on for me; they're right in the pocket. Looks like a nice one, too. I better go rescue him before he changes his mind," I say into the mike, then hang it on the radio.

"You'll have to split that one with me, Partner," he replies, chuckling

I soon have another twenty-pounder aboard, and turn for the back pass. Out in the strait, several boats are making their first haul of halibut gear, and looking south, down toward the cape, I see several more. As I go past Dick he is in his pit, cranking furiously and suddenly my left pole rattles. I let it shake for a couple minutes, hoping he will draw a crowd, but nothing happens. The port pole has stopped wiggling, so I go out and crank the line up. There is a King on the flasher, and a small halibut on the spoon.

Now the other pole is going and as I let the line out I feel it yank again. I crank it back up and land another nice fish. Now I pull the starboard line; it has two fish on it. Things are getting out of hand. I tangle the leaders as I put the line back out and by the time I get them straightened out, I am at the south end of the drag. I turn the boat around and get another hit on the starboard side.

"Man this is fishing!" I shout at Dick as we pass. He just gives me a toothless grin and keeps cranking.

The rest is a blur; I had fish on both lines most of the time for the next hour. Some I landed, some got away, but when they stopped biting, I had fourteen nice fish on deck. Some of the leaders had knots in them, some were in the wrong position, and none of the hoochies were baited. I went through the gear one more time to straighten out the mess, then cleaned the fish and put them in the icebox. The fish had stopped biting like someone had turned off a switch. After I had the mess cleaned up and put away, I made several more passes, but didn't get a wiggle.

About a quarter to eight I said to Dick on the radio, "I don't know about you, Cap, but I'm pooped and hungry."

"Okay, let's call it a day. I'm gonna crank 'em up right now; see you in there," he answered.

I click the mike a couple of times, and go pull the lines aboard. We soon have the hook down, and while the potatoes boil, I fillet the small salmon that we are going to eat. When I'm finished, Dick has his big cast-iron skillet hot, and the spuds are done. We dig into the food, and as we eat we discuss the day's work.

"Not too bad for the first day. I got twenty-six, and all but one is over twenty pounds; one is over forty," I remark.

"I got eighteen; that's the best day I've ever had on Kings," he replies.

"I've had a couple of higher days, number-wise, but I think I got more pounds today than ever before," I say.

We banter back and fourth a while until fatigue finally overwhelms us, and then head for the bunk. Three-thirty will come early and I definitely want to make the morning bite again tomorrow.

10

We have the gear in the water by four the next morning. There is a fair morning bite but the fish are smaller with lots of shakers, fish shorter than twenty-eight inches and illegal to keep. I manage to scratch out seven fish by ten o'clock, then the bite dies. As the late morning passes we grow bored, and after tide-change we troll south past Breakfast Rock, then on down to Poor Man Bay, a wide cove south of town that is open to the strait. There are lots of birds feeding and big patches of needlefish on the surface, so we make a couple of passes through the bay, then continue down to Wooden Island.

Wooden Island is a beautiful, spectacular place. The island is a large rock thrusting up about 120 feet out of the water, several hundred yards SE of Cape Ommaney, which is the southern tip of Baranof Island. The shores of the island are vertical cliffs rising straight up out of the water, and the top of the island is covered with knarled Spruce and Hemlock trees. To the south and west is the North Pacific Ocean, and looking north, the east shore of Baranof Island bounds Chatham Strait, with Kuiu Island to the east. Turning SE, you see Cape Decision and Coronation Island, then directly south are the Hazy Islands, a group of rock piles about fifteen miles out in the ocean.

As we troll along the east side of Wooden Island, I think of Captain Vancouver, who named the island for a sailor who was lost here. They had been anchored in Port Conclusion for several days, waiting out a SE blow. The wind finally went SW, so they tacked down to the cape and then the wind died. The strong currents at Wooden Island were threatening to ground them, so they towed the ship with the long boats till about two in the morning, when a light NW wind came up. As they were hauling the boats aboard, Isaac Wooden fell overboard and sank. In spite of an attempt to rescue him, he was never found. Captain

Vancouver named the island after Wooden, and in his logs he says that Wooden was a good sailor, but couldn't swim. A common trait among sailors of those days.

"Pretty spectacular place, eh, Partner," I say to Dick on the CB.

"Yep, it must be a terrible place in the winter."

"Yeah, the navigation light, on the south end, is sixty feet off the water and it gets wiped out by waves every year," I answer.

"Huh…boy, the fishing sure went dead, I haven't had a wiggle since mid-morning," he says.

"No, me either…might as well go in when we get back up to the other end. I was thinking I would pitch off these fish and get iced back up while it's dead, then we'll be ready for the next bunch of fish that come around the corner," I reply.

"Sounds good to me. I wonder what the price is; hope its two dollars for large reds."

"I heard a couple of halibut boats talking this morning; they were complaining about the halibut price. One guy said that Pelican Seafood was having a strike, and until it was settled they would be paying an advance, but final prices would not be announced till after the strike was settled. We might be smart to hold onto these fish as long as possible, till things settle out. We can talk to John Hughes tonight and find what the skinny is before we sell. I'm okay for a couple of more days if the fishing stays this dead," I say.

"I think fishing will be better when the halibut season is over tomorrow; all these boats running around night and day spook the fish and scatter the feed. Same thing happens over in Clarence Strait when they have a seine opening; you can't buy a fish for the next couple of days," Dick says.

"Okay, well I'm going to drag up to Breakfast Rock, then go in. Sure would like to pick up a couple more today; guess I better go run through the gear if I really want to catch one. I'll see you at the dock after a while; it'll feel good to stretch the old legs on dry land."

Dick clicks the transmit button a couple of times, and I head for the pit to freshen up the bait and shake the brown bombers off the lead spoons. When I finish, I turn into the cookie jar behind Poor Man Point and work the gear along the bottom contour. The flood is just starting and the time is right for an evening bite, if there is going to be one. As I come out of the bay and point toward Breakfast Rock, the port pole rattles good and hard, so I dive for the pit and crank the line up. There is a nice eighteen-pounder on the top spread, and after a wild fight I manage to conk him and gaff him aboard. I put the line back down as I turn out into the strait to circle back for another pass. When the line is down I step into the house and call Dick.

"Don't leave Dick. I just got one right off that big flat rock on the beach. I'm going around for another pass."

"Click click," I hear in reply.

I nose back on the drag up tide of the spot where the fish hit, and follow the bottom closely. Yank, yank, yankety-yank, the port pole takes off again. Then the starboard pole jerks too.

"Right here, Cap," I say to Dick, who is just outside me going the other way.

I go out and crank the port pole. The fish is gone so I put the line back out and run the other one. There are two fish on the line, so I turn out to go around again and as I pass Dick, I see him in his pit cranking furiously. When I am south of the hot spot, I turn in toward the beach and start my pass. I get one keeper on the starboard side and a shaker on the port and the next pass nothing. We try a couple more times, going south to the point and north to Breakfast Rock, hoping to run into the school again, but no luck.

"That was fun while it lasted," I say on the radio.

"Yeah, I got four nice ones and lost a couple more; one broke a hook off a Superior!" he answers.

"That's too bad; I lost two also. One was a no-show and I missed the other with the gaff. I hit the water beside him, he spooked, made one wild run and spit the hook back at me," I lament. "Oh well, got to leave some for seed."

"I've about had it, it's almost eight o'clock, By the time we get tied up it'll be past my bed time," Dick says

"Let's crank 'em up," I say.

"Click click."

When I finish hauling the gear aboard at the rock, there is a sleeper on the bottom of the starboard line that I never saw hit a nice fifteen-pounder. Not such a bad day after all, I think to myself, as I clean and ice the fish while the boat charges for the red can.

As we near the dock we see a hubbub of activity. Boats unloading at the fishhouse, people baiting up along the dock, and as we round the airplane float on the north end, someone is gutting a big halibut on the float. There is only one open spot at the dock, so I wait while Dick ties up, then land on his starboard side.

We eat a simple supper of leftover salmon and bread, with canned peaches for dessert. When we finish, Dick decides to hit the rack, and I take a walk up the dock as the sunsets behind the ridge to the west. The aroma of halibut and half-rotten bait permeates the air, and the dock is littered with tubs of hooks and coils of groundline.

Down toward the ramp, the Celedo is tied on the outside of the dock and the big man is cleaning halibut on deck.

"It looks like you got a few," I say as he looks up.

"Oh, hi, you're the guy that was trolling in Conclusion yesterday. Hey thanks for the tip, that was our best set yet. We got over twenty-five hundred pounds on that haul! My name is Bud Harwood and this is Celia," he says, nodding toward the dark-haired woman standing in the wheelhouse door.

I introduce myself and reply, "I'm glad there were some fish there. This your first time here?"

"No, my son and I fished halibut and salmon here last year. Have you been here before?"

"Yeah, I lived here for a year in the mid-seventies. Been trying to get back ever since but didn't make it till this year," I answer.

We chat while he cleans his fish. They offer coffee, but I'm ready for the sack, so I soon head home and go to bed.

When I awaken it's broad daylight and the Ravens are squawking in the trees ashore. I get up, grumbling to myself for forgetting to set the alarm, and stumble outside.

"Wondered if you were ever going to get up," Dick says from his door.

"I forgot to set the damn alarm, why didn't you wake me up?"

"Just woke up a few minutes ago too. Figured we had already missed the morning bite so I might as well let you sleep," he answers.

I go in and make a cup of coffee, then join Dick on the dock. There are only a few boats in; the halibut season ends at noon and they are all out hauling the last few sets. We enjoy our coffee in the morning sun, then head up to the cold storage to find out what the fish price is. As we walk along the dock a huge fish buyer boat, the Howkan is tying up at the float. There is a big white sign on her pilothouse that says, "CASH BUYER, PETERSBURG FISHERIES"

"Looks like some competition for Pelican," Dick says as we walk by.

"Yup, that'll keep em honest."

We go on up to the store and run into John Hughes on the boardwalk out front.

"Morning, gentlemen. How did the fishing go, you got any Kings for me?" he asks.

"We got a few," I answer, "what are you paying?"

"Well they're having a strike in Pelican and haven't come out with a new price yet; we're still paying a buck fifty for large reds and ninety-eight for mediums. There will probably be a retro payment after the strike is settled. How many do you have?" he asks.

"I have thirty-eight, all large, and Dick has twenty-two, but we sure don't want to sell them at those prices. When do you think they will settle the strike and come out with the real price?"

"I would think any day now, and I'm sure they will match the other buyers," he replies. "I sure want those fish when you're ready to sell."

"We'll see what happens. I was also wondering if you have any good bait; the stuff they gave me is half-rotten. It's costing you and us both money."

"No, that's all we have till the strike is over, and they want me to get rid of the bait leftover from last year first," he says.

"That's too bad; can't do much with rotten bait," I say disgustedly.

"Sorry, that's the best we can do for now. Well, I have to get to work…bring those fish over…see you later," John says, hurrying away.

"That really twists my crank; the cheap bastards are going to squeeze every penny out of us they can. Let's go see what the Howkan is paying," I say angrily, as we watch him walk toward the blast freezer building.

We go back to the dock and climb onto the back deck of the Petersburg buyer.

"Ahoy, anybody aboard?" I yell as we walk up to the galley door.

"Yeah, come on aboard. What can we do for you?" a man sitting at the table says as we step through the door into the galley. "Have a seat, you want a cup of coffee?" he asks, getting up and taking two heavy, white mugs off hooks above the sink.

"Sure," we say, sitting down. "Are you buying King Salmon, or just halibut?" I ask as he pours the cups full from a big enameled pot on the oil stove.

"You bet!" he says, setting the mugs on the table in front of us. "How many you got?" he asks, sitting down.

"Over fifty between us, mostly large. What are you paying?" I ask, sipping my coffee.

"I'll give you two dollars straight across for everything. That's an advance; if the price goes up before I get back to Petersburg, the company will retro the rest to you by mail."

"Have you got any trolling bait aboard?" I ask.

"No, all I have is halibut bait, but I can have some flown out on the company plane this afternoon. Would a case be enough?"

"A case would be great, if it's fresh bait packaged this year, not re-frozen, rotten crap, like Pelican is trying to palm off on me," I answer.

"Okay, you guys pull alongside whenever you're ready and we'll unload you. I've got lots of ice aboard too if you need it."

"All right," I say as we get up to leave, "sounds good to me."

"Pretty accommodating outfit," I say to Dick as we walk back toward the boats.

"It'll probably piss Hughes off, but we can't afford to pass up those prices with the amount of fish we got aboard," he answers.

"That's for dang sure!" I reply.

We fire up the boats and idle over to the Howkan. They weigh up our fish quickly, and help us shovel ice out of totes into our holds. When we are finished, the skipper has our fish tickets ready to sign and imprint with our limited entry permit cards. When the paperwork is finished, he takes a roll of cash out of a bank bag and counts fourteen brand new, crisp, hundred-dollar bills into my eager palm! Not bad for two days work. Of course you have to consider the nine months that have passed with no income, but it feels pretty good anyway.

"I called in your bait order and the plane will be here in about an hour. You can leave it in my freezer until we sail. That will be tomor-row night after all the halibut boats are unloaded," he says as we get up to leave.

"Okay, thanks for everything," I say as we climb back aboard our boats.

The packer crew unties our lines, and we putt back over to the dock. Our spot is still open so Dick ties up first and I tie outside him. When the boats are secure we have a PBJ for lunch, on the Spray, and when we finish Dick says;

"I think it's nap time."

I take the hint and bid him adieu. I'm not sleepy, so I wander down the dock to see what's happening. It's after twelve and the halibut season is closed. The dock is filling up as the boats finish unloading. Groups of exhausted looking people are sitting on the bullrails, telling fish stories and moaning about prices, short seasons, and whatever else is bothering them. In spite of the complaining, there is a sort of festive air present. The pressure is off now and everybody made a few bucks to support their fishing habit, so there are a lot of tired smiles.

As I sit telling fish lies with several acquaintances, we see a small white and green double-ender idle in and tie up on the outside of the dock. It's the Alice May from Petersburg. They had fished in P.A. when I was here a few years ago. I remembered them because they had run out of fuel on the drag down at Poor Man Bay one afternoon, and I had left a good Coho bite to tow them in. Bernie and Dot Oster were nice folks and had thanked me profusely.

After the boat is tied up, Bernie disappears inside and comes back out with a quart of whisky in his hand. He walks right up to me and sticks out his hand.

"Howdy," he says as we shake hands, "I was hoping to run into you again someday. Here's the bottle of whisky I promised you for towing me in a few years ago. A debt is a debt and ain't clear till it's paid. How you been anyway?" he asks, sitting down.

"I'm fine, good to see you again, Bernie, but you don't owe me anything; could have been me out of gas, and I suspect you would have towed me in if it was," I answer, taking the jug and looking up and down the dock to make sure Dirty Dick isn't in sight.

"I would, but I said I'd bring you a bottle, and there it is."

"Well, we better open her up and have a snort, to celebrate it being Wednesday then," I say, breaking the seal and taking a swig. I hand the open bottle to Bernie and he tips it up. When he is finished he hands it to Steve, and the bottle makes several rounds before it is empty. A bottle of white rum magically appears, and several joints of pot make the rounds.

The afternoon and evening are kind of a blur. Sometime after dark, I'm on the Capon with a lot of people and decide it is time to go home.

The next thing I know, I'm in the hold on the Capon with someone else. We reel around, falling down several times trying to climb out, and the next thing I know I wake up out of a drunken stupor, sweating like crazy, with a terrible thirst and a pounding headache.

I'm zipped up to my chin in the sleeping bag with all my clothes on, including hat, coat, and rubber boots. As I struggle to get the zipper down, I discover that my pants are bunched around my boot tops. I must have been trying to get undressed and couldn't get them over my boots and just passed out. How the hell I got those size eleven Extra-Tuffs down in the sleeping bag, and got the zipper all the way up without jamming it, is a mystery that's beyond my few remaining brain cells to comprehend.

After untangling myself and getting my pants back on, I drink all the water I can hold and go back to sleep. Without the boots, coat, and hat.

Sometime around noon, I finally crawl out to face grim reality. My head is pounding like a pile driver, and my mouth feels like bears slept in it. Dick is in his door when I finally appear; he just shakes his head and gives me a rueful grin.

"You never seen anybody with the whisky flue before?" I ask, grinning painfully back at him.

"Looks like you better close those eyes before you bleed to death. Better come over and have a cup of coffee," he says, disappearing inside.

Dick feeds me aspirin, bacon and eggs, and several cups of Taster's Choice. I start to feel a little better. We walk up the boardwalk and back, then visit around the dock for the rest of the afternoon. I compare hangovers with some of last night's revelers, and after a light dinner, hit the rack early to finish healing up. Never did find out who the other person was in the hold on the Capon.

11

The battered, old "Big Ben" jangles its rude racket on the binnacle. I'm jarred out of a deep, dreamless sleep, hours too soon. I stagger into the wheelhouse and turn off the alarm. The tall Spruce and Hemlock trees that line the east side of the harbor are silhouetted by the first streaks of dawn painting the eastern sky. I stir up a cup of coffee and start the engine. When it warms up enough to run smoothly, I untie from the Spray and shove off. As soon as I'm clear of the airplane float, I step out and lower the trolling poles. I've done this so many times over the years that I can almost do it in my sleep, and by the time the red can is abeam, I'm ready to put the gear out. When the fathometer shows twenty fathoms, I go out and put the lines in the water.

The sky to the NE is glowing pink and gold, and the sun is just below the horizon. This is a land of glorious sunrises and this one is a "10" for sure. This is my favorite time of day; the beauty of the light and the promise of a new day more than make up for the missed sleep.

As I finish putting the lines out, I see several other boats coming out the harbor entrance. With the halibut season over, the rest of the fleet will be on the trolling drags today, and I feel a wee twinge of resentment at not having the grounds to myself. The fewer the boats the better the fishing. With several boats working the same hole, everybody must get in line and take turns making passes over the hot spots. Some of the young newcomers in the fishery are unwilling to adhere to the simple rules of the road that the old-timers worked out to avoid conflict.

As I pass Breakfast Rock the starboard pole rattles, and I land a nice fifteen-pounder off the lead spoon. I consider turning around to make another pass, but I decide to go on down to Poor Man Point and have a look. There are lots of birds in the bay and the tide will start to flood in about an hour. There were a few fish here a couple of days ago and Poor Man is one of my favorite fishing holes.

The Juanita H steams by at a full charge off my port side and as he passes the CB crackles to life.

"Nomad, you got this one on?" Jim's voice drawls out of the speaker.

"Mornin' captain, what's happenin'," I answer.

"Oh…I don't know what to do here, I should go out to Larch Bay but I don't feel like rolling in the westerly all day…maybe we'll try it here for a while. Heard you did all right the first couple of days. I hated to miss the opening but I couldn't afford to pass up the halibut season. I wish they would have halibut before King season, while we're all tied to the dock," Jim says.

"Yeah…they don't get it I guess. It's hard enough to make a living with the seasons getting so short. They could at least arrange it so you could fish both," I say as I watch him slow down to trolling speed off my port bow. His deckhand comes out the door and heads for the pit to set the gear.

"We're going to get 'em today anyway. What did you think of that rotten bait Pelican's trying to palm off on us? I raised hell with the manager and he promised to have some of this year's herring in on the next packer. I can't believe those cheap bastards; I've been reminding John all spring to order it. Luckily Pop had a case in the freezer up at Little Port, or I'd of been really ticked off," Jim says.

"Yeah, I was stuck with that crap the first two days. That and the price pissed me off so bad I sold to the Howkan. He paid me two bucks straight across for everything, and had a case of bait flown out to me on the company plane; didn't even charge me for the bait. Nice looking stuff too," I answer.

"Huh, well that's neat. I'd have done the same thing. Pelican will probably match prices when the strike is settled, but that bait business outweighs any sense of loyalty I had," Jim says.

"I don't owe them anything. I sell to the highest bidder for now, anyway, till I see how things shape up. Well I better get off the radio and go run through the gear. Catch you later, thanks for the shout," I say hanging up the mike.

"Click click."

"Ahh…the Moocher, the Moocher, you pick me up, Pop, the Moocher," I hear Jim call his dad, who works at the NOAA hatchery up the beach, at Little Port Walter. Big Jim is an avid sport fisherman and is usually out fishing before work in the morning this time of year. Jimmy tries several more times as I run through the gear, but there is no reply. I finish putting the last line back out, then nose in toward the big flat boulder that is one of my line-up marks on the beach. When the bottom comes up to twenty fathoms, I turn and follow the bottom contour south, down the drag toward the point. As I work my way in and out of the nooks and crannies, there are big schools of needlefish boiling on the surface. The seagulls and diver ducks are having a field day. This is a good sign; it means that the salmon are feeding and have driven the schools of baitfish to the surface.

"RATTLE RATTLE RATTLE." Both poles go off at once as I come out of the last hole before the south point of the bay. I am at the end of the drag so I turn out and head back up the thirty fathom contour, to give the boats behind me the right of way while I run through the gear. I land two fish and lose one. By the time the gear is down again, I'm back up by the flat rock. There are so many boats now that I have to go all the way up to Breakfast Rock before I can turn around for my second pass.

The tide is changing and fish are biting at several places along the drag. I see people in the cockpits of all the boats around me. There are about twelve boats on the drag now, and it requires total concentration to work the gear and steer through the drag without running into another boat. You have to keep track of several things at the same time: the depth under the boat, your course, and what the other boats are doing. Your mind must constantly switch from one aspect to another, because the data is constantly changing. Every other person is doing as many different things at the same time as you are, and all it takes is one person to get involved in landing a fish and paying attention to where he is going, to screw up the drag. It's really frustrating to look up and see another boat cutting across your bow and know that in a moment he's going to have to come back out again or hang up on the bottom. Your only option is to turn out and let him pass on the inside.

The bite lasts till about ten-thirty and then dies to nothing. I have ten fish aboard, and as I pass Dick he steps out on deck and flashes me five fingers. I show him both hands and he waves disgustedly at me, then go back inside. I will have to try to convince him again to use bait, although I suspect it will be a waste of breath.

As the morning drags on, I stir up some scrambled eggs for breakfast and listen to the radio chatter, trying to stay awake. You can always tell when the fish stop biting, because the radio traffic increases proportionately. Most of the conversations are like a broken record: complaints about prices, speculation about whether the Fish and Game people are trying to put us all out of business, or somebody who's been rude on the drag. I finally turn it off in disgust. The food has made me sleepy, so I go out and run through the gear to wake up.

This is a difficult time of day; the boredom brings on a tendency to space out. Your mind starts to drift and hours can slip by unnoticed. One of the things that makes a successful fisherman is the ability to stay focused, to keep the gear free of kelp, jelly fish, and trash fish. The baits need to be freshened up every half-hour or so, and by experimenting with different colors and types of lures, sometimes you can get the fish to bite briefly between the major feeding periods. The fish see the same lures going by at the same speed hour after hour and get wise to them and won't hit them. Something unusual behaving differently will sometimes trigger a fish to bite, and that can excite several others into hitting also. These little one or two-fish clatters between the bites add up over the course of a season, and make a significant difference in the paycheck.

The boats are starting to scatter out now, some trolling down to the cape and others up to Conclusion. I know that the fish will probably feed here again sometime later in the day, so I force myself to keep working the main feeding spots. I have learned from experience that if I wander off I may miss the bite. Sometimes though, another school of fish might be feeding a mile up or down the shore, so I keep an eye on the other boats. If they start bunching up somewhere, it may mean that the fish have moved or another bite is starting.

The afternoon wears on, I work the gear up and down a couple of times each hour and scratch out an occasional fish. About four o'clock the Juanita H goes by heading north up the drag. Jim comes out on deck and flashes me twenty-two fingers. I signal three handfuls back. Jim is power trolling and is permitted to run four lines and haul them up with hydraulic motors. I figure I'm doing okay; he is a good fisherman and has twice the gear in the water. He pretends to talk on the radio then goes back inside. I turn the radio back on and say into the mike, "Feels like nap time."

"Yup, this feels like the harbor tack; I can feel the red can pulling on me real hard. Looks like a good afternoon for a barbecue," he replies. I know this routine. The idea is to convince everybody that the fishing is so poor that we are going to quit early. Everyone else is just as bored as we are and having to force themselves to stay on the drag. If they think we are going in, they can justify quitting early and avoid the embarrassment of giving up first. If one boat actually hauls his gear and goes in, several more might be caught up in the frenzy and go in also. The fewer boats on the drag the better the fishing for those of us who tough it out.

"Yeah...(yawn...) can't hardly stay awake. Can't even remember the last time I caught a fish. What you got to cook up?" I say to keep it going.

"We could toast up some halibut; I think Karen saved one back there...yup, she did. I don't know though, maybe just a nap would be the thing to do (long drawn out yawn followed by pregnant silence)."

"Yyyyaaahh…pretty boring, just wasting fuel out here today, might as well tie her up till some fish come around the corner. Maybe the next set of tides will bring something in," I drawl into the mike.

"YAWNNNN…man, I can't stop yawnin'. Yep, that's what I'm goin' to do, enough of this. Hey, Karen, throw them aboard, were outa here," Jim hollers out the door without letting go of the transmit button. Karen is probably standing in the galley trying not to laugh out loud.

"I won't be far behind ya, Cap. Soon as I get up to the rock I'm going to crank mine aboard too. I need a nap, bad," I say, yawning into the mike one more time for effect.

The power of suggestion is almost irresistible and outside of us I see a boat steaming full-bore toward town. Within the next hour or so, several more disappear into the harbor. The ruse has worked and by tide-change there are only a handful of us left on the drag. I see the Spray steam by with a bone in her teeth and black smoke streaming out the stack.

"Quittin' kind of early, ain't ya, Cap?" I say as he rolls past.

"Ah, you guys convinced me; might as well sleep tied to the dock as out here," he answers.

"Okay, I'm going to stick it out through the tide-change, see what happens. Got to keep my momentum up. If I go in this early today, I'll want to quit early tomorrow, and the next day, and the next. Bad habit to get into."

"Gettin' pretty hard core there. First thing you know, you'll be goin' in debt on a bigger boat and a powertroll permit."

"Not bloody likely, Cap, I can barely keep this operation going. Last thing I need is more work to do," I answer.

Dick chuckles and says, "Okay, I'll see you in there after a while. I'm coming up on the entrance, so I better go pull up the poles before I forget."

I click the mike button a couple of times then go out to run through the gear. The evening bite doesn't amount to much; I get one little clatter and land five fish in three short passes. By seven-thirty I'm burned out. I haul the gear for the last time at Breakfast Rock, then head for the harbor. As I approach the red can, I feel a sense of satisfaction through the fatigue. The season is off to a good start and the pre-season anxiety is gone. I'm catching fish and starting to get into the groove. As the boat plows through the glassy, calm waters of the harbor, there is no doubt that this is the life. I live an adventure that most people only dream about!

As I cruise by the dock in the lengthening shadows of evening, I decide to anchor out for the night rather than tie to the dock. Sometimes it's easier to go out early and stay focused if I don't socialize on the dock. You tend to pick up other people's moods, the dock is noisy at night, and it's hard to get to sleep before eleven or later.

I anchor south of the fish plant near the entrance, and after watching the sunset I hit the bunk about nine-thirty for a much-needed rest.

12

The days begin to run together in a blur of early mornings and late nights. The fishing is on again, off again and as the days turn into weeks, May becomes June. The spring run of King salmon to the mainland Alaska rivers is starting to wind down, and some days produce no fish at all or only a few. The Coho run won't begin in earnest till late June or early July, and by then the Canadian, Washington, and Oregon Kings will begin passing through. But for now things are pretty slow.

One sunny, flat-calm morning I head out early, full of what is probably mis- placed optimism. Outside the entrance, I see a strange object floating off Crow Island. It is silhouetted in the morning sun, and I have never seen anything that looks quite like it. After the gear is out, I troll over to it to investigate. The thing turns out to be a brand-new, yellow wheelbarrow, floating there pretty as you please, without a drop of water in it. It's too new to just let it fend for itself on the briny sea, but I haven't room for it aboard. I look around and see the Juanita H coming out the harbor entrance.

"Hey, Jim," I say into the CB, "Guess what I found floating over here—a new yellow wheelbarrow!"

"Ahemm, right," he answers.

"No, I'm serious, there is a wheelbarrow floating over here. It's brand-new and floating high and dry. I'd pick it up but I don't have room for it. You ought to check it out," I reply.

"You're kidding. A wheelbarrow? Oh yeah, I see it floating there now, we'll swing by and try to pick it up. I wonder where the heck that came from?"

"I don't know, but it's a dandy, that's for sure," I say, pointing the boat toward Breakfast Rock to give them room.

93

"Huh, you weren't joking, it is a dandy," Jim says breathlessly, a few minutes later.

"It was a struggle but we got it aboard. It's a beaut' too, not a scratch on it. Thanks man, I can really use it, my old one is about shot."

I click the mike in reply, then go out to land the fish that is rattling on my port pole. The fish is a humpy, but I throw it aboard anyway for the eggs, which are worth a buck a pound.

As I work, I hear Noel Johnson on the Ruthless say, "Gee Jim, you could keep that wheelbarrow aboard, then Karen could prop you up with cushions so you're nice and comfy. When you wanted to go out on deck she could just wheel you out, you'd never have to get up; think of all the energy you'd save."

"I was thinking about that. We could mount an umbrella on it to keep the sun and rain from ruining my complexion," Jim says back.

I have to put in my two cents worth so I go inside and pick up the mike. When Jim keys off I say, "Yeah, you'd have to mount the CB on it though, so you could talk on the radio. Probably need a coffee pot too."

"Then there's the remote for the auto pilot, so you could steer. Hell, I wish I had room for one in my wheelhouse," Noel says.

"Heck, maybe I should start manufacturing them to sell to the fleet. The way fishing is this morning I'd probably do better at that. 'Little Jim's Patented Wheelhousebarrow, The Troller's Friend, just ninety-nine-ninety-five plus tax.' I'd get rich. Why I'd be able to support my trolling habit without having to borrow money from the State," Jim replies.

"Hey, I found the wheelbarrow, you got to cut me in for half," I shout back.

"Wait a minute, it was my idea, I should get a third at least," Noel says.

"Oh yeah, then there would be expenses and capital gains tax and all the other complications of running a business. I think I'll just take it home and haul beer in it or something; keep life simple," Jim says.

A new voice breaks in, "Are you guys talking about a wheelbarrow? I left a yellow one on the beach last night and the tide floated it away. I've been looking for it all morning. It doesn't even belong to me; I borrowed it from a neighbor. I'd sure like to get it back," the voice says earnestly.

"Yeah, I got it, we found it at Crow Island a while ago. You can pick it up at the dock tonight when I come in," Jim answers.

"Hey, thanks a lot man, I thought it was gone for good. Thought I was going to have to buy a new one for the guy I borrowed it from. I'll see you tonight when you tie up, I'm out."

"Ah, too bad for you, Cap, so much for the big plan. I guess you'll just have to make it fishin'," Noel says sympathetically.

"Yeah, it was close there for a while. I could see the light shinin' at the end of the tunnel, but it slipped right through my fingers," Jim replies sadly.

More days slip into the past and one morning Dick and I are standing on the end of the pier drinking coffee, trying to come up with a legitiment excuse for not going fishing. The Kimshew is tied to the pilings on the face of the fishhouse dock, and as we stand there we see Little Jim climb down the ladder, then step carefully aboard. He did something in the cockpit for a few minutes then climbed off the Kimshew and went back up the ladder. After a few minutes he came sauntering down the pier toward us with a satisfied grin on his face.

"What the hell you up to now?" I ask as he walks up to us.

"Oh, Cap Skeel was bragging last night about some big bite he was in at Katz Bay last year. He was going on and on about having a big slug on every hook, so I gathered up a coffee can full of garden slugs this morning and I just put one on every one of his hooks. I covered them back up with the burlap bags he had over his gear, and he'll never know it till he goes to put his lines out. I'd like to see the look on his face when he finds them this morning," he says, chuckling.

"You should have seen him last fall at Home Shore, up in Icy Strait. One night "Smiley" and I, and Berney Oster, switched his leads for these cute little one-ounce sinkers we bought in the store at Hoonah. They were about an inch and a half in diameter and had a swivel molded in; looked just like tiny trolling leads. We hid his cannonballs under the deck ahead of the pit, and tied the sinkers on to the breaker straps, then set them in the cannonball holders just like the real thing. He was the last one out of the harbor that morning, and we saw him slow down on the drag and go back to the pit to put the gear in the water. He was right beside Smiley, and I guess he didn't notice what we had done. Smiley said he grabbed the wire to heave the first lead over the side. He was expecting a heavy weight, and when the little sinker came out of the holder it swung around and smacked him in the forehead. Smiley could hear him cussing up a blue streak and fumbling around looking for his real cannonballs. Finally he went in the wheel-house and took off for town; couldn't find the leads, they were right there under some stuff in the pit. Boy was he pissed; he was mad at us for the rest of the summer. I can't wait till he sees those slugs," Jim says, laughing, as he heads on down the ramp.

John played it cool and didn't mention the incident for a long time; he was getting used to being the butt of Jimmy's humor and got in a few licks of his own now and then. To this day Jim still asks him once in a while if he has been catching any big slugs lately.

June turns into July, and a few Cohos are starting to show up. The Salmonberries are ripe, and rumor had it that someone was going to roast a whole pig underground on the Fourth of July. There would be free beer and a big picnic in Back Bay, a small cove east of the board-walk.

In the twenties and thirties, there were a lot of people that worked in the canneries, whaling stations, and herring reduction plants of lower Chatham Strait. Port Alexander was town to most of these people, and it was really booming. There were sometimes as many as two thousand people living in P.A. in the summer and many more scattered up and down the strait. P.A. was always famous for it's Fourth of July celebrations, and people came from all around to celebrate the holiday.

One year, a big boxing match was scheduled between a couple of semi-famous prizefighters from back east. It was the talk of the whole area that summer, and on the morning of the big day a huge crowd had gathered. There was standing room only around the ring that had been built on the cold storage property, and the bars were doing a sellout business. Most of the sports fans were pretty well oiled, and about an hour before the fight was to start, an argument broke out in the waiting crowd. Such a terrible fistfight ensued that the ring was wrecked and several people were hurt. So much damage was done to the ring and the nearby business that the match had to be canceled. Things have mellowed out some around P.A. lately, but if you mix enough booze and enough fishermen, who knows what might happen. I decide to go fishing.

By two o'clock I only have five small Cohos aboard, so I decide to go in and partake of the festivities after all. When I arrive at the party most of the pig is gone, but the beer keg is still producing. I tap a beer and wander around, mixing with the crowd. Everyone has a pretty good buzz on, including Dirty Dick, who has homesteaded the beer keg. When he thinks nobody is looking, he sticks the tap in his mouth and guzzles beer till it runs out of his mouth. One of the women spots him and begins to protest his disgusting behavior. Dick makes a crude remark and takes another blast off the beer hose. Bernie Oster, off the Alice May, spots him and yanks the hose out of his hand.

"What the hell's the matter with you, Dick? For God's sake, get a cup; nobody wants to drink your slobber!" he says angrily, rinsing the hose off in a tote of half-melted ice with cans of pop floating in it.

"BUWHGHAAAAAAA!" Dick laughs his guttural laugh and says something unprintable.

"I think you better leave, Dick; there are wimmin' and kids here, and they don't need to listen to your drunken filth," Bernie says, getting right in Whitham's face. Dirty Dick gives him a shove and the fight is on. It's not much of a fight, mostly a shout and shove match, and Bernie finally tips Dick over and drags him bodily, by the leg, through the narrow band of woods to the main boardwalk.

"If I see you here again, I'm really going to kick your ass!" we hear Bernie shout through the woods. Things mellow out after that and we pass a pleasant afternoon visiting and enjoying the good food and the beer.

When it starts to get dark I head back to the dock to hit the rack. The Betty B is tied at the foot of the ramp, on the outside of the float, and I can see Greg Smith in the lighted wheelhouse as I walked down the ramp. On the dock beside Greg's boat is a wet spot and one of Dirty Dick's deck slippers.

"Hey Greg," I yell at the Betty B.

"What's up," he says, stepping out of the house.

"This looks like Dick Whitham's shoe; I wonder if he fell in or something," I say, pointing to the shoe.

"Oh yeah, he was on the Talon acting like an ass a while ago, and Bob threw him overboard. I was down here reading and heard something thumping against the hull. I came out on deck to see what was making the racket, and found Dick in the water between the boat and the dock. He had paddled all the way down from the Talon, trying to find a place to climb out. I let him soak till he promised to go home and sober up, then I helped him out on the dock. He laid there at the foot of the ramp for a while, singing and shouting, till I had to offer to throw him in again. He finally left. I don't know why he left his shoe; probably too drunk to notice it was missing," Greg says, laughing.

"Okay, I just wanted to make sure he was a lright. 'Night Greg, see you out there tomorrow."

"I'll be there," he says, as I walk off up the dock. I go on home and crawl into bed, congratulating myself for staying sober and looking forward to the next day of fishing.

13

July is fog month in Lower Chatham. Fog really makes trolling interesting if you are alone on the boat and have no radar. I'm a couple of miles offshore, tacking back and forth between Eagle Rock and Cape Ommaney, working a tide line. I've been getting nice little clatters of Cohos all morning, and by ten o'clock already have about twenty-five fish aboard. It's easy fishing, just troll west for an hour or so, then turn around and fish back east. I'm out in the ocean far enough that my sixty-fathom depth sounder isn't even registering the bottom. The rest of the fleet is scattered out enough that I hardly have to pay attention to anything but running the gear up and down, and avoiding the occasional kelp island.

There has been a fog bank on the southern horizon all morning, and as I run a line up I notice a cold, damp breeze coming from the direction of the fog. It has been a warm, windless morning so far, and the wind gets my attention immediately. I look south and realize that the fog is only about a half-mile off, and it looks thicker than before. By the time I finish running the gear, the sunlight has started to pale and the fog is just a few hundred yards away. I look toward the cape and realize that there is no way I can make it back into Chatham before the fog catches me. Even as I think, the first tendrils begin wafting past on the chill breeze. I feel a moment of panic but soon realize it isn't that much of a problem if I keep my wits. I turn the bow toward Cape Omanney and Wooden Island, and when the compass settles down from the turn, I write the heading to the cape on a piece of scrap paper on the binnacle: 026 degrees.

Within minutes I can see nothing. The sky is a featureless gray and the water is a gray, green disc that disappears into the mist a few yards away in all directions. It's like being inside a wet pearl. The only visual references are vertical and the compass needle.

"Let's see, I'm about three miles off the cape. All I have to do is stay on this heading until I'm in twenty fathoms. The tide is ebbing, so the current should carry me to the NW. When I pick up the twenty-fathom contour, I can turn right and follow it around Wooden Island into the strait. I am familiar enough with the bottom in Chatham that I can follow the twenty fathom line all the way to the red can if I need to." My confidence begins to come back and I concentrate on keeping the compass needle on 026 degrees, looking out the window frequently to avoid kelp islands.

There are fish on both lines, so I go out and haul them up. It's hard to stay on course because the boat has a tendency to turn away from the line I have up. I have to step into the house often to put the boat back on course. When I'm finished and the fish are cleaned and in the hold, I make a cup of coffee and sit at the wheel, watching the compass needle and the fathometer. It seems like hours have passed since the fog moved in, and I glance at the clock, wishing I had written down the time when I took the bearing on Wooden Island. It's 11:45 and I esti-mate that about an hour has past.

"Should be picking up bottom any time now," I think, turning up the gain on the depth sounder. Nothing…

More time passes. It's 12:30; still no reading on the meter.

"Maybe I'm going the wrong direction! No, I was SW of Wooden Island when the fog came in. Just trust the compass and keep your eyes peeled for the beach," I tell myself, peering out the windows. I look at the clock, check the depth sounder, and look at the compass. I'm starting to get a headache from concentrating so hard. It's almost one o'clock and still no bottom.

"Damn! Something's wrong here." I suddenly see what looks like surf ahead, barely visible through the fog. I glance at the meter; still no bot-tom.

"This isn't right. If I can see surf, the fathometer should be registering bottom. Where the hell am I, anyway?" Suddenly I see what I thought

was surf is only a line of foam along a tide rip. Now I'm really confused; I start not trusting the compass. I look around into the fog. Out the port window, off in the distance, I see a tug with two barges in tow, about a mile away.

"What the...I must have been going the wrong way and I'm clear out in the shipping lane, five or six miles farther out than I was! Something must be wrong with the compass." I point the bow at the tug, and in a few minutes it resolves into a seagull and two card board boxes! Suddenly another troller idles out of the fog. As we pass a few yards apart, Dave Gifford steps out on deck of the Col. Lindy.

I lean out the window and shout, "Where the hell are we, anyway?"

"Damned if I know. I was heading east a couple of miles off Eagle Rocks when the fog settled in," he yells back.

"Is your fathometer showing bottom?" I ask.

He looks inside."I'm showing about ninety fathoms," he answers. Dave shrugs as the Col. Lindy disappears into the fog.

"Well I'm not the only one lost anyway," I think to myself. I put the compass needle back on 026 degrees and make another cup of coffee.

The next time I look out the port window I see the top of a mountain through the mist. I can't see enough of it to tell which one it is, and as it disappears again I realize it is west of me (?). If I'm coming up on the cape from the SW, I should see Ommaney Mountain ahead, to the NE. I check the compass...it still shows 026 degrees. I look at the depth sounder...its still blank! Now I'm really confused. I can't think of anything to do but stay on the original course and hope the fog burns off soon.

Suddenly the sky turns blue overhead, and in a few minutes I come out of the fog into clear air. I'm almost straight east of Poor Man Point! Went right by the cape without seeing it and up into Chatham Strait. The reason the fathometer isn't showing bottom is because I'm a couple of miles offshore, in about two hundred fathoms. Dave must have been right on the corner, at Wooden Island, when I passed him.

WHEWWW! I heave a big sigh of relief and turn toward the Poor Man drag, glad to finally be out in the world again. As I troll in toward the beach, I remember a few years ago on a very similar day.

I was fishing between Poor Man and the cape one morning when the fog rolled in like it did today. I was heading north toward town on the twenty-fathom line, when the fog caught me. It was no problem to stay on the twenty and follow it to Breakfast Rock, then to the harbor entrance. I was very familiar with the bottom here, and never lost track of where I was.

When I had almost reached Breakfast Rock, I heard an engine at running speed coming up from behind. In a moment, a big double-ender charged out of the fog. She was making about six knots and crossing my stern, heading straight toward trouble. There is a reef that extends from Dude Ranch Point out to Breakfast Rock, like a series of jagged black teeth, and she was heading right for it. In a moment he disappeared into the fog. I grabbed the mike and shouted on channel five, the local calling frequency.

"HELENA! STOP! YOU'RE HEADING FOR THE REEF!"

I heard the engine on the other boat slow down suddenly and heard the transmission clunk into reverse at too high an RPM. The engine screamed at full throttle for a few seconds. I expected to hear the boat crash on the rocks any second. I shifted into neutral as the other engine sound faded away to nothing. In a couple of minutes, I heard it idling toward me, then saw the bow of the other boat emerge from the fog, going dead slow.

They stopped alongside and the shaken skipper came out on deck.

"Do you know where we are?" he shouted across the few yards separating our boats.

"Stay on my stern while I pull my gear and I'll lead you in. We're just south of Breakfast Rock," I answer.

"Okay, thanks. I've never been here before; I'll stay right behind you," he said as I put the boat in gear, then went out to pull the lines.

The fog was lifting by the time we entered the harbor, and when we were finally tied to the dock the three young men came over and thanked me for leading them in. They didn't hear me on the radio; they were standing by on a different channel. They had seen the bottom come up suddenly on the fathometer and reversed hard to stop just short of one of the rocks. They were lucky the skipper happened to look at the meter when he did; in another few seconds they would have hit the rock at six knots. They would have been lucky to survive. I gave the young skipper a short lecture about the irresponsibility of running at full speed toward a strange harbor in the fog with no radar. I hope they learned something that day.

There are quite a few boats in; the fishing has been dead on the inside drags and the fog has made the outside un-fishable for anyone without radar. Dick isn't aboard the Spray, so I walk down the dock to see what's happening. The old timer is visiting with Bud and Celia. They are sitting on the bullrail beside the Celedo, soaking up the morning sun..

"There he is, Mister Hard-core himself. What are you going to do with all your money?" Dick asks with a feisty grin.

"A couple more years of hard-coring it and I figure I'll be able to lounge on the dock all day with the rest of you ner'-do-wells," I reply, lowering myself to the dock in the shade of Bud's boat with a sigh.

"Any fish on the outside?" Bud asks.

"Well, there were a few before the fog came in, but nothing to write home about. You could probably scratch out forty or so, if you could stay all day. It's too spooky in the fog though; you can only see a couple hundred feet. With all those other boats wandering around just as blind as you are, I'm afraid of running into somebody while I'm in the pit. It's also hard to keep the boat going in a straight line when you can't see where you're going." I tell them about getting lost, and they chuckle at the image of the seagull and the two boxes.

"I have enough trouble keeping track of where I am when it's clear, I sure don't need to fish in the fog," Dick says.

"Be nice to have a radar, just to find your way back to the harbor if the fog moves in. Maybe someday..." Bud says with a sigh.

"What I want first is one of those new Furuno chart recorders. I'm tired of keeping track of how many times the damn blinker on my old fathometer has gone around," I say. "I heard Dave on the Col. Lindy can order one on his business license for about four hundred bucks," Dick says.

"Really!" I reply with sudden interest. "I think I'm going to order one; that's the best price I've heard anywhere."

"Yeah, talk to his wife; she does the ordering. I've been thinking about getting one too. We might as well have her order them both at the same time," Dick says.

As we chat, Celia comes off the boat and says, "I'm going to the store, can I get anything for either of you?"

"No thanks, I've been there already," Dick answers, and I decline also. As she climbs the ramp to the pier, we hear an airplane approaching from the north.

"Fog must have finally lifted in Sitka, the mail-plane has been on hold all day," Bud says, as we watch the Beaver fly past, then turn and land from the south.

As the plane is unloading, we hear Dirty Dick's guttural laughter from the airplane float, and soon we see him heading down the dock toward us.

"Where has that old shit been?" I ask. "I haven't seen hide nor hair of him since Bernie ran him off from the Fourth of July party," I ask as he approaches.

"I heard he had to go to court for stealing a front-end loader and driving it over the top of a taxi cab down in Craig last winter," Bud answers.

"Too bad they didn't lock him up for a while," Dick says with disgust.

When he arrives where we are sitting, he stops and stands over us, weaving drunkenly and looking at us with a maniacal grin on his face.

He is wearing a brand-new, gray, wool coat, new deck shoes, and a brilliant white, snap-brim halibut hat, set at a jaunty angle on his Neanderthal brow. He has a case of beer under one arm and a half- gallon of rum in his other hand. He is obviously drunk as a lord, and I dread dealing with him for the rest of the day around the float.

"Hello, Mr. McConnell," he growls, spit flying out of his mouthful of rotten, nicotine-stained teeth. The phlegmy goo runs down his stubbled chin and he wipes it on the sleeve of his new coat.

"Well, it's the 'Taurantasaurus Dick'. I was hoping they had locked you up and thrown away the key," I say. Several people have gathered to watch the show and a chuckle ripples through the crowd. "Why don't you take your booze and head for home, so we don't have to look at you making a fool of yourself all afternoon," I add. He gazes at me stupidly.

"It's really a shame what you're doing to yourself with liquor, Dick. You are a pretty decent guy when you're sober. Hell of a good fisherman, too, but when you're drunk you're nothin' but a royal pain in the ass," I pontificate self-righteously.

"Ya know, Mr. McConnell, I been trying to bring you up to my level for years now, but I think you're just a little bit too slow. BUWAGHAAAGHHHG!"

We all bust out laughing. This statement is so out of character with the image of this drunken baffoon standing before us with snot running down his chin, that it's impossible to not appreciate the humor of the scene. About then, Steve Preston, whose boat the Celeste is moored at the foot of the ramp behind the Celedo, walks up from the direction of the airplane float. He's carrying a box and a backpack and is also wearing a wool jacket and a white halibut hat similar to Dirty Dick's. As he passes, Whitham follows him and they go aboard the Celeste. We laugh some more at the antics of this backwoods jester and from time to time we can hear his guttural laugh issuing from the wheelhouse of the Celeste.

Soon we see Celia strolling down the pier, carrying a sack of groceries. She comes down the ramp, and as she passes the Celeste at the bottom, she says in a pleasant tone to the figure sitting in the wheelhouse window with its back to the dock, "Hello Steve, welcome back. How was your trip to town?"

Unfortunately it's Whitham and not Steve sitting there, and as she speaks he turns and gives her a black-toothed, lascivious leer and lets go a bellow of drunken laughter. With a shriek of terror, Celia's groceries go flying, and in the blink of an eye, she is aboard the Celedo and in the wheelhouse.

Now Celia is a very cultured and refined lady. She is a concert cellist and plays professionally in a famous orchestra in Seattle during the off-season. The sight of Dirty Dick's gruesome countenance leering from the window, and the guttural bellow of maniacal laughter, coupled with the fact that she has never laid eyes on the "dirty" one before, is more than she can stand and still maintain her composure. We can hear her crying in the cabin and Bud goes in to comfort her. The other Dick and I round up Celia's groceries and take them aboard the boat. Bud is rubbing her shoulders while she cries and laughs at the same time.

"Thanks you guys, I'm sorry I lost it out there, but the sight of that horrible man when I was expecting Steve was too much! And that laugh! It really frightened me. I lost my grip on reality for a few seconds and all I could think of was to run," she says, blowing her nose and drying her eyes on a handkerchief.

"That's okay, the sight of him is enough to freak anybody out. I don't think you need to be afraid of him. He's not dangerous, in spite of his looks; just obnoxious and annoying when he's drunk. Actually, he's pretty likable when he's not drinking, but when he's on the booze, he's a total pain," I say as she puts the food away.

"Thanks, I just hope he stays away from me, I don't like him. Would you guys like to stay for dinner? I'm making spaghetti with meat sauce and garlic bread. There will be plenty for all of us, and I'd like you to stay," she says, starts to pull herself back together.

"You bet! Sure!" we reply in unison and without hesitation, glad of the opportunity to eat something that Dick didn't dump out of a tin can, for a change. Bud makes coffee for everyone and we exchange yarns and fish stories while the food cooks.

Bud is an interesting man and has lots of good stories to tell. He was a mining engineer for many years and has worked all over the world. He entertains us with tales of the Australian Outback, the mines of Peru, and the jungles of Brazil. The food is as good as the company and we all enjoy a pleasant dinner and evening. Dick and I say good-night about nine-thirty and as we head home, we can hear Dirty Dick singing "Allouettahhh, allouettahhh," somewhere off in the distance. As I climb aboard and hit the bunk I am thankful that he has gone home for the night.

14

"**A**hoy there, mates, there's a big white vessel with a red stripe down the side headin' our way. You better put out them joints and throw all those eatin' fish back in the lake," an anonymous voice drawls out of the speaker on the CB. I look north up the strait, and sure enough the Coast Guard Cutter is steaming our way with a bone in her teeth.

In the past they pretty much left us alone while we were fishing, but this year, because of budget cuts by the Federal government, they have started doing fisheries patrols for the State of Alaska. The State is paying them, so the money they provide offsets the funding that the Coast Guard has lost. It also benefits the State in that they don't have to buy, maintain, and equip as many patrol vessels and officers.

Many of the crew members on the Coast Guard vessels have done tours of duty off the coasts of Florida and in the Caribbean where they have had to deal with all manner of drug smugglers, pirates, and illegal immigrants. They seem to see every one of us as a threatening, potential criminal and so they come aboard our boats armed to the teeth and loaded for trouble.

You combine their zeal with a fleet of hard-core, freedom-loving individualists who are just trying to eke out an honest living and the mix is volatile, to say the least. There is something about the idea of government gun-boats crewed with uniformed storm troopers, who have the right to board you anytime they wish whether you like it or not, that tends to tighten the jaws of men, many of whom fought in Vietnam and whose fathers fought the Nazis.

Adding fuel to the fire is a new regulation passed by the State limiting handtrollers to two lines instead of four. In the early-seventies there was a great influx of people into Alaska, brought on by the building of the oil pipeline from Prudhoe Bay to Valdez. SE Alaska, being closest to the Lower 48 caught a lot of people who heard about the fantastic wages being paid on the pipeline. They checked the map, picked the nearest part of Alaska, and spent their last few dollars on a ticket to Ketchikan, or one of the other fishing or logging towns, along the ferry routes from Seattle. What they failed to notice was that Ketchikan is hundreds of miles from the pipeline. The upshot was that many of them took jobs as deckhands on fishing boats and became hooked on the lifestyle.

In those days you could buy a license to fish Salmon or Halibut for fifty bucks, and if you had the resources to put together a skiff and outboard motor and a little bit of gear, you were in business.

Within a couple of years the fish stocks, which were in trouble anyway because of several factors such as decline in feed stocks and overfishing, started to feel the impact of the increase in gear pressure. Something needed to be done and the response of the wildlife managers was to shorten the seasons, but this was not enough. The old timers, who were feeling the pinch, started to complain about the shortened seasons and the crowding on the grounds, and after a couple of years of bitter debate, a limited entry program was created that limited the number of boats that could participate in the Salmon fisheries. A point system based on past participation and residency was established to determine who got a permit and who didn't. In the troll fishery there were two gear groups: those who used some type of power to crank their lines up and down, and those who did it by hand.

Handtrolling had a long history in the fleet, and the first commercial trollers were probably handtrollers. Anyway, when the dust finally settled in the mid-seventies, there were a 947 powertroll permits and about 2157 handtroll permits issued, and most of them were transferable. You could sell them.

The powertrollers formed an organization called the Alaska Trollers Association, which handtrollers were not allowed to join. For the next few years the ATA fought to eliminate the handtrollers completely.

Whenever the Fish And Game wanted to shorten the season or limit us in anyway, there was always a big battle with the powertrollers, trying to get rid of the handtrollers and the handtrollers fighting for their rights to fish.

In 1980, in order to lower the gear pressure on the fish, the ADF&G decided to limit the handtrollers to two lines. The handtrollers knew in their hearts that the government officials had caved in to pressure from the powerful ATA lobby, and so there was al of hard feelings in the fleet.

Part of the duties the State passed on to the Coast Guard was to enforce the new regulation and see that the handtrollers were not fishing with four lines. They would hit a drag with a mixed fleet and single-out the handtrollers to board, not even stopping the powertroll boats. Needless to say, we were not too happy about it. This unfortunate situation created a lot of hard feelings toward the Coast Guard. The boarding procedure, which was designed for a more hazardous environment, tended to fan the flames. Some of the boarding officers had a chip on their shoulders, and their attitude tended to bring out the rebel in us, which was already simmering just under the surface because of the radical cut in gear we were having to get used to.

The ninety-foot cutter Cape Romaine slows to an idle just outside the drag, then turns and stops perpendicular to the line we are working. They unload a big Zodiac skiff while the cutter is completely blocking the drag. The noise and sheer bulk of it kills the nice Coho bite we've had going all morning. I consider this a rude and unnecessary display of power and keep my boat pointed right at its starboard side amidships, then turn to pass astern of it at the last possible moment. As I pass by the bridge several officers step out on the wing bridge with M-16's prominently displayed. I guess they think I'm on some kind of Kamikaze suicide mission in my twenty-one foot wooden boat, but instead of ramming them, I just step out of the wheelhouse and shout, "GET OFF THE F_ _ _ _ ING DRAG, WE'RE TRYING TO MAKE A LIVING HERE!" The last thing I see as I turn past their stern and head on down the drag is one of the officers stepping into the wheelhouse. I must have got my point across because the Cutter soon backs out into the strait until it is clear of the line of boats working the drag.

The Zodiac is in the water as I idle back north and is approaching the Sad-Eyed Lady. Steve still has bow poles on his boat and that got their attention right away. The gray, rubber skiff idles alongside him for a long time before I finally see two of the boarding party climb over into his trolling pit. They are on Steve's boat for a long time and I never see Steve come out of the house. Finally they board the Zodiac and head my way.

"Afternoon skipper, we'd like to come aboard and check your papers," one of them says politely, as they come alongside. There are six of them in the raft, all armed to the teeth with shotguns, assault rifles, and pistols.

"Do I have any choice?" I ask in the same phony, polite tone that he used.

"Well, you could refuse, but we'll just have a warrant sworn out for your arrest, and the State troopers will come down and serve it," he replays with a grin.

"Come aboard, then. We had a pretty good bite going here, so I would appreciate it if you would get this over with as soon as possible so I can get back to earning a living."

Three of them climb aboard and the one doing all the talking asks to see my fishing license and boat registration. I invite him into the wheelhouse and offer him a seat opposite the helm. I sit behind the wheel and hand him the papers he asked for.

"Before we start, do you have any loaded firearms aboard?" he asks.

"Why do you want to know?" I ask in return.

"I'm following procedure mandated by the Commandant of the Coast Guard, and that is the first thing I am required to ask," he answers.

"Yes, I have one pistol that is loaded," I say pointing to the Smith and Wesson, 9mm automatic hanging on the throttle handle in its holster.

"Would you unload it now, please," he asks.

"Why should I? You are here at my invitation, this is my home, and the Constitution of The United States guarantees me the right to keep and bear arms. I have not been found in violation of any laws, and have made no threatening gesture toward you or your men."

"I would feel more comfortable if you would unload it, so we can get on with our inspection," he says.

"Well, you're all armed with pistols; I see the hammers are cocked, which leads me to believe that they have a round in the chamber. That not only makes me uncomfortable, I also consider it rude to enter another man's home with a loaded weapon. How do I know that one of you won't misinterpret my actions and start shooting, or that one of the weapons won't discharge accidentally? I'll tell you what, if you unload yours, I'll unload mine," I offer politely.

"I'm not allowed by regulation to do that. If you won't unload it, my only choice is to end the boarding and report the incident to my superior officer. Once again, the next step is a warrant for your arrest for refusing to cooperate," he threatens.

"Well, I'm tempted to let you do that because I think these regulations are too severe and my rights are being infringed upon. However, since I can't afford to loose the fishing time going to jail and court, I will unload the weapon."

"Thank you. I'll make a note of your protests in my report and talk with my superiors about this; maybe the rules can be modified somewhat in this area."

I pull the pistol out of the holster and drop the magazine out in my lap. Then I pull the slide back, catching the round that is in the chamber as it falls out the magazine well in the bottom of the handle. I put the cartridge on top of the compass, lock the slide open, and hand him the pistol butt first. He looks it over and gives it back the same way. I take it from him, shove the clip into the handle, and drop the slide closed. As the slide falls shut, in plain sight of all three men, it strips another round from the magazine into the firing chamber. I lock the safety and shove the pistol back into the holster. For all their training, they all three miss the fact that the gun is now loaded again, with a round in the chamber just like it was to begin with. The only difference being it now contains only fourteen rounds instead of fifteen.

I gloat with boyish satisfaction at my small victory while he records the data off my papers and hands them back.

"Everything seems to be in order, but what is this black substance in your bilge, it looks like fuel oil to me?" he asks, reaching down under the motor and sticking his finger in the water for a sample.

"It's fish blood. The cockpit bilge is common with the engine compartment; it runs through the floorboards into the bilge and collects here. Considering the fact that this is a gas engine, if the bilge was full of fuel we would have probably exploded by now," I answer, pointing to the spark plugs that are prominent on top of the engine. He takes a paper towel out of his pocket and carefully wipes his fingers, saying nothing more about the bilge.

He steps over the engine and exits the wheelhouse and I follow him out. As he and I and his two minions stand in the cockpit, he says officiously, "Well, everything seems to be in order, except this halibut." He points to the small fish lying on deck.

"I'm going to have to cite you for that," he says with a note of triumph in his voice.

"I don't think so. The second halibut season opened at noon today, and according to the regulations, handtroll gear is legal for halibut. I am allowed up to twenty percent of my load to be halibut on a troll license," I reply confidently.

"Well, I think your wrong. I'm going to call the skipper of my boat and have him check," he says. I reach in the pilothouse for my copy of the regulations and open it to the page that states that I'm legal. I hand him the book and he reads the paragraph I have indicated. He hands the book back curtly and motions the Zodiac alongside. They board their skiff without another word and roar back to the cutter. All the other handtrollers have scattered to the four winds, and as soon as they have the Zodiac aboard, they steam off looking for better pickings.

I feel a twinge of regret for giving the young lieutenant such a hard time; he really wasn't that bad and probably deserved better treatment. However, those boarding officers are the pointy end of the stick and are here by choice. They are the main contact point between those who rule and those who are ruled. It's never been an easy relationship.

Soon the boats start reappearing out of Conclusion Bay and Port Lucy where they have hidden while the boarding party was busy with Steve and I. The bite we had going has tapered off to nothing, so I pull the lines aboard about four and head for town. The conversation on the dock this evening is centered on the boarding, and those of us who experienced it directly compare notes. Apparently, Steve's method of dealing with them was to stay in the wheelhouse and ignore them. During the whole encounter he never made eye contact or spoke a single word. They looked in his hold and poked around in his trolling pit for a while then finally gave up and left. They wrote him up for several infractions and left the ticket on his dash. His was the only boat they were able to find any violations on. Their time and the taxpayers money could have been better utilized than flexing the government muscle before a bunch of people who were not in violation of the law, and had no intention of being so. The ticket they gave Steve was for fire extinguishers being out of date and having a halibut aboard, which was legal at the time.

Once again, I want to make it clear that the heroic search and rescue and navigation aid work, along with the countless other services the Coast Guard performs, is deeply appreciated by those of us who make our living on the water. What is unfortunate is that the State and Federal Governments have turned them into fish cops, to police our own fleet. This creates undeserved hard feelings and really accomplishes little to preserve the fish stocks.

While the incidents related above are happening Korean, Japanese, and other foreign vessels are fishing with illegal gear in violation of international agreements concerning fisheries management. The miles long, monofilament, gill nets they are using are so devastating to the salmon stocks that the few fish caught by handtrollers fishing four lines doesn't even merit consideration. It is common practice by these foreign fleets to dispose of worn out nets by dumping them overboard at sea. These nets continue to fish for months, even years, after they are abandoned. Birds, whales, and other predators also become trapped while feeding on the fish caught in these grotesque, floating, carrion bundles and the damage to many species can only be guessed at. During the early-eighties, the by-catch by trawlers and high-seas gill-netters was estimated to be double the amount the American and Canadian fishermen were allowed to catch. Not only were they stealing the fish, often the fish were winding up on the same international markets that we were dependent upon. That's where management should be concentrating its efforts, not on the lowest impact fishery in the country.

The talking and complaining helped us vent our frustration and I eventually drifted off home to bed. Tomorrow was to be a better day.

15

When the alarm goes off I get up and begin my morning routine: starting the engine, untying the lines, and lowering the poles. By the time I clear the red can, I can see several boats ahead of me and others are pulling away from the dock. I decide to try fishing at Wooden Island today. I had heard a rumor around the dock that fishing was better there than north of town, where I had been trolling the last few days.

When the engine is at operating temperature, I throttle up to running speed and point the bow to pass through the gap between Breakfast Rock and the reef. There are boats scattered everywhere, with no particular group at any one spot, so I figure I might as well run down to the cape before putting the gear in the water. It's a beautiful, calm morning and I savor the golden sunrise and a second cup of coffee as the boat hums her way south toward the ocean.

I finish my coffee just past Poor Man Point and decide to put the gear down before I get to Wooden Island. There are several boats bunched up there and I figure it will be safer to get the lines fishing before I reach the heavy traffic.

I lift the starboard cannonball out of its holder and let it hang on the brake while I snap on the bottom spread. I feather the line down to the two-fathom markers and reset the brake. As I throw out the second lure and reach for the wire with the snap, the wire pulls back sharply and starts to bounce. I snap the leader back on the gear tray, and as I start to crank the gerdy, a big Coho leaps into the air behind the boat. The fish dances across the shimmering surface on his tail then disappears beneath the surface. My heart pounds with sudden excitement, and after a short struggle I throw him aboard. As I let the line back down and start to reach for the second spread, the line takes off again. I crank it back up and land another nice fat Coho. As I let the lead down for the third time, another fish hits the spoon, and it finally registers on my brain that the thing to do is get both lines down as soon as I can, so the other nineteen lures can start fishing too.

As I let the lines down I change out the flashers and replace them with all

Coho spoons. The spoons are faster in a heavy bite, and less likely to tangle in the frantic confusion. If the fish are really clattering, they will bite anything that moves, and the faster you can run the gear, the more fish you catch. This is where the powertrollers really have an advantage over hand-cranked gear. The hydraulic motor hauls the line steadily and all you have to do is unsnap the leaders as they reach the surface, and coil them down on deck. Powertrollers are also allowed to fish four lines, so they have twice as many lures in the water and are really able to clean up in a hot bite.

By the time both lines are down, the poles are pumping up and down frantically, so I go back to the starboard line and run it up as fast as I can. There is a fish on every hook! Some of them escape at the gaff, but I am able to land most of them. As I let the line back out, I can feel the fish hitting the spoons as they disappear beneath the surface. I ignore them and when the line is back down. I go run the other one. There is a fish on every hook here also, and as I put this line back out I can feel the spreads loading up.

The Nomad is so small that it has no deck in front of the cockpit to land fish on, so I have to bring them into the cockpit where I stand as I work the gear. Soon the deck is covered with fish and blood is flying everywhere. I wasn't expecting this kind of fishing today, so I hadn't bothered to put on my rain gear. By the end of the first hour, I'm soaked to the skin and covered with blood. The slaughter bin, under the gear tray, is filling up fast and the deck is so slick with blood and fish that I can hardly stay on my feet. The Salmon are feeding on Needlefish and are so full that the small fish are spewing out of the Coho's mouths and adding to the mess under my feet.

I'm running the gear up and down so fast that some of the leaders are starting to get knots in them, but there is no time to change them out. I run another line and as I pull the first fish toward the boat, two others are attacking it, trying to take the spoon out of his mouth. I throw the fish that is on the hook aboard and the other two are still following along behind the boat, just below the surface. I shake the fish off the hook with a twist of the gaff, then flip the lure out in front of the followers. One grabs it immediately and the fight is on. I get him aboard also, then go on running the line.

Looking around, I can see schools of fish finning on the surface and slashing through schools of feed. Gulls are diving into the swirling mass and eagles are soaring overhead, occasionally swooping down to grab a talon-full of the millions of bait fish that have been driven to the surface by the feeding Salmon.

The Celeste is just off my starboard side, with the majestic cliffs of Wooden Island in the background. I can see Steve frantically cranking his gear and snapping the leaders on a wire above his head. The leaders are trailing along behind the boat as he works, and as I watch, a big Coho slashes through the trailing gear, hooking itself on one of the spoons. As the fish fights the hook, he braids the other leaders into a terrible tangle, and when Steve discovers what has happened, I can see him cussing a blue streak. Some lessons must be learned the hard way; the small amount of time saved by not bringing the leaders aboard is hardly worth the risk of tangling a whole side. I learned this lesson the hard way too.

The bite goes on, and by mid-morning I have over fifty fish aboard. I haven't cleaned any of them, and Cohos spoil very fast when their bellies are full. Finally around ten-thirty, I have to just let the lines rattle and start cleaning, wishing all the while that I had a deckhand to do the butchering so I could keep hauling fish. It takes me over an hour to clean the fish and get them on ice in the fish box.

When I finally finish, I realize that I am starving. I have eaten nothing all morning, and the hard work is starting to take its toll on my energy reserves. I go inside and throw together a quick sandwich and as I sit at the wheel, eating, looking out the wheelhouse window, I notice a small school of fish following the stabilizer. The water in every direction is seething with Salmon and schools of Needlefish, and people are working frantically in the cockpits of every boat in sight. The sky is full of birds and Sea Lions are ripping through the masses of fish.

After I finish eating, I go out and start running gear again. Nothing has changed; both lines have a fish on every hook. I've been in some good bites before, but nothing like this! Within a couple of hours the slaughter bin is full again. There are about ten fish flopping around on deck and both poles are rattling. The bite is still going full blast, but I'm starting to get exhausted. I'm tangling leaders, miss-gaffing fish, and about fifty fish behind on my cleaning. The boat is a mess, there is blood splattered all the way in the wheelhouse door and on the inside of the windshield. I look like I've been swimming in it; my pants are so wet with blood and seawater, that my boots are starting to get full. My little operation just isn't set up for coping with this volume of fish. I look with envy at the bigger boats around me who, at least, have a deck to land fish on, and maybe another pair of hands to share the labor.

At twelve-thirty I stop again to clean fish and try to restore some semblance of order to my work area. When the fish are cleaned and put in the hold, the icebox is completely full. I can't even close the lid all the way. I run through the lines a couple more times, then finally give in to exhaustion. I have lost track of how many fish are aboard, and I'm too tired to care. I pull the gear and charge for town with the intention of unloading, then coming back out for a few hours.

I round Breakfast Rock, and as I head for the red can I pass Dave Gifford idling slowly along. I slow down and as I come alongside I ask, "Are you in 'em, Cap?"

"I got about fifteen," he answers with a shrug. "I've been in Conclusion all day; it's totally dead up there," he adds.

"They're really biting at the cape; I'm completely plugged and last time I ran the lines they were both full. You might want to haul your gear aboard and charge down right now. I'm going back as soon as I pitch these off, so that I have some place to put more. It's wild!" I say.

"Okay, thanks! I'll see you later," he replies and heads for the pit.

When I get to the fishhouse, there is a packer tied to the pilings, blocking the unloading hoist. I tie alongside and climb over his deck, then up the ladder to the dock. Sharon, the buyer, is talking to John Hughes and the crew off the packer. They all greet me as I walk up.

"Do you need to pitch off?" John asks.

"Yeah, the fish are really biting and I'd like to get back out this afternoon, if possible. I'm totally plugged and have no place to put another fish," I answer.

"We can unload him across my deck. I can sling the bucket from him across to the grading table, then when we're finished we can sling them back into my hold. It will save moving the boats," the skipper of the packer says to John.

"Okay," John says, "sounds like a plan to me."

I climb back down to the deck of the packer, then over onto the Nomad. They soon have the bucket hanging over my cockpit and I fill it with the icy cold, silver fish. I fill the big aluminum box three times. There are 132 Cohos and five Kings. They are all nice big fish, and I can already smell the greenbacks. This is the best day I've had in the six years since I started, and I know the check will be over a thousand dollars.

When the last bucket of fish is hoisted to the dock, I scoop the bloody slush out of the fish box, then scrub it out with Clorox and seawater. When the hold is ready for ice, I scrub down the rest of the cockpit, then climb up to the fishhouse to get the scale ticket.

975 pounds of Silvers and 53 pounds of large red Kings! I take the scale ticket to the pay window at the store and the accountant counts fifteen crisp, new, hundred dollar bills into my hand, along with some twenties and small change. Not bad for about ten hours work. After I add the wad of cash to my roll in the Band-Aid can in the first aid kit, I untie from the packer and slide over to the ice shute. The iceman soon

has a stream of ice coming down the chute, and in a few minutes I'm ready to head back out.

As I pull away from the fishhouse, I suddenly realize what a wreck my body is. My hands are cut to pieces with leader cuts, and my arms ache from the miles of wire I have cranked. My back hurts and my clothes are wet and stiff with slime, blood, and salt. As the boat idles toward the entrance of the harbor, I realize that I just don't have the stamina left to crank any more fish.

"How much money do you need to make anyway," I say to myself as I turn around and head for the dock.

Dick and Bud come down the dock to help me tie up. When we finish fastening her to the dock they look me over and Dick asks, "What the hell happened to you; ya fall in or something? Looks like you been wallowin' in the blood and gut trough at the slaughterhouse. Looks like we missed the bite."

"I suppose you ne'er-do-wells were lounging at the dock all day while honest, working folk were slaving before the crank. I got a hundred-thirty since daylight and they were still biting like bulldogs when I left. I was plugged; only place left to put fish was the bunk, and I was about worn down to a nub. Made fifteen-hundred bucks today," I reply, sitting down tiredly on the bullrail.

"Jeez, I figured something was going on down there when we came around from Conclusion and saw all those boats by the island. The radio has been dead quiet all day too; we should have guessed. I'm tempted to go back out for a while," Bud says disgustedly.

"It's too late for me; they'll probably be there tomorrow. I think I'll wait and go after them with a good night's sleep under my belt," Dick says.

"Yeah…I suppose that's the best idea. It's already after four and by the time I got down there it would be time to quit," Bud says, relieved that reason has prevailed over conscience.

"Boy I'm pooped; I'm going to go take a bath and get out of these clothes. Put your rain gear on before you put the gear in the water, tomorrow. If they're biting like today you'll never get a chance after you start pulling fish," I say, struggling stiffly to my feet with a groan.

"I feel about ninety years old," I complain climbing aboard the boat to get my shower gear and a change of clothes.

I feel better after I get cleaned up. Celia feeds us on the Celedo and we all turn in early so we can get up at the crack of dawn. The night passes in an instant and it seems like I just closed my eyes and the alarm goes off.

I am so stiff and sore I can hardly get out of the bunk. My hands are swollen and stiff and my arms feel like lead. By the time the engine is warmed up, the boat untied, and the poles down, my body is starting to loosen up. As I pass through the entrance, I can see a bank of clouds across the strait and there is a light north wind blowing; a sure sign that the weather is changing. I charge down to Poor Man Point and put the gear down. I get a small clatter on the first pass but it is soon obvious that the fishing is not going to be like yesterday.

As the morning passes the wind gradually increases from the north. By ten-thirty it is blowing about twenty knots and has whipped up a nasty, five-foot chop. As I turn around at Wooden Island, I realize that it is time to head for the harbor. The boat is plunging over the foaming crests and into the troughs between the steep, blue waves. The boat is hobby horsing so badly in the short chop that I have the engine at half-throttle to keep moving at trolling speed. Pitching over the waves makes the poles whip fore and aft, and you couldn't see a fish hit if they were biting, which they aren't.

I can see several other boats heading for the harbor and finally give up. It is difficult to get the gear aboard with the boat pitching over the waves; hard to keep it heading straight into the seas while cranking and coiling down the gear. The wind catches the leaders and blows them back out of the gear tray as I try to coil them, and by the time it is all aboard and covered with wet burlap bags, it's a tangled mess.

When I finish with the gear, I go into the wheelhouse and angle the boat so that it quarters the waves toward the beach. It looks calmer along the shore, and I'm making little progress bucking straight into it.

I am about four miles from the entrance when the last spread comes aboard, and it takes two and a half hours to crash my way up into the shelter of Conclusion Point. By the time I pass the red can into the harbor, the whole southern sky is gray and foreboding and clouds are blotting out the mid-day sun.

I soon have her snugged up alongside the Spray, with spring-lines fore and aft, and a couple of extra lines to the dock. The harbor at P.A. can be a real blowhole and I don't feel like putting more lines on later in the rain. By the time I finish the whole sky is overcast and the north wind is lying down. I walk down to the Celedo. Dick and Bud have their noses in their coffee cups, telling fish lies and feeling smug with the wisdom they had displayed by heading for the harbor at the first sign of wind.

"There he is, Mr. Highliner. Must be a real bitch, to have a reputation to live up to," Dick says with a twinkle in his eye as I enter the wheelhouse.

"Coffee?" Bud asks as I sit down on the bunk.

"Sure," I reply as he gets up to make it.

"Are the fish still down at the cape?" he asks, handing me the steaming cup.

"Well I got a few on the first pass but as the wind came up I couldn't go slow enough going with it, or fast enough bucking into it. I think the poles were yanking so hard in the swells that it was pulling the hooks out of their mouths. I got a couple of handfuls, is all," I answer, sipping my coffee.

"I never can catch anything in a north wind," Dick adds.

"No, me either. This storm will probably make them take off for the rivers too. I expect it will be different when we get back out. It's almost the first of August, so they will be getting the spawning urge pretty soon," I say.

"Look, the wind is switching to the south and it's starting to sprinkle," Bud says pointing out the window.

The top of No Name Mountain is shrouded in steely-gray clouds and small puffs of white fog are racing past the dark-green slopes below the overcast.

"The old timers say when the white horses are running on the mountains, she's goin' to blow," Dick says, lighting a cigarette. We talk for a while enjoying the warmth of the oil stove in Bud's galley. The south wind is getting gusty and rainsqualls are lashing the water of the harbor.

"Well, I've got to go up to the washhouse and help Celia; she's doing laundry and the bag is too heavy for her to pack," Bud says, tamping out his cigarette in a black plastic ashtray.

"Yeah, I should go tie some leaders to replace the ones that got ruined yesterday," I say, finishing my coffee and getting up to leave.

The wind whips a shotgun blast of high-velocity raindrops in our faces as we step over onto the dock. Dick and I pull our caps down tight on our heads and turn our collars up as we scurry down the dock toward the boats.

"Come on over for dinner after a while; I'm gonna make stew," he says as we climb aboard.

"Yeah okay," I reply. Making stew means heating up a can of "Dinty Moore" and probably throwing in a can of green beans, but anything I might concoct probably wouldn't be any better, and the company will be good. I tie up enough leaders to replace the ones that wore out in the big bite yesterday, and then head over to Dick's about five-thirty. It's flogging down rain and blowing about thirty knots from the SE. Dinner is good, in spite of coming out of a can and we top it off with peaches that I bring over. When we're finished eating, we brave the storm to head down to the Celedo for a couple of games of chess and a yarnin' session.

16

The sunrise illuminates the underside of the clouds with pink and yellow light; the water looks like polished, hammered gold. Gulls wheel and dive along the rips off Wooden Island; brilliant white against the foreboding blue-gray sky. The Nomad rises and falls in the SE groundswells left over from the recent storm. I pull in a nice ten pound Coho and as the boat hesitates at the bottom of a trough I conk him and throw him aboard.

It's a wild morning to be on the edge of the ocean in my little boat. I am pushing the envelope of safety, but there are no fish on the inside drags and they are biting in the rips between Wooden Island and the cape. The tide is ebbing and the bite gradually moves NW to Eagle Rocks and then into Larch Bay.

This is spectacular country. Ocean swells spend their energy crashing on the boulder-strewn feet of towering cliffs that rise vertically from the sea. At Eagle Rock, a tiny island a few hundred yards off Bobrovi Point, the Stellar Sea Lion colony is a brown mass draped over the top of the barren rock. The great seas break upon their precarious perch, throwing spray into their midst. Their restless movement makes the rock seem alive.

Eagle Rock marks the SE corner of Larch Bay, a large open bay just NW of Cape Ommaney. It is a primal place of strong currents and surf breaking on rocky shores. The great swells rolling into the shallows become steep and treacherous. In spite of its violent rips and crashing breakers, Larch Bay teems with life. There is a great school of herring that resides here, feeding on Krill and Plankton, which are abundant in the clear, cold water. All species of birds common to the North Pacific can be found here, and Humpbacked Whales spout and wave their tails as they sound.

As the morning wears on, the sky gradually clears, and by noon when the sun is overhead, the sea is aglitter with silvery reflections. The fish are in small, scattered schools, and come aboard in twos and threes, with time in-between to keep up with the cleaning and icing chores.

At one-thirty the tide begins to flood. The tremendous volume of water flowing into Chatham Strait creates a strong current across the mouth of Larch Bay and across the shallow ledges at Eagle Rocks. When, like today, there is a big SE swell, the current running against the seas causes a particularly vicious tiderip to form. I'm busy with a small clatter of fish and fail to notice that the increasing current has carried me to Eagle Rock. Without realizing it, my little boat is sucked into the rip that suddenly has formed just west of the rock. I'm facing aft, gutting fish, when the boat pitches violently. I look up, and all around me the sea is being torn apart by breaking seas whose crests are ten to fifteen feet above the bottom of the troughs. A cross swell, running at an angle to the deep groundswell, has appeared out of nowhere and the crosshatch pattern is causing an area of pyramid-shaped waves to develop. The rip is literally forming around me, and the sea has changed from large, smooth, evenly spaced swells to a confused hell of foam, kelp, and logs being tossed and tumbled by the vicious wave pattern.

I dive for the wheel and look quickly around for the nearest edge of the rip. Off to the SE, about a half-mile away, where the water is deeper, it is calm. I realize it is impossible to turn around, and that my only hope is to try to keep the bow pointed into the chop and let the current carry me through to deeper water off the cape.

The distance between the waves is very short, barely longer than the boat. She rises up the steep face of the wave, bursts through the crest, and plunges into the next trough, only to immediately pitch up the face of the next sea. Because I'm going with the current and pitching up and down so badly, it seems like I'm sitting in one spot rocking and rolling over the waves. Cross-swells coming from the SW cause the boat to roll sickeningly along with the violent pitching motion.

Because it's impossible to maintain any headway relative to the surface of the water, the trolling lines are hanging straight down. As the boat rolls, the lines go slack then snap tight, alternating from one side to the other in an irregular rhythm. Occasionally a stabilizer is pulled clear of the water, and I am worried that one of them will swing into the side of the boat and puncture the hull. I consider trying to get the gear aboard, but realize that if I want to survive I better stay at the wheel and take it one wave at a time until the current carries me into calmer water.

The boat pitches up onto a great pyramid of a wave and as it falls off the crest it rolls to port. The line on that side goes slack then as the boat rolls back the tag line breaks with a loud crack. The trolling line snaps against the side of the boat with a thud. This is really getting out of hand! The line now hangs about three feet from the prop, and with the boat rolling like this there is a danger of it tangling in the wheel. The boat leaps up another wave and crashes down the other side, then up the next one and down again, over, and over, and over. The floor is strewn with stuff that has been thrown off the dash and in the foc'sle the teakettle has jumped the sea-rail on the stove and spewn its contents onto the galley deck. Coffee cups, charts, books, food, and fishing gear are strewn everywhere.

POP! The other tag line breaks. The nightmare seems to go on and on. I start to worry that any water in the fuel tanks will get stirred up, clog the filters, and the engine will stop. I keep checking the bilge to make sure the pump is still working, and that the violent twisting and pitching haven't opened up a seam. What seems like hours has only been about twenty minutes. The current has taken me past Eagle Rocks, and as the boat breaks over the next crest, the relatively smooth water a half-mile ahead beckons tantalizingly.

"If I can make it another few minutes, I'll be in the clear," I mutter out loud to myself. More waves, violent pitch and roll, recover and repeat, over and over, till my arms burn from wrestling the wheel, and my feet ache from clutching the deck through my boots. Finally I realize that the waves are becoming farther apart and not so high and steep. Within minutes the current spits me out of the standing waves of the rip, and back into the long, gentle groundswells. I go out into the pit and haul the gear aboard. The leaders are tangled and knotted from the violent up and down motion with no forward speed to keep them streamed out behind.

By the time the lines are in I am at Wooden Island. I point the boat between the island and the cape and head for town to straighten out the mess. The water inside the cape is calm as glass, and I sag into the seat exhausted and relieved. At Poor Man Point I have recovered enough to go out and finish cleaning the fish that I pulled before the rip caught me. After the pit is tidied up, I pull the poles and retie the tag lines to the big metal snaps that clamp them to the wires.

I am lucky to be alive. I knew about the Eagle Rips, and had intended to stay on the NW shore until the next tide-change. But I had become so involved with fishing that I had wandered into the current without realizing it. It has cost me an afternoon of good fishing, and almost my life. Staying alive on the water requires constant presence of mind. Sometimes, like today, luck smiles on you if you let your guard down and get into trouble. But luck is fickle, and depending on it will eventually bring you to disaster.

Dick and Bud had been fishing in Conclusion for a couple of days, and I hadn't seen them as they were anchoring in Ship Cove at night. When I round the airplane float, The Spray and Celedo are tied one behind the other on the inside of the dock. My two friends help me tie behind Bud's boat, and as we finish fastening her to the dock, Dick says, "In kind of early, ain't ya?"

"Yeah, I wasn't paying attention this morning and got mauled by the rips at Eagle Rock. I'm lucky to be alive. It was the worst slop I've ever been in. Big pyramids of water, some of them fifteen feet high or so. Broke both tag lines, and I was afraid the wires were going to get into the wheel. The galley is a wreck, my leaders are all tangled, and I'm worn out. What have you gentlemen been up to the last couple of days? Laying on the hook in Ship Cove like a couple of tourists, I bet." They look at each other with a twinkle.

"Well, while you were out there beating your brains out in the ocean, we've been conkin' in calm water. We saw a school of fish on the surface when we came out of the cove yesterday morning, so we put the gear out and started catching right off. Bud got a hundred and ten and I got eighty-three; best fishin' I ever had. There was nothing there today though, so we came in to unload," Dick answers with a grin.

"I think those fish are still up there somewhere, we're going to go back up in the morning to look for them. There's no one else fishing up there and it's flat calm," Bud adds.

"I'll probably join you. It's pretty good fishing on the outside, but I'm tired of rolling in the slop. I could use a day or two of calm water to rest up," I say, sitting down on the bullrail.

"Celia is cooking a roast; she said to invite you over for dinner. Dick is coming too," Bud says.

"Alright, real food; I'll be there."

We chat for a few minutes, then go our separate ways. I go back to the boat and attack the mess in the gear tray. Some of it is tangled so badly that I have to cut the hardware out of the mess and tie new leaders. As I work in the warm afternoon sun, my mind drifts back over the close call of the morning. I'm lucky to be alive and it makes life seem sweeter. Nothing like a brush with doom to whet the appetite for life.

I remember another incident that happened to me a few years ago. I was working my way down the outside of Baranof Island one afternoon. I was in the mouth of Red Fish Bay, right outside Ten-Fathom Anchorage, dragging twenty fathoms of gear in what the chart said was thirty fathoms of water. Unknown to me, there are a couple of pinnacles in that area that come up to fifteen fathoms. They are so small that the cartographers missed them when they were collecting the data for the area. Consequently, the pinnacles don't appear on the chart.

It was a nice afternoon: windless, warm, and there was a long, glassy, smooth groundswell rolling in from the SW. The crests were so far apart that the ten to twelve- foot height of the waves was hardly notice-able. Fishing was slow and I was spacing out in the wheelhouse, think-ing about cranking up and charging for town.

Suddenly the port pole rattled. I glanced at the depth sounder, which was showing fifteen fathoms. What the...! The pole bounced again then pumped up and down. All right, I thought, must be such a thick school of feed that the meter is reading off it instead of bottom, and there must be a bunch of Cohos feeding on them. As I step out the door the port pole bends way back and the tag line breaks with a pop. The wire snaps over to the side of the boat, and as I dive for the gear-shift, the other tag line breaks too.

When the transmission is in neutral I try to crank the port line, but it is hung tight. I try the starboard line and it is free, so I haul it aboard as fast as I can. There is a current setting to the west, and by the time the starboard line is aboard, the port line is tight as a fiddle string, and each time the boat rises on a passing swell, ten or twelve feet of line is stripped off the gerdy. I try cranking it but the pressure of the current on the boat is too much for the leverage in the crank handle. I step in the door, shift into forward, and try to steer into the current to slack the line, but it doesn't work. The current is too strong, and the pur-chase point that the wire has on the boat makes it impossible to get the bow pointed in the right direction.

Finally I give up and go back out to try the crank again. The extra line on the gerdy spool is almost gone, and every swell peels off another ten feet. I stand there helplessly, trying to come up with a solution, and watch as the last few feet disappear off the reel.

As the boat rises to the next swell the gerdy stanchion, made of one-inch galvanized pipe, bends like rubber until the pulley on its outer end is in the water. The line slacks a little in the trough, and as the next crest picks the boat up, I hear a creaking groan where the stanchion is bolted to the gunnel of the boat. The next one starts pulling the side of the boat away from the pilothouse wall.

I suddenly snap out of the unconscious daze I've been in and dive for the toolbox to get the wire cutters, realizing that if I don't get free fast it's going to pull the boat apart.

As I rummage frantically through the tool box, I remember that a few days ago I had dropped the cutters in the bilge and had been unable to find them. I grabbed a pair of pliers and dove for the pit. I gripped the wire with the wire-cutting part of the pliers, but they were too worn-out to cut the one-sixteenth inch, nine strand, stainless steel cable. I twist a loop in the wire with the pliers and twist it around and around, trying to fatigue it enough to break.

Every swell is flexing the side of the boat more than the last, and the cap-rail is splintering where the stanchion pipe comes through it. The screws holding the chock at the bottom of the stanchion have torn out of the deck and the leverage on the side of the boat and the cap-rail is enormous.

PING! The wire finally snaps where I'm twisting it and disappears into the depths. I lean panting against the gear tray, trying to collect my wits. After a few moments I recover enough to lash the bent stanchion to the side of the wheelhouse to keep it from flopping around, then put the boat in gear and head for town.

As I cruise toward Cape Ommaney, I mentally kick myself for not using breaker strap to fasten the cannonball to the wire, like everyone else. But I, in the wisdom of inexperience, had decided to fasten them on with a metal snap. I thought there was a better chance of saving the twenty-dollar lead ball if I hung up on bottom. Another lesson learned the hard way. With the power of the whole North Pacific Ocean pushing up on the bottom of the boat, and the lead stuck in a crack on the bottom, something has got to give and it's not going to be the relentless sea! The old-timers tie the lead on with cord or a leather strap that has a considerably lower breaking strength than the wire. Better to sacrifice a twenty-dollar lead than the whole line. Or the boat!

I finish rebuilding the lines about five-thirty and head over to the Celedo for dinner. I have been smelling the delicious odor of Celia's roast for the last couple of hours and am hungry enough to eat a skunk. Dick is already aboard playing chess with Bud, and they are discussing the rumor of a closure that has been the main topic of discussion on the radio for the last few days.

"Hey, there he is. You get your mess straightened out?" Dick asks as I enter the galley.

"Yup, ready for the next round. What are you two old fossils lying to each other about now?" I ask jokingly. Celia chuckles behind her hand. She has led a very sheltered life in the world of classical music and higher education, and I reckon that hanging around with a bunch of earthy fisherman is quite an experience for her.

"I heard they are going to announce a closure tomorrow at noon, and it's going to be ten days. Their excuse is to allow enough escapement to inside waters so the seiners and gill-netters can catch them," Bud says, moving a pawn on the chessboard.

"I thought they were supposed to target on Humpys and Dogs, not Cohos. I suppose they will be having a seine opening out here next," I reply, sitting down at the table.

"Well, what the heck. I could use a few days off," Dick says looking up from the game with a mischievous expression. He loves to come at a serious complaining session from an oblique angle, inserting a pearl of crazy wisdom into the conversation that usually opens our eyes to the humor of the situation. It keeps worry-warts like me from taking life too seriously.

"Since when do you need the government to tell you can take a vacation? You've already spent most of the summer loafing at the dock while the rest of us have slaved away on the restless sea, trying to eke out a meager living," I ask with a snort of disgust.

"Whaddya mean, 'loafing at the dock'? I been out almost every morning. Just because I've got the good sense to come in at a reasonable time, doesn't mean I'm lazy. I'm just doing my part for conservation. If I was to get serious, the rest of you amateurs wouldn't have a chance. They would have to have a special closure just for me, so the rest of you could make a few bucks. Hell, you guys ought to pay me not to fish," Dick replies with mock seriousness.

"Well by golly, Dick, I guess I owe you an apology. All this time I thought you were just taking life easy for your own selfish pleasure. I didn't know you were taking care of us ne'r-do-wells," I say.

Bud is grinning at us over his glasses and Celia is looking at us with a puzzled frown, trying to figure out if we are joking or are serious. Finally she shakes her head and announces that dinner is ready.

We dig in to a beautiful roast, with spuds and carrots cooked in the juice, and homemade rolls hot out of the oven. Now that's heaven after weeks of Alpo and Dinty Moore stew.

17

The morning dawns clear and calm, and as I untie and head for the harbor entrance I marvel at the amount of sunny weather we have enjoyed this summer. SE Alaska is notorious for its rainy weather and so we savor every clear day, knowing that the rain and wind will soon sweep in off the ocean.

I head north up the strait, hoping to run into a school of Cohos that nobody else is working. The early mornings and the constant swell in the ocean are beginning to take their toll on my energy reserves, so I look forward to a day of calm water and some different scenery.

I put the gear in the water at Crow Island and let the flood tide sweep me north across the mouth of Port Conclusion. I work the Miner's Cove drag above Port Armstrong, then troll up to Port Lucy, dipping in across the pinnacles on the south point, then across to the slide on the north shore. It's really dead, and by noon I'm at Port Herbert and still haven't caught a single fish. I make a few passes at Codfish Cove, then when the tide starts to ebb I point the bow south. I consider pulling the gear and running for the cape but it is so pleasant motoring along, enjoying the scenery and the calm water, that I never quite make it.

At Miner's Cove I get a nice double-header of twenty pound Kings—the first fish of the day. The rush of suddenly seeing the poles bounce and the excitement of the battle to get them aboard shakes me out of the complacent daze I've been in all day. I put on more King gear, thinking I have stumbled upon a school of hatchery fish heading for the NOAA experimental hatchery at Little Port Walter. I work the Miner's Cove to Port Lucy drag for the rest of the afternoon, hoping for a bite at tide-change, but nothing happens. I'm gradually lulled back into my lazy mood, and about nine o'clock I troll down past

Armstrong, intending to fish my way around the backside of Conclusion and anchor at Calm Cove for the night.

About a mile south of Port Armstrong there are a series of small coves. Between the first and second little bays there is a cliff with deep water right to its base. In the middle of the wall there is a crack that opens up into a small grotto with a tiny sand beach in the back. The water in the mouth of this crack is so deep that with a small boat like mine, you can drag eighteen fathoms of gear so close to the cliff face that the pole tip is almost scraping the rocks. Sometimes salmon will lay in this crack and flash out to grab feed that swim by with the current. I have pulled some nice Kings out of this spot in the past, and so decide to give it a good rub on the way past. It's about the right time of year for the Little Port fish to be heading for the creek, and sometimes they will stop here to feed for a while before heading for the spawning stream.

I come out of the first cove, then turn to follow the bottom contour as close as possible. When the bottom falls off at the crack, I turn sharply into the mouth of it and then turn right back around to the left, to dangle the lures along the south point. The left line, which is on the inside of the turn, stops for a moment until the boat straightens out of the turn, then pulls back as it starts moving again.

Suddenly the pole pulls down so hard it looks like the tip is going to break off. The pole straightens out, then pumps up and down furiously! I look at the fathometer, thinking that the lead is dragging on the bottom, but I'm already in twenty-five fathoms and the bottom slopes off rapidly here. The pole is still rattling so hard that the whole boat is shaking.

As I dive for the pit the line wings out away from the boat then goes ahead until it is angled out forward of the pole! "My God," I think, "what the hell have I caught?" The line goes completely slack, drifts back behind the pole, then snaps tight in a series of hard yanks that make the whole boat roll.

I carefully start cranking in the line. The yanking has stopped for the moment, but the line is dragging back so far that the leaders are breaking the surface out of reach behind the boat.

My mind is racing. It feels like a big King. A halibut fights the wire differently. The tugs are slower and after a couple of jerks they usually just pull aft on the line. A King will shake his head from side to side furiously, trying to throw the hook, then will make wild runs out to the side away from the hook or forward, probably because it relieves the pull of the hook in his mouth.

I crank up slowly and whenever the fish starts fighting the line, I give back slack, trying to keep an even pressure, but not give him a solid purchase to break the leader or pull out the hook. On a big fish, the lure may be far enough back in the mouth so that the leader drags across the teeth when the fish shakes its head. This makes tiny cuts in the nylon line that weaken it significantly.

I'm running 100 pound test leader and it doesn't hold up well to abrasion. A few small cuts can quickly turn a 100-pound leader into a 50 pound leader, which won't hold a forty or fifty pound fish for long. With a sport pole, the springy action of the rod acts like a shock absorber, and it is possible to land a fish that is much heavier than the breaking strength of the line. On the commercial gear, however, there is not much give in the line. A big fish can put a significant shock load on the leader and it's not unusual for a big King to break the leader, or straighten out the hook and escape.

I feel the huge fish fighting the line as I crank up the wire and remove the leaders as they come within reach. Suddenly the wire goes slack, then wings out away from the boat. There is a "whanging" sound and the wire goes slack. I crank1 again but feel nothing on the line. The next leader has no lure on it and the bottom spoon is empty. *"Damn, lost him,"* I think to myself. I swing the boat back toward the beach for another pass. I put the line down with only the bottom three spreads, leaving off the Coho gear, and changing the lead spoon out for a plug the same color as the hoochie that the fish took. I replace the broken tail leader on the second spread and put another plug on the third leader.

By the time the line is back down, I'm lined up for the second pass. I nose into the crack, trying to duplicate the first pass as closely as possible. On1ce again I turn sharply around and come out along the south shore of the bight. Both poles take off! Big fish again, and it feels like they are going to tear the rigging off the boat. I head out for deeper water to give myself lots of room to fight them. I'm thankful that there are no other boats on the drag so all I have to do is concentrate on landing the fish.

The port pole seems to have the larger fish on it, so I decide to run the other side first to let the big one tire himself out fighting the pole. The starboard line comes up easily, and after a short fight I throw aboard a nice thirty-pounder hooked on the lead spoon. I run the line back down, leaving off the Coho gear, then start cranking up the port line.

At first, there seems to be nothing on it, but as the bottom spread nears the surface the line pulls back sharply and suddenly a huge King leaps into the air behind the boat! He is enormous, at least fifty pounds. He falls back into the water with a great splash, then charges the boat. I crank up to the snap and grab the leader. It goes under the boat, and off toward the other side, right past the prop. I start pulling on the line slowly, trying to encourage the fish to come out from under the boat. The leader goes slack in my hand and I see the fish streak by, heading out to port. When he hits the end of the leader, the wire bows out away from the boat so far the cannonball comes clear of the water for a moment, then swings back and bumps the side of the boat. The fingers of my right hand are caught in a half hitch of leader, and when the leader snaps tight it peels a half-inch of skin off my little finger.

As I stand holding my bleeding, smarting fingers in my other hand, I realize that the fish is gone. I push the rudder handle to starboard with my foot and point the boat back toward the shore. I have come out into the bay quite a distance while fighting the fish, so I take time to put some Buckley's Ointment and a Band-Aid on my finger. I dig out a pair of rubber gloves to protect my hands, which I should have been wearing all along, then replace the broken leader and put the line back out.

Nosing into the crack again, I duplicate the other two passes and pick up two more big fish. I manage to land a twenty-five pounder but lose another monster. The 100 pound-test leader just isn't strong enough, and I make a silent vow to buy some heavier line to have ready next time I run into a school of fish this big.

On the fourth pass I hook what is probably the biggest fish I ever will catch. I get one look at him leaping completely out of the water behind the boat, then he charges straight at the other line taking the port lead with him. I see the starboard line bounce, then the fish goes aft and charges up the port side, taking the wire forward with him. When the wire swings back it hangs straight down. I crank up to the snap and find the hook on the six-inch plug jammed so tightly into the jaws of the line snap that I have to use pliers to get it off the wire. The fish must have scraped past the wire on the last run and snagged the hook in the snap, ripping it out of his mouth.

As I head back toward the drag I notice that it is getting dark. I look at the clock on the binnacle and see that it is ten-thirty. I line up for one more pass, hoping for another chance to boat one of the big kings, and as the port line stops in the hole, the pole takes off again. After a fifteen-minute fight I land a nice forty-five pound fish. By the time I have him aboard it's too dark to see the line markers, so I head across the bay to the anchorage. After the other line is aboard I throttle up, then gut and ice the three fish. They are beauties no doubt, but I am pretty grumpy over the loss of the other bigger ones. At two dollars a pound, the ones that got away would have thickened my wallet considerably. I will definitely buy some stronger leader.

By the time I have the anchor set it is completely dark, so I take a couple of aspirin for my throbbing hand and fall into the bunk, exhausted. Morning comes about thirty seconds after I fall asleep. "Big

Ben" rattles it's obnoxious tune on the binnacle and I struggle up out of a dream about driving the boat around on dry land, hoping the cannonballs don't hang up and trying to keep the boat going fast enough so that it doesn't fall over.

When the engine is warmed up, I pull the anchor and charge across to the Crack- in-the-Wall drag, hoping that the fish are still there. It's completely dead; I catch nothing. After tide-change, I troll over to the cookie jar on the south side; maybe they have moved over there. By noon the "skunk" is still on the deck, so I give up and haul the gear aboard. I decide to go pitch off at the fishhouse and get a good night's sleep. The radio has been mostly silent all day and I suspect they are catching Cohos at the Cape or Larch Bay. It's too late today to run down there, and the fish box is about full. I'll get an early start tomorrow and if the silvers are really biting, I'll have room for them. That's the best excuse I can think of to take the afternoon off. One of the advantages of working for yourself.

Selling the fish is routine and while I'm at the store picking up my money I buy a roll of 120-pound test leader, the heaviest they have. The dock is suspiciously empty of boats, even the Spray and Celedo are still out. After I tie up I have an egg sandwich for lunch, then spend the afternoon cleaning up the boat and changing the motor oil.

About five I hear an engine rev up and look out to see Bud and Celia pull alongside the dock across from me. Beyond the Celedo, out in the harbor, I see Dick stopped, raising his poles. I go out and catch a line from Celia, who is on the bow of the Celedo, and as the stern swings in Bud steps off with the centerline.

"What's happenin', captain?" I ask as we tie the lines to the bullrail.

"Where have you been? There's been a good bite at Wooden Island all day. We got sixty-three and I think Dick has about fifty," Bud says, straightening up with a hand on his lower back, which obviously hurts.

"I trolled up to Jerry's Harbor and back to Conclusion yesterday. It's deader than a doornail north of here. No Cohos at all. I did scratch out a handful of pretty nice kings, though. I got into a school of hogs at the crack below Armstrong last night just before dark, but lost most of them. They walked through my hundred pound test leaders like it was sewing thread. A couple of them were well over fifty pounds. I just couldn't hold them. Every time I'd stop cranking to unsnap a spread, the fish would go wild, and by the time I'd get them to the surface, the leaders were worn out, full of tooth cuts. Pretty frustrating," I reply, heading up the dock to help Dick tie up.

"There ya are," Dick says, tossing me a line, "we figured ya fell in and the sand fleas ate ya."

"Nope, I been holding down the light-weight drags in Conclusion for you guys while you get in the way of real fishermen down at the Cape," I reply as I throw a clove- hitch around the rail.

"Anything doing up there?" he asks, as we finish tying the Spray to the dock.

"Nah, I caught a couple of Kings last night but they were gone this morning. Sounds like there's a few Silvers at the Cape, huh?"

"Yeah, I think I broke fifty today; it's mostly a morning bite, but I scratched a few this afternoon. Better be down there at the crack of dawn, they were clattering pretty good during tide-change," he answers.

"That's my plan," I say as we drift toward the Celedo. Bud comes out of the house with a can of pop and we sit down on the bullrail. There are tantalizing odors issuing from the galley, and in a few minutes Celia comes out and invites us in for curried halibut.

"Any word on the closure yet?" I ask as we enjoy Cilia's excellent food.

"You didn't hear? It starts on the tenth and re-opens on the twentieth. Didn't you hear all the moaning on channel five yesterday?" Bud asks, surprised.

"I was channel-surfing yesterday morning. I listened to a conversation on nineteen about somebody's dog jumping out of a pickup and forgot to switch back. Boy, ten days is a heck of a chunk of our best fishing time. I wonder if they will shut the seiners and gill-netters down too."

"Nope, just trollers. In fact rumor has it that there will be a seine opening from Cape Ommaney north to Warm Springs Bay, starting on the thirteenth," Dick says, scooping up more fish and wiping his chin on a paper towel.

"What?! They've never let them fish south of Lucy before. That's crap. It'll ruin the fishing for weeks here. Is anybody trying to stop it?" I ask incredulously.

"There have been some phone calls made, but the ADF&G conveniently made the announcement Friday evening just before quitting time, and now nobody will be in the office till Monday morning. Fishing closes at midnight tomorrow night. Everybody is really bummed. I bet the phone at the Dept. of Fish and Game is going to be ringing all day Monday," Bud says, reaching for another helping.

"I came back out here to get away from the seine fleet in Clarence Strait. Now we will have to put up with it here too. You know damn well they will be targeting on Kings and Cohos, so not only will the fishing go to hell, but we'll have to sit tied to the dock while they flood the market with our fish. We really need to talk the Alaska Trollers Association into letting the handtrollers in, so they have more clout. It's really dumb to split the fleet up like this; we should be together, fighting for our fishing rights as a single group instead of fighting each other," I say disgustedly.

Dick and I say good night about eight. I want to hit the drag early, since tomorrow is the last day we can fish. As I crawl into the sleeping bag there is a feeling of impending doom in my gut. I have a premonition of the fishery turning into a political struggle between the government and us with the gear groups fighting each other and losing everything in the end.

The alarm jars me out of a fitful sleep at three-thirty and I do my startup routine in a daze. It has clouded up overnight; the damp morning is full of mist and the leaden sky looms a few hundred feet overhead. The short, restless sleep hasn't dispelled the feeling of doom and the dark, heavy sky contributes to the mood.

I charge down to Poor Man before putting the gear in the water, and in a few minutes both poles are rattling. One line has five nice fish on it and the other line has three. As the morning passes the fish come aboard steadily, and by noon I have fifty-one. The good fishing has pushed away the black mood and the overcast has thinned. Maybe there is some hope after all.

I go in at four, to avoid the rush at the cold storage, and only have to wait about an hour to unload. There is a lot of chatter on the radio about the closure and the rumored seine opening. Everyone else seems to share my feelings of frustration and gloom. After the boat is tied up and scrubbed down, I join Dick for hash and eggs. Over dinner we discuss the idea of heading home early, before the fall southerlies start, but decide to stay through the closure and try the fishing when it re-opens.

As I head home there is rain in the air and the clouds have thickened again. I crawl into the sleeping bag and pull the covers up over my head. I drift off, lulled by the sound of water dripping from the rigging and the gentle squeak of the fenders working against the dock.

18

I awaken with the feeling that something is wrong. Sunlight is streaming in the porthole over my bunk!

"My God! I must have forgotten to set the alarm!" I think, leaping out of the bunk and standing up in the wheelhouse. Big Ben says five o'clock. I look down the dock, expecting to see all the boats gone already, but everybody is still in. Boats are tied two and three deep down both sides of the dock, and as I stare blankly at them it gradually dawns on me that we can't fish for ten days, and I don't even need to be up this early. I consider going back to bed for a while, but realize that I'm wide-awake and might as well stay up. I make a cup of coffee, pack my jaw with Copenhagen, and climb out on the dock to enjoy the morning sun.

The small, low-pressure area that brought rain and wind the night before has given way to the summer high, and the sky is clear. The sun, which has just cleared the trees to the east, is warm on my back as I sit on the bullrail sipping my coffee. I think about the closure and realize that I can really use some time off. I've been hitting it pretty hard and already have enough money saved to see me through the winter, so the pressure is off. I drain the last of the coffee from my cup and go make another. When I'm back on the dock I see Bud stirring around on deck and walk over to yarn with him for a while.

"I could get to like this closure business; it's the perfect excuse not to fish. Dock time without guilt and the government takes the blame," I say as Bud looks up at my approach.

"Yeah, but it's not doing my pocket book any good. I was just about to break even, and now we have to sit here for ten days while the fish feed past. I sure hope there are still some left when it opens up again," he answers.

"Hard to say what will happen. I think there is supposed to be a run returning to the hatchery at Little Port Walter this fall; maybe they will lay in here and feed for a while before they hit the creek," I reply, hoping to cheer him up.

"What are you two lying about?" Dick asks, walking up with a cup of coffee in one hand and a Marlboro in the other.

"We were talking about you; whaddya think, we was talkin' about fishin' or somethin'?" I answer, grinning at him.

"I suppose you were bitching about not being able to fish. Myself, I was thinking about callin' the Fish and Feathers and thanking them for the vacation," Dick says.

"Well ask if they will consider vacation pay, will ya? They all get a paid vacation every year, so we should be entitled to the same perks," I say.

"Yeah, they pay farmers not to grow crops, why shouldn't they pay us not to fish?" Bud adds.

The conversation lags for a few minutes as we enjoy the leisure of the morning.

We sip our coffee and watch the activity begin to increase along the dock, as other people wake up and come out into the sunshine to exchange complaints and speculate on the government conspiracy to run us all out of business. It's interesting how many of us believe in that notion. Many think there should be no regulation at all, but were it not for the regulating agencies, there wouldn't be a fish left in the ocean to catch.

"Well, what are you guys going to do with yourselves for the next ten days?" Dick asks, firing up another smoke.

"Catch up on my sleep for one thing. Then maybe climb the mountain, or do some beach combing. Little Jim was mumbling something about a trout fishing expedition to Little Port Walter; I might get in on that too," I answer.

"I've got to paint my wheelhouse roof with Silver Seal. It drips on my bunk when it rains. It can drip anywhere else but I can't stand the sound of water dripping on my sleeping bag in the middle of the night. Drives me up the wall. I better take advantage of the nice weather and start on it today," Dick says.

"I've got to do some fiberglass repairs on my fish box; the hoist bucket at the fish dock has broken the edges and water is starting to get into the insulation. Also, I have to overhaul my halibut gear; never took time after the last opening and I have to get it done before we leave in September," Bud says.

"You fellers are too ambitious for me. I'm on vacation. I'm going to go play before one of you tricks me into some kind of work," I say, getting up to leave. They chuckle as I head over to my boat.

I go aboard and whip up some breakfast, then head for Little Jim's house to see if the trout fishing expedition is still on. Jim lives in a small house on Back Bay, a small bight east of the harbor. I push my way through the salmonberries that have overtaken the trail from the main boardwalk, and bang on the half-open door, hollering, "Ahoy! Anybody home?"

"Enter," a voice shouts back from inside.

I walk through the entry way into the kitchen. Jim is siting at the table working on a cup of coffee and a Camel cigarette.

"Hey, what's up?" he asks as I walk in. "Grab a cup, coffee's on the stove," he adds.

I take one of the heavy, porcelain mugs off a hook under the cupboard, and fill it from the pot simmering on the old, wood-fired, cook stove.

"You still want to go trout fishin'?" I ask, sitting down across from him and tasting the coffee.

"You bet; you want to run up today? We could hike up to Round Lake this afternoon and camp out tonight. Looks like the weather is going to be nice for a few days, and we can leave the boats tied to the dock at Little Port. My pop can keep an eye on them while we're gone," Jim says with obvious enthusiasm.

"Sounds like a plan to me; we could be up there by noon or a little after. How long a hike is it?"

"Takes about two hours to get to Round Lake. There's a good trail to Sashun Lake, then all we have to do is climb a few hundred feet to some muskegs and it's easy going the rest of the way. I know where there is an old cabin we can camp in; it's pretty well caved in, but we can throw a piece of plastic over the walls to keep the dew off," Jim answers.

"Okay. Did you talk anyone else into going?" I ask.

"No; I asked Steve and Dave but they have stuff to do at home, so it's just us. How soon can you be ready to take off?" he asks.

"I'm ready now, just have to fire up and go. How about you?"

"Give me about an hour. I have to get Karen and the kids up and everybody down to the boat. I'll meet you at the dock after while," Jim says.

"Sounds good. I have to go to the store and get a few things, but I'll be ready to go when you get down there," I say, finishing my coffee and getting up to leave.

"Okay, see you down at the dock about ten o'clock," Jim says as I walk out the door. I push back through the bushes to the boardwalk and head for the store.

I buy a few candy bars for trail food and a couple of cans of snoose then saunter back to the boat. I rummage around digging out my spinning rod and box of lures, then I get out a box of 45/70 cartridges for my rifle. Baranof Island is Brown Bear country and the creek we will be following is a major Salmon spawning stream. Even though the heavy, Marlin lever-action is a burden, it will be a comfort walking up that brush-choked, narrow trail. I take the rifle out of the gun rack and work the action a couple of times, then push four of the shiny, brass shells into the magazine. I drop several more into my pants pocket, then put the box away. As I inspect the fishing gear and handle the rifle, a feeling of pleasant anticipation comes over me. I'm tired of the grind of the daily routine, and this little overnight adventure is just what I need to break the monotony. My favorite thing to do is to ramble around in the woods with my rifle in my hand and new territory to explore.

My only regret about fishing for a living is that it uses up the summers. I often catch myself daydreaming, as I watch the green mountains passing by, wishing I was walking slowly up some cool, green valley exploring a creek, or looking for a deer to hunt.

I see Jim and Karen loading gear on the Juanita H. a few boats up the dock, so I check the oil and fire up the little four-banger. While it warms up, I walk over to the Spray to tell Dick where I'm going and when I'll be back. He is busy on his wheelhouse roof, smearing a liberal layer of sealer on the old canvas-covered wood.

After I've filed my flight plan with the old skipper, I untie the Nomad from the dock and shove off. Jim's boat is faster than mine is so I decide to get a head start. When I'm around the north end of the dock I idle slowly by the Juanita H., and as I pass I ask Jim what channel he wants to use on the CB radio.

"How about 22," he answers.

I nod affirmatively and point the bow at the red can. I throttle up as I pass the fishhouse and twist the dial on the radio to 22. When the red can is abeam, I turn left and head for the strait. I settle back in the driver's seat and run the throttle up to running speed. The water is glassy calm and the mountains shimmer in the late morning sun. When I'm clear off Point Conclusion, I aim the bow stem at Toledo Point and settle in for the hour and a half run to Port Walter.

"Ahhhh, one two, one two, the Nomad, you got me on this one, Cap?"

"Yeah, you betcha, Jim. Looks like perfect running weather," I answer.

"I don't know, it looks pretty dangerous to me. I just took one over the waterline. Maybe we better turn back," Jim replies in his best radio drawl.

"That's the trouble with those big smoker boats. Even these six-inch swells can get ya. Now a little ship like mine can rise up over the crests, whereas yours just plows right through. That's why she takes them over the top of the boot stripe."

"Yahyaheyah, that's probably it, by golly. I better trade her in this fall, get me a real sea boat, like that one of yours," he says.

"Tell ya what, Cap, since you're a family man and I wouldn't want you risking their lives, I'll trade you straight across. How's that for big-hearted?" I reply.

"You would do that for me? Man, that's really nice of you. Does that mean you'll take over the payments too?"

"Well now....I don't think that's part of the deal. Here I am willing to risk my life so your family can be safe, and you want me to make the payments too," I answer.

"Heh heh, aghhh boy...it's nice out here. We should be there in about an hour and fifteen minutes," Jim says.

I click the mike a couple of times then space out for a while. The calm water reflects the deep blue of the sky, and heat waves shimmer off the hills in the late morning sun. We soon pass Toledo Harbor, then round the point into Little Port Walter.

Little Port is a narrow inlet in the south side of Big Port Walter. As you round the point into the entrance of the bay, the first thing you see is a big, three-story, white house. As you approach the building, the channel narrows until it is only a few hundred feet wide. As you pass the house, the bay widens left and right into a beautiful lagoon with a large creek running into the west end. On the left side, a mountain rises in a series of steps to a couple of thousand feet elevation, and on the right is the NOAA experimental hatchery. The white house contains a small lab, bunkhouse and galley for the crew, and a large apartment, where Jim's parents live. Jim's father is the maintenance man for the facility.

Just west of the big house is the dock and rearing pens, and along the north shore are the generators, the hatchery, warehouse, pier, and housing for other full-time workers. The buildings and grounds are well maintained, and there is an air of calm efficiency about the place. As we idle toward the dock, I see Big Jim waiting to help tie up. Jimmy is ahead of me and after he is fastened to the bullrail, I tie alongside the Juanita H.

"Hi Mike, hear you guys are going up to Round Lake to catch a few rainbows,"

Big Jim says as I step off onto the dock.

"Yep, busman's holiday. You been catching any kings lately?" I ask, shaking hands. Big Jim is an avid sport fisherman and one of the best King fishermen in the country.

"I've been pretty busy lately, haven't been out for a while. How about you?"

I tell him the story about the big Kings at the crack a few days ago.

"Figured there was some around. I almost went down to Armstrong about that time, but we had company from Juneau, so I had to hang around," he said as we climb the ramp and enter the house. We go up the stairs to Jim and Nita's apartment and head for the kitchen.

As usual, there was the odor of food cooking. Nita is the best cook in the world and an invitation for a meal is always the high point of a trip to Little Port. She makes superb cream puffs and so we call her kitchen "Cream Puff Corners." We gather around the table for lunch, and when we finish eating Jimmy and I go back to the boats to get our gear. When we have our stuff packed, we say good-bye to Karen and the kids, who will be staying behind, and we head around the north side of the bay, through the hatchery, and up the gravel trail to the weirs. They trap the returning experimental fish here and separate them from the wild fish that spawn in the stream. The hatchery fish are not allowed to spawn in the stream, but are spawned by hand in the hatchery, then raised in the net pens.

As we cross the creek on the weir, we load our rifles. The Dog Salmon are already in the creek, and there are piles of rotting carcasses lying along the banks where the bears have been feeding. The bears here are Alaska Brown Bears, a member of the grizzly family, and are not to be taken lightly. They have no predators and are not afraid of people. Almost every year, someone in SE Alaska is attacked. They are very territorial over fishing spots, and sows with cubs are especially dangerous.

The trail to Sashun Lake is a bear highway this time of year, so it must be traveled cautiously and with presence of mind. The last thing we want is to have to shoot a bear, but the twelve-gauge shotgun Jim is carrying and my heavy caliber rifle are a comfort, as we navigate the path through the Alders and Devil's Club. The hot, midday air is heavy with the smell of rotting fish, the distinctive odor of Devil's Club, and an occasional whiff of the musky scent of bear. Ravens squawk from the Spruce and Hemlock trees, and the shrill cries of Eagles echo from the hills as we work our way up the path.

It's hot work in the August sun, with sweat burning our eyes and "no-see-ums" chewing on exposed skin, but this is the stuff of adventure. The small discomforts we suffer and the danger from the bears add spice to the memories we'll share of this day for the rest of our lives.

The ground gradually rises, and after a while we reach the vague path that branches off the main trail, up the steep slope to the north. As we struggle up the hill, we occasionally see Shashun Lake shimmering in the valley below. Eventually we come out on the ridge into open muskeg, then wind our way around ponds of brown water with Lilly pads floating on their surfaces. The trail winds off to the left, toward a notch in the hills, and after a while we strike a creek that leads us through a pass to Round Lake.

The lake is about three-quarters of a mile across. The south side is against a steep slope and there is a low hill to the north. We walk along the north shore to a gravel bar, then stop and put down the packs and guns.

"This looks like the spot to me, I'm going to give it a try here," Jim says as he rigs up his pole.

We soon have spinners clipped on the end of our lines and are casting out into the lake. I work my way slowly along the north shore, casting into likely looking spots, but nothing happens. I change lures several times, and I can see Jim doing the same.

As I retrieve another cast, I hear Jim yell, "EEEHAAHHH!"

I look over at him and his rod is bent in a circle as he fights a fish. After a short struggle, he lands a nice ten-inch rainbow, which he holds up for me to see, grinning triumphantly. I wave back and continue casting and changing lures, but I can't seem to get a bite. After a while, I wander back to the packs and break out a Snickers bar. As I lay there in the warm, afternoon sun, I can see Jim fighting another fish. He has worked his way down along the south shore, and as I watch he signals that this is the fourth fish. I shake my head and get up to try again.

The sun is heading for the horizon, and as evening settles over the lake fish begin to dimple the water, feeding on the insects that hover near the surface. I eventually catch a couple of fish, and as the evening approaches I begin to think of food. Before long, Jim comes back along the bank carrying a forked-stick with several nice trout hanging on it.

"How many did you get?" he asks, walking up and laying his fish and pole on the ground.

"Three, couldn't seem to get them to bite," I answer.

"Huh, that's weird. I got ten. I wonder what you were doing wrong. This is what I caught them on," he says, showing me a yellow spinner.

"I don't have one of those. The ones I got were on a black and white Dare Devil, but they were barely interested in that either. They would follow it in but wouldn't bite," I say.

"We got enough for supper, anyway. We better go make camp; I'm getting hungry, and it'll be dark in a couple of hours," he says.

We gather up our gear and head down the creek a couple of hundred yards. After some looking around, Jim finds the tiny log hut, hidden in a grove of Yellow Cedar trees. We unload our gear and make camp. There are three walls still standing, so we throw a plastic tarp over the walls and support the front with a pole. I lay a fire in front of the open side, and then we build our beds with moss.

When the fire is making coals, Jim heats up the iron skillet that he packed up, and we fry and eat trout until we are stuffed. When we've finished eating, we make a pot of coffee and spend the evening yarning around the fire. As the color goes out of the Western sky and the night settles over the muskeg, we huddle closer to the fire, basking in its warmth. The air is cool and damp and smells of Yellow Cedar smoke, fried trout and Jim's cigarette.

"Is it my imagination or is it clouding up?" I ask, looking at the southern sky.

"Looks like clouds to me; hope it don't rain," Jim answers, looking up also.

"Well, I've about had it. Think I'll roll up in my blanket and call it a day," I say, tossing the dregs of my coffee into the ashes at the edge of the fire.

"Yeah, me too, it's been a long day," Jim says, tossing his cigarette butt into the fire and getting up.

We bank up the fire and turn in. As I lay for a while, staring into the embers, remembering other fires, I think of the comfort it must have brought to primitive people when they first learned to use it. Eventually I drift off and sleep for a while. Sometime later, I awaken to the sound of Jim shuffling around. The fire has burned down to coals and I'm starting to get cold. As I throw more wood on the fire I notice that it has started to rain lightly.

Jim coughs, "Rainin', ain't it?"

"Yep, I'm afraid so," I answer, pulling the rest of the firewood into the shelter, so we can get the fire started in the morning.

"Great, I hope the wind doesn't come up; we don't have much shelter here, and if this plastic blows away we're going to be wet by morning."

I burrow back into my wool blanket, trying to avoid the staub that is poking me in the hip. The night seems to last forever. Eventually the wind comes up and we have to get up to tie the tarp down better. The rain comes and goes but by daylight there is a steady soaking drizzle. I finally give up on sleep as the first gray light of dawn begins to lighten the leaden sky. After several tries, I manage to get a smoldering fire going and the coffee re-heating. Jim stumbles over to the fire, lights a smoke, and he hunkers down to warm his hands in front of the small blaze. When the coffeepot is steaming, I wipe the dirt out of the cups and fill them with the foul looking brew. I hand Jim a cup and he takes a sip.

"Damn, that's good. Take the hair off a bear skin," he says, smacking his lips. I taste mine.

"Turpenhydrate number three, guaranteed to get your heart started on the dampest of mornings."

"Genuine panther piss, take the paint off a battle ship," he says.

"My enthusiasm for trout fishing isn't what it was yesterday. Wonder what your ma is fixing for breakfast this morning," I say.

"I don't know about breakfast, but if we take off now we can be there for lunch," he says, flinging the dregs of his coffee into the bushes and grinning sheepishly at me.

We pack up our gear and head off down the mountain. It's raining harder now and between the wet bushes and the steady rain, we are soon soaked to the skin. We are not cold though, and take a perverse pleasure in the wet windy day. Back down on the Sashun Lake trail, we shelter under the roots of a big Spruce that has grown on top of an old stump. The stump has long since rotted away, leaving a semi-dry hollow under the new tree. These places are common in heavy, old growth timber, and can provide a semblance of shelter. I munch a candy bar and Jim has a smoke while we rest. We soon begin to feel the cold from our wet clothes, so we take off again. About mid-morning we walk out of the woods at the weir and head for the boats and dry clothes.

At the boat I strip down and dry off. There's nothing like dry clothes when you have been out in a soaking rain. I wring out my wet stuff and put it in a plastic garbage bag. The boat is too small to hang it all up, so I will take the clothes to the laundry at the fish plant and use the washer and dryer when we get back to P.A.

About noon, Jim comes down from the house and tells me lunch is ready, so I follow him back to Jim and Nita's apartment. She fills us with soup, homemade bread, and banana cream pie for dessert. We discuss the weather and decide to stay till the next day. The wind is suppose to swing to the SW by morning and the swells will be smaller. Jimmy and I tag his dad around for the afternoon, helping him with a couple of chores, and spend some time snooping through the warehouse. Dinner is venison roast followed by cream puffs for dessert. After supper we play cards for a while, then hit the rack early. We didn't get much sleep the night before and the warm, dry, soft bunk is like heaven after a night on the ground, wrapped in a wool blanket with water dripping in your ear.

I wake up about six-thirty and it's still raining, but the wind is coming out of the west, gusting down the bay, toward the entrance. The west wind is a good sign that the front has passed and the weather is changing. I stir up a cup of coffee, then go out to look at the salmon fry in the big net bags that hang through large holes in the floats. There is several, each containing a different size or type of Salmon. This is an experimental hatchery, and has been instrumental in the development of rearing techniques that are being used all over the world to raise King Salmon and other species. During part of the summer and fall, there are runs of Kings and Cohos returning here that we have the privilege of fishing on, so we whole-heartedly support the experiments conducted here.

The net pens are about twenty feet in diameter and about twenty feet deep. Each one contains thousands of tiny fish, which mill in a dark cloud in the green water.

As I walk around looking at them, one of the workers comes out on the float and does the first feeding. Each pen gets a measured amount of feed several times a day. The man walks around each pen, throwing scoops of the brown pellets into the water. The small fish turn the surface into froth in their frenzy to feed.

I watch for a while, then wander up to the house to see if Jim has come up with a plan for the day. As I climb the steps at the head of the Tide Bridge, Jim and his dad come out the door.

"Hey, why didn't you come up for breakfast?" Big Jim asks.

"I got to looking at the fish and forgot about the time. Looks like the storm is about blown out," I answer, as we stand under the big Spruce trees and look out over the bay.

"Yeah, I think we should take off pretty soon. There's another low coming through tonight and I need to get home. It might be a little lumpy on Conclusion Point, but we should be able to make it all right. Karen is rounding up the kids and their stuff, and I'm on my way down to warm up the boat. I gave Pop the rest of the trout; he really likes them for breakfast, and I don't have any ice aboard to keep them anyway."

"Sure, I had my fill up on the hill the other night," I say as we walk down the ramp to the boats.

Karen and the kids come down in a few minutes, and after everyone is aboard we untie and shove off. As we idle past the white house, Nita sticks her head out the window and waves goodbye.

"Stop by again when you're up this way, I'll make cream puffs!" she yells.

"Okay, I will. Thanks Nita," I yell back.

The seas aren't too bad in the strait, big but far apart, and we make fair time. We are bucking the tide because on the ebb, when there is a southerly swell, there are several nasty tide rips between Little Port and P.A.. As we cross the mouth of Port Lucy, several hard squalls blow out of the bay, making the boats heel over and pelting us with violent rain showers. The water is whipped into a white froth, but the waves are small.

"Boy, I'm glad were not crouching under that tarp in this crap," Jim says on the CB.

"Yeah, me too. I wonder what it's going to be like crossing Conclusion?" I ask, noticing that the swells are getting bigger.

"The swells are a long ways apart. It'll be windy but we should be okay. It's still flooding, so there shouldn't be any rips," Jim answers.

"I hope not, there isn't any place in Conclusion to get out of this westerly wind. I guess we're committed one way or another," I reply.

The wind mellows out some as we run in the lee of the mountain, between Lucy and Armstrong. When we come out from behind it, into the mouth of Conclusion, another vicious squall hammers the side of the boat with horizontal rain, and I have to fight the steering to stay on course. After the squall passes, things settle down for a few minutes and I only have to contend with the ten to twelve-foot SE swell coming in off the ocean and growing bigger with each mile we run.

We are off the small, timbered island on the south side of Conclusion when the next squall hits. This is by far the worst yet. The boat almost lays on its side as the tremendous gust swoops across the bay in a welter of rain and foam ripped from the crests of the choppy waves. I top out on a swell and watch the Juanita H. roll so far to port that it looks like his trolling pole is going to go under water. I skid down into the next trough and when I come back up on top of the next sea, the whole world has disappeared in a fog of rain and wind-blown water.

I yank back on the throttle, then turn into the wind. This puts my course at an acute angle to the big swells from the south, but at this point I am forced to pick the lesser of two evils. When the next swell comes, I turn into it, and when I'm over the crest, I turn back to starboard into the wind and ride down the swell at an angle. I repeat this maneuver for the crest of each swell until the sky finally lightens and the squall moves on to the east. In a few moments the rain lets up to a drizzle, and the wind lays down to about fifteen knots. I point the bow south again and throttle back up a bit, so I can make some progress against the tide.

"Man, that was something else. My wind-speed gauge showed fifty-eight knots in that one. I almost dipped a pole a couple of times there," Jim says on the radio.

"That was some squall. I'll talk to you in town, I gotta pay attention here; these swells are getting pretty big and I need both hands to steer," I answer, hanging up the mike and angling into the crest of the next one.

"I'm going to go behind Crow Island. It'll get us out of the swells faster, and it's not so far to the red can that way. If you don't know your way through there, just follow me," Jim answers.

A few more swells and another small squall and we finally make the turn in behind the island. Another ten minutes and we clear the red can and head for the dock. This trip has been a memorable adventure from start to finish, and is one of many that I will share with Little Jim over the years.

I'm soon tied to the dock and enjoying a cup of mud on the Celedo. My trout-fishing trip makes for an evening of good story telling. It's one time I'm really glad to be tied to the dock; adventures really are more fun in the telling than the living!

19

The next morning dawns clear and there is a hint of fall in the rain-scrubbed air. The main topic of conversation on the dock this morning is the seine opening, which starts today. Everyone is up in arms and ideas about what should be done include everything from political action to downright anarchy. Many phone calls to the Fish and Game office and to State Legislators are made with little satisfaction gained. The word is that the opening will happen and nothing can be done about it.

Management claims that the seiners will catch only Pinks and Dogs, but we know that the fish school in the same places and that the boats will target on Kings and Cohos because they are worth more money. We are also afraid they will flood our markets with cheap fish while we are languishing in port, and that this will drive our prices down after the closure.

Several people decide to go out in skiffs and photograph the fish they are hauling aboard to document the claim that they are not only catching many Kings and Cohos but are sorting them out of the haul and icing them in totes on deck. These fish will be sold as troll caught fish on handtroll licenses the skippers have on their seine skiffs. This is a common practice which the Fish and Game refuses to admit is happening.

It is obvious to most of us that the management people would like to eliminate trolling and use net boats to harvest fish as they enter spawning streams. It would make it easier to control the amount of fish taken from each run, and eliminate all the gear conflicts that occur between different gear groups. This type of management probably makes a certain amount of sense, but there would be such a hue and cry from the trollers and the buyers that market their fish that management doesn't dare broach the subject openly.

For quite a few years the Cape Ommaney/Port Alexander area has been closed to seining and gillnetting, and the troll fleet has had the area to itself. The two types of fishing don't mix, and the trollers believe that some areas should be set aside for trolling only. Meanwhile, the net fleet is pressuring the ADF&G to open these areas to net fishing. One of the sad parts of our lifestyle is the growing necessity to participate in the politics of these issues. Most people who seek out this type of lifestyle aren't very interested in politics, and it really is hard to concentrate on fishing when there is always some ominous cloud hanging just over the horizon. The threat to our life style is a reality that must be faced, but most of us just wish it would go away.

By late morning I feel I've had enough politics and decide to take a walk in the woods east of town. It's too nice a day to waste listening to arguments and the perpetual complaining that dominates the dock talk these days.

I pack a lunch, load up the old Marlin, and head for the beach. I go up the boardwalk a ways, then cut off to the right on Woody Ave., a foot path that leads out into Back Bay. It's only a few yards through the trees to the small bight, and in a moment I come out into the open cove. I walk around the north end, climbing over the hundreds of driftwood logs piled there, and enter the woods again behind Blueberry Island.

The forest is dark and cool; it's like entering another reality after the hubbub of town and all the human energy there. I stand just inside the trees for a few moments, letting the tension drain out of me and adjusting to the new world before me. Soon the mystery draws me in; my feet pick their way along the faint trail leading up a gentle slope. I climb over fallen logs covered with green moss, and pass root masses of giant Hemlocks that have blown down in some forgotten storm. The wet places are torn by the hoof prints of deer, and in a muddy spot, among huge Skunk Cabbage plants, there is an old bear track that is as long as my size eleven boot. I move on up the slope past a dead tree with a brilliant, orange and yellow Chicken Of the Woods Mushroom clinging to its crumbling bark. The color of the fungus is a startling contrast to the blacks, browns, grays, and greens of the surrounding woods.

After a short climb I top out on a low ridge that marks the divide between Back Bay and the next cove to the east. I can see the blue and silver water of Chatham Strait shimmering through the trees, and as I stand for a while, the Red Squirrels scold me from the trees overhead. Ravens croak in the distance.

I turn left and push through the Huckleberry brush along the top of the ridge. Ahead, I see a rock wall that looks too steep to climb, but as I approach through the trees I see a gap with a deer trail leading into it. I climb up into the gap, and stop to look around in wonder.

A great force has broken the spine of the ridge in some ancient upheaval creating a narrow pass between vertical walls twenty feet apart. The walls of the pass are green with several kinds of mosses that thrive in the water trickling down the rocks. Great Hemlocks tower above on top of the ridge, and one has fallen across the pass. The trail meanders between large, angular boulders that have fallen from the cliffs, and there is sign that deer and bears frequently use this break in the wall to pass from one side of the ridge to the other. In the middle of the pass is the stump of an old Hemlock that has been dead for many years. All that remains is a ten-foot tall rotting column, surrounded by piles of punky wood that has sloughed of the trunk over the years. Its four-foot diameter and the length of time it has been dead are a clue to the time that has passed since the upheaval broke the ridge and created the pass.

I climb down the trail into a grove of small Spruce and Hemlocks, and cross a tiny stream trickling between moss-covered banks. I kneel on a stone, scoop up a handful of the cold water, and suck it into my mouth. It tastes of earth and rocks and mystery. I scoop up more and drink again and again until my thirst is quenched. I kneel, listening to the brook chuckling over the stones in its bed, and feel the water trickle out of my beard and down my neck. I wipe my chin on the sleeve of my shirt, and rise up to head on down the trail.

In a short distance the path turns down to the right and into an open park among a grove of ancient Spruce trees that line the shore of a tiny cove. The trees are not tall but are very large in diameter, with long, knarled limbs hanging out over the gravel beach. Their trunks are lumpy with burls, and on the shore side they bleed sap from wounds that mar their bark. The wounds are made by logs tossed against them during the great storms of winter.

I sit on a log in the shade of one of the limbs and look south, past Crow Island toward Cape Ommaney and Wooden Island in the distance. The water shimmers in a light westerly breeze and twinkles like diamonds in the noon sun. The sky is cloudless and deep blue overhead. As I sit with the ancient forest at my back and the sea at my feet, I feel a deep sense of wonder and oneness with the universe that I can only find in these magical places. As I bask in these feelings, I realize that true wilderness is necessary for the soul, and that humans are working diligently to remove the last traces of it from the planet. In our obsessive lust for wealth, we are destroying the real treasure. The beach at my feet is littered with plastic and other junk. It reminds me of the old saying "You can't see the forest for the trees." True wilderness is not a few isolated patches of trees with rangers to charge admission.

I shake off these thoughts as I get up and crunch across the gravel beach toward the next point. There is a narrow, low ridge of an unusual shale-like stone jutting out into the bay. As I climb around its end, I notice that the formation stops abruptly at a deep crack that runs parallel to the shore, and that it does not continue on the other side. I look both ways, left and right, and realize that what I see is a fault line. The continuation of the ridge is offset about two hundred feet to the east. To the west, the crack disappears into the woods, and I realize that the pass from Back Bay is part of this fault line. Now I know what caused the break in the ridge that I climbed through to get to this beach. I shake my head in wonder and cross another tiny pocket of beach toward the point.

I climb up and around the rocky bluff that forms the east point of the cove, and as I round to the other side of the point, the shore falls away to the north. Looking up the narrow inlet, I see a gravel beach, strewn with hundreds of logs at its head, about a quarter mile away. The first half of the distance is a scramble over boulders and rocky points, then a rock shelf with sedge grass and pools of brackish water. Several huge logs lay parallel with the timber, and one has been there so long its back is covered with moss and a small Spruce tree is growing out of it. The beginning of the gravel beach is marked with a huge boulder, which has a cap of moss and several knarled trees on its top that look like Bonsai trees.

I pass the great rock and step onto the gravel. There are hundreds of deer tracks, and many logs and other pieces of flotsam piled on the shore. I sit for a while in the shade of a Spruce that hangs out over the beach and drink in the beauty of the place. After a while my curiosity gets the best of me and I get up to poke through the piles of driftwood and other debris. There are plastic bottles, pop-can holders, net floats, trolling plugs, and many other items cast off by humans, scattered among the loose strands of giant kelp. There are thousands of pieces of wood, from tiny sculpted bits and pieces, to logs fifty feet long and four feet in diameter. I notice that most of the wood has some mark or other, indicating that its presence is a result of man's activity. I also see great pits dug into the gravel and kelp mixture, and logs that have been rolled out of their resting-places, where bears have been rooting for sandfleas.

Perched precariously on the crest of a gravel wave, sculpted by the swells at some past high tide, is a round, blue-green, glass ball, about four inches in diameter. It is a Japanese net float, made of blown glass. A beachcombers prize! They are one piece of human trash that actually adds to the beauty of the place. I wonder how far it has traveled to this deserted shore, and how it has survived being smashed on the rocks by the waves that deposited it here. It is like a frozen bubble of sea foam, its symmetry a contrast to the bed of olive-drab kelp upon which it rests.

I pick it up and turn it over in my hand. Inside is a shiny round ball of glass the size of a marble, which is part of a disk of glass that is the point where the ball was attached to the glass blower's pipe. When it is the right size, he twists the tube to seal the hole and cuts the ball off with a knife. Before it cools, he brands it with his mark, which appears as one or two characters on the flattened disk where it has been sealed. After looking at it for a few moments, I grin and put it back on the kelp. I have found many glass balls over the years, and have several on the boat, so I will leave this one for someone else to find. I hope they enjoy it as much as I did. The joy is in the finding not the possessing. As I look at it laying at my feet, I remember the first one I found years ago at Happy Harbor.

I had traded a 16-Gauge shotgun for a 14-foot double-ended skiff, and had just finished installing a 16 hp Briggs and Stratton engine in it. Late one evening I decided to putt out of the harbor, for no other reason than just for the fun of it. As I steered through the narrow entrance, I noticed several Sea Lions rolling around on the surface a few hundred yards out. As I got nearer, I could see that they were playing with something and I soon realized that it was a giant, glass ball the size of a basketball! The Sea Lions swam away as I approached, and as I idled past I reached down and scooped it up. It was beautiful. It was a deep, aquamarine blue and possessed a magical quality that totally captivated me. As I held it in my hands and looked at it against the backdrop of mountains and sea, I felt a sense of wonder. This delicate, beautiful glass had traveled thousands of miles in the currents of the North Pacific, surviving storms and near-beachings on distant shores, to come to this spot, at this time. What motivated me to come out of the harbor? If the Sea Lions had not found it first, would I have seen it?

This country has woven a spell around me. It constantly reminds me of the mystery of life, and it never lets me forget for long that there is more to being than the petty struggles that we perpetuate upon ourselves in the everyday world. This is why we need to live in the world with as little disturbance as possible. The natural world, if you immerse yourself in it, will lead you to experiences of being that have a value that you can't measure in dollars and cents. I realized in that moment that I truly love this magic universe and best of all it loves me!

Eventually I tire of beachcombing and wander into the woods at the NE corner of the gravel beach. There is a well-used deer trail leading up a small valley and I follow it slowly, hoping to see a deer. The trail gradually climbs up a series of steps, then leads through a notch in a rim that runs east and west. The timber here is mostly Yellow Cedar and the sun beating down on their boughs brings out their pungent odor. As I near the break in the ridge, the trail crosses two well-defined deer beds. I examine them for signs of recent use, but find no evidence that deer have been there lately. They are probably winter beds, used when the frigid, arctic wind howls out of the NE across the muskegs higher up.

I push through a clump of runty Cedars, up a steep bank, then out onto an open muskeg. There is a mound to my right, so I clamber up it to get a better view. To my left the rim curves away to the NW and ends at the foot of a hill that rises a couple of hundred feet. This knob is the highest point on the peninsula that Port Alexander is inlet into. To my front the terrain falls away in a jumble of small hills and valleys, with patches of scrub scattered here and there and many small ponds of various sizes. The ponds are full of lilly pads, and many of them have bright yellow flowers. To the north and east, the land gives away to Chatham Strait, and its brilliant, cobalt blue is a sharp contrast to the dark green of the mountains. Far to the NE, I can see the white, snow-capped mountains on the mainland that forms the boundary between SE Alaska and Canada.

I turn to the south and look at Cape Ommaney, Wooden Island, the Hazy Islands, and Coronation Island to the SE. To the west, No Name Mountain shimmers in the heat of the afternoon sun. The beauty that surrounds me is stunning. It takes my breath away. It must be seen to be understood; there are no words adequate to properly describe it. I follow the rim around to the base of the hill, stopping at each new viewpoint to savor the magnificent scenery.

At the base of the hill I cross a small creek that runs off to the east, through a deep narrow channel. In some places the tiny stream disappears under the moss and then reappears farther down hill. I push my way up a steep slope through a thick grove of Yellow Cedars, and top out in an open basin just below the summit of the hill. Down to the right is a small lake filled with flowering lilly pads. The water reflects the blue sky between the green leaves of the Lilies.

I cross the basin and climb the last hundred feet to the top of the hill. The highest point is one of several mounds that rise ten or so feet above the rounded top of the hill, and I climb up onto the highest one.

A rugged, saw-toothed ridge looms behind Port Conclusion, which cuts inland to the west. At the back of Conclusion is a low pass to Larch Bay, and to the south of the pass is No Name Mountain, then Ommaney Mountain and the Cape. Along the shore at Poor Man Point, I see about ten seine boats, their nets forming huge circles marked by the white floats that hold the top of the nets on the surface. I also see several trollers and skiffs moving among them, and the magic of the day is swept away by the feeling of conflict emanating from the boats. Here they are, in the middle of this spectacular, natural beauty, and their total focus is on catching as many fish as possible as fast as possible before someone else gets them. Or before the powers that be tell them to stop so someone else can take a turn.

I shake my head and look away to the north, toward the snow-capped peaks of Admiralty Island and the mainland to the NE. As I stand there trying to reconnect with the spiritual high that has dominated the rest of the morning, I realize that I have made enough money for this year. I have $5,500 saved up and it will see me through the winter easily. I believe in only taking what I need, and I have enough. There is still some summer left, and what I want most is to spend it wandering around in the woods in Kasaan Bay. To savor it before it is ruined forever by over-exploitation.

I climb down off the mound and go down into the basin, back down the way I have come to the rim, then drop down into the Back Lagoon. I am just traveling to get there now, hardly seeing my surroundings, the mood of the morning lost. I'll talk to Dick about leaving, but offer to stay if he wants to. I have a feeling that he is burned-out too, and will probably welcome the idea of starting home before the September gales start blowing in off the Pacific. I cross the mud flats in the lagoon, then cross the point into the back harbor, and onto the rickety old boardwalk at Dick Whitham's house. By the time I'm on the main boardwalk I'm pretty much back into the reality of town, and hurry on down to the front dock to the boat. I put the rifle away and head for the Spray.

Dick is at the galley table with a cup of coffee in front of him and a cigarette in his hand.

"Hey, how was your walk?" he asks as I climb down the galley steps.

"It was great. Found a glass ball at Judy's Cove," I answer, pouring hot water into a cup and sitting down to mix in the brown crystals of instant coffee.

"You didn't miss anything around here but a lot of complainin'. Seems like that's all fishermen ever do is sit around and bitch. I get tired of it sometimes," he says.

"Yeah, I know what you mean. You know, I was thinking about heading for home; I've got a winter stake saved up, and I'm about fished-out for this year. Be nice to get down there while the weather is still nice, too," I say.

"Sounds good to me. When do you want to leave?" he asks with a twinkle in his eye.

"I hadn't got that far yet. I need to change oil and get a few things at the store. I could probably be ready by morning if the weather is nice."

"The forecast is for clear skies and light and variable winds for the next few days. If we are going to do it, now is the time. I need to change oil, too. We could go over and fuel up now and do the oil changes when we get back; the engines would be warm and we could kill two birds with one stone," Dick answers.

"Okay, let's go for it!" I say, finishing my coffee and rinsing out the cup.

I head back to the Nomad and start up the engine. We untie and idle over to the fishhouse to fuel up. When we are finished and tied back at the dock, I go through the messy oil change routine, and when the dirty chore is finished, Dick and I walk up to the store to buy a few things and pay for the fuel. We run into Bud and Celia on the way back and inform them of our plan. They are disappointed that we are leaving, and invite us over for dinner later. We return to the boats and finish preparing them for the 150-mile trip home. By dinnertime I'm finished with my chores and head for the Celedo. Dick is there ahead of me, and good smells are issuing from the galley. We enjoy an excellent dinner as usual and an evening of good conversation. It's been a busy day and I go home early, excited by the prospect of heading back to Happy Harbor, and a change of pace.

20

"**A**hoy there, the mud scow!" Dick shouts. "You gonna sleep all day? We need to get goin' if you still want to leave today."

I struggle up out of a dream about trying to land a big fish with a gaff that has no hook.

"Yeah okay, I'll be right out," I yell back, heaving myself out of the bunk. I yank on my pants and stand up into the wheelhouse. Ole "Ben" says eight o'clock and I notice that I forgot to pull up the alarm button before I went to bed last night. I check the oil then start the engine. When it's ticking over smoothly, I mix up a cup of heart starter and take a dip of snoose.

"Forgot to set the alarm. You should have hollered sooner," I say, climbing over onto the dock and sitting on the bullrail with Dick and Bud.

"I've only been up for a half-hour too; getting lazy in my old age," Dick replies, taking a drag on his Marlboro.

"It looks like you guys will have good running weather today," Bud says.

"Anybody heard the forecast?" I ask, looking up at the sun which is just coming up over the trees to the east.

"More of the same, light and variable winds in the three day out-look," Dick answers.

We sit quietly for a while, enjoying the warmth of the sun and the good company.

"You running the boat south this year, Bud?" I ask

"No, I'm going to leave it in Ketchikan this year. Celia and I are thinking pretty seriously about moving up there in the spring."

"All right, maybe we can run up together next year," I say, pleased at the thought of having them close enough to visit in the winter.

"Well, Partner, we better hit the trail if we're going to get out of here today," Dick says, standing up.

"Yup, got a long ways to go to a good anchorage. You want to try to make Baker today, Dick? The tide will be with us all the way up Sumner Strait," I ask, getting up too.

"Well, you guys have a good trip home and a good winter," Bud says, shaking our hands. We wish him well too, then untie the boats and shove off. As I pass the cold storage on the way toward the red can, I feel a small sadness at leaving. I really like P.A., and have given some thought to wintering out here next year. Kasaan bay is being logged off, and many of the places that I have hunted and hiked in the past are gone. The feeling of wildness that has kept me there so many years has disappeared. P.A. still has that unspoiled, untamed feel that I seem to need, and it draws me strongly. At the red can I take the camera off the binnacle and snap a couple of pictures of the harbor.

The ocean is calm as we point the bows east across the strait. The morning passes slowly as we grind steadily toward Decision Pass at six miles per hour. I feel like a bug crawling along the surface of a blue ball, always moving but never getting anywhere. Eventually the hills on South Kuiu Island begin to look bigger than the ones on Baranof, and at about twelve-thirty we finally pass the lighthouse on Cape Decision. The deep bellow of the foghorn reminds me of the trip out when I thought the horn was my engine making strange noises.

When I'm clear of the cape, I put the bow stem on Calder Peak, over on Prince of Wales Island. This course will take me out to the red can on Saint Albans Reef, and the turn north toward Point Baker. Sumner Strait is calm as a lake; even the ground swell coming in off the ocean is blocked by Coronation Island. The only disturbance on the silver-blue surface is the current boils caused by the tide starting to flood over the un-even bottom. Long lines of kelp and other flotsam are trapped in the eddies and whirlpools along the lines separating bodies of water that are of different temperatures and salinity. Plankton and algae also accumulate along these rip lines, attracting herring and needlefish to these rich sources of feed. This in turn attracts birds, seals, salmon, and other sea life. I have never fished here because of the distance to a buyer, but the richness of life has always piqued my curiosity. The area just looks fishy. We are soon abeam the Fairway Islands. The Fairways are a string of small islands and rock piles, which lie in the mouth of Affleck Canal, the first inlet east of Cape Decision. I can just make out the buoy ahead at Saint Albans Reef.

"Ahoy there, Cap, you still awake?" I say to Dick over the CB.

"Barely," he answers.

"We're making good time; should be in Baker around six or so. The tide is flooding, so we should get a nice boost up the hill. You realize this trip is twice as far because we have to run north twenty-five miles, then back south twenty-five miles. Too bad there isn't a channel through Prince of Wales; save us a whole day's run," I say wistfully.

"Maybe you should write a letter to The Army Corp of Engineers and complain.

They dug a canal through Panama, why not Prince of Wales Island," he answers.

"Now there's an idea; we're just as important as them Panamaniacs, involved in commerce and trade, and contributing to the grotesque national product, ain't we? Heck, think of the fuel and air pollution it would save; even the Coasties could use it to get here from Ketchikan to make sure our fire extinguishers are up to date," I reply.

"Heh heh, now that's the wildest scheme I've heard out of you yet. You should have been a politician; you'd be good at spending the taxpayers' money."

"Yeah, but think of all the jobs a project like that would create. Why, the economy would boom, it would be bigger than the pipeline. They could take all the deadbeats off welfare, give them a shovel, and tell them to start digging. Be good for their souls, teach them a work ethic. Hey, this is sounding better all the time. I'm gonna write my congressman as soon as we hit town," I say.

"But what would you do with the dirt they dug out of the ditch?" he asks.

"Well, I don't know. How about instead of a canal we build a railway? You could haul the boats out at Hollis on the east side, put them in cradles on flat cars, and haul them over to Craig. Prince of Wales has 500 miles of State highway; might as well build a railroad, too," I answer with mock enthusiasm.

"Yup, you should run for congress; with an idea like that you'd get elected for sure. I can see you now in a three-piece, shark-skin suit with a big, rotten ce-gar in the corner of your mouth, tellin' the voters how you're going to put a chicken in every pot, and a new car in every garage," Dick says, getting into the spirit of it.

"Well, Partner, I'd make you Commissioner of Railroads and give you your own train so you could run back and fourth on the line keeping everybody honest for me. You could have a couple of good lookin' secretaries, and a cook to fix your Alpo every night," I offer.

"Now you're talkin'. This idea is sounding better all the time. I'd want summers off though, so I could go fishin', and a new boat so I could take them secretaries and my Alpo chef," he says.

"Hey, no problem. You'd be the boss, you could do whatever you want," I answer. The St. Albans can comes abeam and I swing north toward Point Baker, twenty miles away. The buoy is leaning way over in the current as we enter the strong tidal stream. I can feel the boat picking up speed. In a few minutes the can is growing smaller behind us.

"Boy! It must be running about three or four knots here; if this keeps up we'll be in Baker in no time," I say into the mike.

"Yeah, she's really running; I could hear my governor lighten up when we came around the can. We might be able to make Salmon Bay, over in Kashaverof Pass, if this current holds," he answers.

"It might; the tide just changed about an hour ago and it's a big tide today. We might as well go as far as we can before dark. Salmon Bay is a good anchorage and if we get an early start in the morning, we can ride the flood through the pass and catch the ebb down Clarence Strait. Heck, we could be at Grindall Island by noon. You ought to stop at Happy Harbor for a couple of days; I want to stop there to see if anyone needs anything from town, and then run across in a couple of days to fuel up and get a bunch of grub," I say.

"Yeah...I guess there is no hurry. I've never been in there before, wouldn't mind checkin' the place out. I might even spend part of the winter out there. There's a dock I could tie to, isn't there?" he asks.

"Yeah, lots of room. My floathouse is tied to an old, log raft with a standing boom to the beach. You can tie there anytime, for as long as you want. The guy that owns it moved down south and left me pretty much in charge, so help yourself," I answer.

"Okay, I'll stop with you and look the place over, then we can run into town together in a few days. Man this tide is really running. I can see that buoy in the middle of the strait already; that's about halfway, isn't it?"

"Yeah, pretty close. We must be making ten knots or more over the bottom. We picked a good day to make the trip. Well, I think I'm going to whip up a peanut butter sandwich and a cup of mud. Never did eat breakfast; my stomach is starting to think my throat's been cut," I answer, hanging up the mike.

"Click click," Dick answers.

I duck into the foc'sle to whip up some lunch, and then settle back in the driver's seat to eat it. As I sit munching my sandwich and sipping my coffee, my mind drifts into the future. I examine an idea that has appeared in my daydreams several times lately. I have been wanting a small skiff and outboard motor for a long time, but never had the extra cash before. This year, however, it looks like I can swing it and still have enough money to get through the winter. I run through my finances in my head, and decide to buy one if I can find something suitable for around two thousand dollars. That will leave me thirty-five hundred for the winter, which should be plenty if I'm careful. The thought is exciting and I can hardly wait. Happy Harbor is on a small island in the mouth of Kasaan Bay, and a skiff of some kind is necessary for gathering firewood and getting off the island to hunt. There are also some good beachcoambing spots in the bay, and that's one of my favorite pastimes.

I dream away the hours, and with the tide pushing us, we are soon approaching Point Baker. I can see Mariposa light ahead and realize that we are going to be at Baker before five. I get the chart out and step off the distance to Salmon Bay with dividers. *"Ten miles; we could be there before seven if the current keeps pushing us at this speed. Tide-change isn't till seven; heck we could go through the pass on slack water and make Coffman Cove before dark. If we get through Kashevarof tonight we wouldn't have to get up till seven in the morning to catch the ebb down the strait."*

I put the chart away and watch the beach go by. We are off Port Protection already and coming up rapidly on Baker. I unhook the mike and holler at Dick.

"You awake, Dick?"

"Yeah, we're going too fast to snooze. I'm afraid I'll miss Ketchikan and wake up in Prince Rupert, the way this tide is running," he says back.

"I was just doing some calculating on the chart, and it looks like if the current holds we could get all the way to Coffman Cove before dark. Then we wouldn't have to get up so danged early in the morning to catch the ebb south."

"Sounds good to me; be a long day today, but a short one tomorrow. What are all those white things up on the corner?" he asks. "Looks like net floats."

"Yeah, looks like. I hope they don't have the whole strait blocked off with gillnet. It would spoil my plan if we have to spend a lot of time dodging nets," I answer.

We are right off the entrances to Point Baker now, and as I talk on the radio, a whale rolls onto the surface right in front of the boat. I yank back on the throttle just as it blows a misty breath into the air and dives straight down a few yards ahead. As the whale sounds, its huge black and white tail rises ten feet above the surface for a moment then disappears under the water. A wide, black streak appears on my depth recorder as the boat crosses the patch of bubbles where the whale has disappeared.

"Wow! Did you see that?" I shout into the mike, as I push the throttle back up to running speed.

"Yeah, I thought you were going to run right over it," he answers.

"I got a picture of him on the paper machine. It shows a thick black line heading for the bottom. I've heard guys from here talk about a whale that hangs around all summer every year. They call it "Ma Baker;" I wonder if that was her?"

"I don't know, might be. Boy, were still making about ten knots; look at that beach race by. Must be hard to fish here with this current."

"Yeah, I was halibut fishing with a guy here a few years ago. We made a set one afternoon over by The Eye Opener. The current was pretty strong, so we decided to haul it in the dark, at slack tide. We got the first anchor up about tide-change and were happily taking off hooks and throwing an occasional fish aboard. All of a sudden we could hear this roaring noise, east of us up the strait. It sounded like a jet or something and kept getting louder. We just kept taking off hooks and all of a sudden, this one-foot high wall of foam, kelp, and other junk came roaring down on top of us. It grabbed the boat and spun us around a couple of times, then started sweeping us down the strait like a piece of driftwood. We hauled frantically, trying to get the line up before it snagged on the bottom, but it got us anyway. The groundline set in a crack, under a boulder or something, and we were hung fast on the bottom. The current was so strong we thought it was going to pull the stern under water. We finally had to cut the line. Went back the next morning to look for the other end of it, but never did find it. We were lucky it didn't roll the boat under or something," I say.

"Sounds pretty scary. Where did you say that was?" Dick asks.

"Right a head of us about six or seven miles. Scared the heck out of us. We went on into Petersburg the next day and I got off the boat and went back to Ketchikan. Ray wound up in P.A. later that summer and stayed. He wrote me a year later and told me about the free land out there; that's why we went out in '76," I answer.

"Huh…I'll be darned. I wondered why you went out there. I guess you still got a couple of stories I ain't heard yet," he replies.

"Yeah, you better stay tuned. Heck, we're living one even as we speak. Maybe I'll write a book someday and tell this one, too. You'd be famous; have your name in print for posterity," I say.

"You sure have the gift of gab alright; shouldn't be too hard to write it down."

I click the mike a couple of times and hang it up.

We're almost abeam Point Colpoys light, which marks the turn south into Kashevarof Pass. I get the chart of the pass down from between the roof beams in the wheelhouse, to refresh my memory. The pass between Prince of Wales and Zarembo Islands is full of dangerous shoals, and I have only been through it three times in the past.

Entering from the north, it's about four miles across. There are two routes through: Snow Pass on the east side and Kashevarof on the west. Snow Pass is deeper, wider, and better marked, but takes us miles out of our way. Kashevarof is narrow with several complicated turns, but will save us time. It's five o'clock and tide-change is in an hour. We don't want to buck the current so we must be across the summit before slack tide. I step off distance with the dividers and find it's ten miles to West Rock, where I figure the summit is. I look for Dick and he's right behind me as we turn in behind the first reef just inside the pass.

The current is still running with us and we are really moving. Before long we are passing Salmon Bay, and I can see Fire Island a couple of miles ahead. At Fire Island we have to cross an eleven-fathom bar, then pass down the west side of the island. The current is really running here and we sweep quickly into deeper water. We pass Exchange Cove, then point toward West Island, which has a day marker on a rockpile in the middle of the channel. Shrubbery Island lies to the east, and as we pass it and approach the day marker, we hit a crosscurrent coming from the south side of Shrubbery Island. It's really running and I have to point into it at about a forty-five degree angle, and throttle up a couple of hundred RPM to stay on course. I look back at Dick. The Spray is moving sideways across my stern! We are both pointing into the current and barely able to move toward the day marker. I realize that the current is pushing us past the narrow channel between West Island and the reef. I grab the chart with one hand and check the depth on the west side of the marker. It shows five fathoms, which is enough, barely. Dick's boat draws about five feet and the chart may be wrong.

I look up and we are getting close to the reef, but I see that to pass it on the correct side, we will have to turn and buck straight into the current. I realize that our boats won't go fast enough, so I hold my angle to pass on the other side of the marker. I lay the chart on the dash and call Dick on the radio.

"I'm gonna pass on the west side; it shows five fathoms. We should make it alright."

"Okay, we're almost through. The current should let up just as we get to the reef," he answers. I click the mike button a couple of times and let it dangle by its wire, too busy to hang it up.

As we near the rock, the current does let up and we suddenly sweep across the shoulder of the reef. I can see clamshells on the bottom as we cross the sand bar that have built up behind the reef. The bottom line on my depth recorder merges with the surface noise for a couple of heartbeats then drops off to five fathoms. I look back at Dick and he crosses a little to the west.

"Whew! That was exciting," I say into the mike.

"Yeah, I thought it was suppose to be slack tide about now; what happened?" Dick replies.

"Well, this is such a squirrelly place with all these shallows and water from Clarence Strait coming in from one end, and water from Sumner coming in from the other, that anything can happen. I bet it's different every tide. Don't forget that we're in the biggest tides of the month right now, too."

"Yeah, you're probably right. Well, we made it anyway, and you got another story for that book, if you ever write it," Dick says.

"Heh heh, yeah one of many. Hey, how do you feel about trying to make Ratz Harbor?" I ask. "It's only another ten or twelve miles; we'd be there about nine-thirty."

"Yeah, it's okay with me; we got lots of daylight left, and the tide should be in our favor," he answers.

Unfortunately, it doesn't work out that way. We buck a two or three-knot current all the way, and it is more like eleven-thirty when we finally get the hook stuck in the bottom of Ratz Harbor and fall exhausted into the racks. I set the alarm for seven o'clock, and we indulge in breakfast before we leave the next morning.

We pull out into Clarence Strait about eight. The water is calm and the ride down to Grindall Island is pretty boring. We do get a boost from the tide and turn into Grindall Pass about two o'clock. It feels good to turn into the pass that leads to Kasaan Bay, and as we come out the west side of the pass, I can see Kasaan Island several miles inside the bay. Happy Harbor is a small bight in the SE corner of the island, and the harbor is protected by two small islands on the east. After another hour, we turn in the narrow entrance and idle slowly to the log raft, where my floathouse is tied. We soon have the boats tied up and stretch the kinks out of our muscles while we look around.

It feels damn good to get off the boat and not have to listen to the motor anymore.

21

As we stand there looking around, enjoying the silence after the many hours of listening to the engines, we hear a shout from the beach.

"Hey! Coffee's on, come on up." We turn and look toward the sound.

"Boots" McAlester is waving from the porch of her small house. I wave back and yell, "Okay, be right up."

"Come on, Dick, I'll introduce you to Boots," I say as I head up the log bridge to the beach. At the head of the ramp is a small log cabin that Elden Heib built a few years ago. Weeds have taken over the path, and the place looks abandoned and forlorn. We walk along the gravel beach for a few yards, then step up onto the stone bulkhead. Boots has built the bulkhead up over the years to keep her property from washing away in the winter storms. There is a well-maintained gravel path along the top of the stone wall that leads past the shed-roofed, pole and shake woodshed to the small, gray, Cedar-shingled cottage. The house is surrounded with a lush vegetable garden and many flowerbeds.

As we climb up the plank steps onto the covered porch, Boots meets us with a delighted grin and says, "You're a sight for sore eyes, didn't expect to see you back for another three weeks or so. Come on in."

"Hey Boots, good to see you too. This is Dick Upward, my runnin' partner," I say, stepping into the warm kitchen.

"Hi Dick, glad to meet you. How about a cup of coffee," she says with the usual twinkle in her eye. We both accept and she points at the kitchen table and says, "Pull up a chair, I'll get the coffee."

As we sit down, Boots gets two white mugs out of the cupboard at one end of the table and moves to the shiny, black and white, wood-burning cook stove. She pours the cups full of coffee that looks like it would float a battleship, then puts them on the table in front of us. She fills her own cup and sits down.

"Well how did it go out there, you guys get so rich you quit early?" she asks, stirring creamer in her cup.

"That's about it. We hit it pretty hard all summer and the fishing was good. I had some of my biggest days ever, on Kings and Cohos both. We've made our winter stake already, so we decided to come home and enjoy what's left of the summer. How you been, anyway? The garden looks nice, been lots of sunshine this summer for a change," I answer.

"Yeah, it's been pretty nice, but the slugs are horrible. I'm afraid my cabbages are a total loss. Every head I've cut into is full of the damn things. I hate them; who wants to eat cabbage that you have to pick twenty slimy little critters out of first," she says, grimacing with disgust

"You ought to get a couple of ducks. My mother used to keep a few around for slug patrol. The ducks love 'em, and the duck crap fertilizes the garden," Dick says seriously.

At first I think he's pulling her leg, you can never tell with Dick, but Boots picks right up on the idea. She has heard of it also, and they launch right into a conversation about ducks, slugs, and cabbages that eventually evolves into brief family histories and life stories. They eventually figure out that they are related through marriage, but the lineage is too complicated for me to follow. Both of them have been married several times. It's good to see them hit it right off, I figured they would. Dick drove log trucks all over the west coast and Boots was married to several tramp loggers. They have lived in many of the same towns up and down the coast. They know a lot of the same people and enjoy telling stories of drunken escapades and wild characters that they have known.

After we have been there an hour or so, a red Lund skiff glides in through the back entrance of the harbor. It's Henry Hamer, who lives with his wife Arlie, in a beautiful log cabin across the harbor from Boots. As the skiff goes by, Hank recognizes my boat and swerves over to the beach in front of Boots' house. He lifts the lower unit out of the water as the skiff grounds on the gravel beach, then steps nimbly out of the boat and throws out the anchor. He's very agile for a seventy-five year old man. His little black lab Phoebe sits obediently in the skiff until he motions her out, then she runs forward and jumps out onto the beach.

Henry and the dog come up on the porch and walk into the kitchen.

"Hey…welcome back, did you bring any whisky?" he says, grinning around a brown, plastic cigarette holder with a half-smoked, hand-rolled cigarette stuck in the end of it.

"Hi, Henry. Nope no whisky. How you doin'?"

"No whisky! What the heck you good for, if you didn't bring any whisky?" he says, pouring himself a cup of coffee.

"Well, I didn't go by any whisky stores," I answer, chuckling.

"That's too bad. Who the hell is this character?" he asks, pointing at Dick.

I introduce them and Hank sits down on the old threadbare couch along the east wall. Now the stories really begin. I can hardly get a word in edgewise, but enjoy the yarns as the afternoon drifts by. Boots tells the one about the yarder engineer that slips off into the woods to take a dump one-day at lunchtime. One of the other men sneaks up behind him as he squats behind a bush doing his business and catches it on a shovel.

When the engineer finishes he turns around to admire his handi-work, and its not there! Mystified, he heads back to his machine and finds a package on the seat.

Then there's the guy who decides that there is not enough excite-ment in Ketchikan one night, so he sets the bed on fire in his room at the Gilmore Hotel, then climbs out the window and jumps into the ally behind the hotel. He forgot that the police station is right across the alley, and two cops were coming out the back door of the cop shop as he dropped to the pavement. They could see the flames in the room, so one of them collared the guy while the other went to call the fire department. The fire was confined to the bed, and the gent was confined in the town jail for a few days. Some of his pals bailed him out, but the night before his court date he was arrested for picking flowers from a planter hanging from a light pole downtown. I suspect he had a hard time explaining himself to the judge, but I suspect his explanations were creative.

Dinner time rolls around and Hank heads for home. Dick and I stay for clam fritters and more stories, then head back to the dock about dark.

"Well, Partner, what do you think of Happy Harbor?" I ask as we stand on the float, listening to a Loon chuckling down at the south end of the harbor, and watching the first few stars come out in the darkening sky.

"Seems like my kind of place, think I'll come back and hang out here for a while this fall," he answers.

"Good, I was hoping you would. See you in the morning."

"Night."

The next day we check with Hank and Arlie and Boots to see if they need anything from town. Henry has a couple of propane tanks that need to go in and Boots decides to ride in with Dick to do some shopping.

It's hard for these people to get freight out from town, as there are no roads to the island. The three of them are the only ones living here, other than myself, and the only boats they have are small, outboard-powered skiffs. The thirty-five mile trip is too dangerous most of the year. Most of their groceries and other goods come by mail-plane to Kasaan Village, which is about four miles up the bay. Airfreight is extremely expensive, and they jump at every chance to get a boat ride into town, or back out, with freight. My boat is so small that I can't haul much, but every little bit helps, and I'm glad to bring out what I can. Dick's old Spray has a regular fishhold below decks and plenty of deck space, so it will be nice to have him here this winter.

It's almost noon, by the time we get everything rounded up and take off. It is about a six-hour run to Ketchikan. The water is calm, so we make good time. By two o'clock we run through Grindall Pass, then out into the strait for the thirteen-mile crossing to Tongass Narrows. This part of Clarence Strait is at the convergence of Behm Canal to the east, Tongass Narrows to the SE and Kasaan Bay to the west. These three large inlets make the area treacherous to cross in small boats. There are shallow ledges on the northwest side and many conflicting currents. These currents, combined with the swells coming in off the North Pacific, can whip up spectacular rips. I have had a few wild rides across here over the years and always dread this crossing.

Today, however, the water is calm as a lake, and in a couple of hours we are across. We enter Tongass Narrows at Guard Island, and as we pass into the Narrows, the traffic increases significantly. Ketchikan is the hub of activity for the south end of SE Alaska, and the channel is busy with tugboats serving the pulp mill at Ward Cove and the fishing boats that sell their catch to the many fish buyers.

It's been several months since we left in the spring, so I feel a kind of culture shock start to set in as we plow our way down the narrows. The closer we get to town, the more houses we can see along the shore. As we pass Ward Cove, with its smoking pulp mill and brown water, an Alaska Airlines jet rumbles overhead, gliding in for a landing on the airport runway, which parallels the channel on the west side. At Sunny Point, the old cannery that has been closed for a couple of years now, sits crumbling on its pier, which sticks out into the middle of the channel.

Beyond Sunny Point, the channel widens out, and along the east side the business and houses of Ketchikan line the waterfront. Homes climb part way up the mountain behind town, and their windows reflect the glow of the late-afternoon sun as it sets behind Gravina Island, to the west.

I follow Dick into Bar Harbor and tie alongside him after he is parked in his stall. We all heave a sigh of relief after the engines are silenced, and Boots goes to call a cab to take her to a friend's house for the night.

"Well, Cap, I'm going to take a walk up the street. I need to stretch my legs and I got a craving for ice cream. You want to come?" I ask, as we stand on the dock gawking at the sight of all the activity up on the street.

"Naw, I'm too pooped to pop, think I'll stay here. Watch out you don't get hit by a car or mugged by some drunk," he answers, grinning at me.

"Okay, maw, I'll be careful, see you in a while. You want some ice cream when I get back, or are you going to hit the rack?"

"Does the bear shit in the blueberries? Damn right I want some ice cream," he says with mock indignity.

"All right, I'll see you in a while," I say, heading off up the dock toward the ramp to the street.

I turn right on Tongass Ave., then saunter slowly along, watching the cars stream by on the street. Their windshields reflect the pink evening light as the sunsets behind Gravina Island. I wonder where they are all going. Nowhere probably; they all seem to have a sort of glazed look in their eyes. Trapped on an endless road to nowhere. The old town gloom starts to settle over me as I walk along, and I long for the peace and serenity of some sunny Cedar ridge that smells like deer, or a muskeg meadow, white with October frost and the promise of fresh venison.

As I pass Timber and Marine Supply store, I look in the window at the rows of shiny new outboard motors, and my mood suddenly lifts as a wave of pleasant anticipation washes over me. First thing in the morning, I'm going to come here and see if I can deal these guys out of a new skiff and outboard!

I head on over to Sea Mart and buy a half-gallon of vanilla ice cream, then stroll on back to the dock. I'm glad for the little piece of home that the boat provides. The town energy is muted somewhat on the dock. Town is something that you have to ease into gradually, after being out in the real world for a while, and it's nice to have the sanctuary of the boat to fall back on, to regroup. I climb aboard the Spray and down into the familiar world of Dick's galley.

"Well, you made it back in one piece anyway," Dick says.

"Yeah, it almost sucked me in, but I managed to get away in the nick of time. I got hypnotized watching the zombie parade on the road and thought I was a goner there for a minute, but the thought of ice cream brought me back to reality and I managed to snap out of it. Seems like every time I come here, there's more cars. Pretty soon they'll have to build more road to fit them all in at the same time."

"Yep. Cars, bars, and churches," Dick says, digging a couple of big scoops of ice cream out of the box.

"Something for every taste. Used to be whore houses too, but they did away with those, except "Dolly's" old place down on Creek Street. Made a tourist trap out of that one. Charge them tourists five bucks to take a tour. Why would anyone spend two or three thousand dollars to travel all the way up here to look at an old whorehouse? Some people will buy anything," he adds, gesturing with his spoon.

"You got me, Partner. It's a weird world. You hear about the boys from the Arctic Bar a couple of summers ago? They were sitting there one afternoon when the longshoremen were warping one of those love boats up to the dock, down by Tongass Hardware. Don Dennis and a couple of others got in Don's ski boat and idled along the side of the ship, banging on the hull with a splitting maul. When they had the whole load of passengers and crew hanging over the side to see what was making all the racket, the boys roared back by and mooned them. They made three or four passes before the Coast Guard started chasing them with a forty-footer. Don's boat was faster and a jet drive to boot. He played with them for a while here in the channel, then led them over the shallows at the north end of Pennock Island. The Coasties almost ran aground, and Don took off for Nichols Passage and laid low till dark. There was a heck of a stink. Big write-up in the paper about how the tourism industry boosted the economy and all. They never did figure out who did it. Most of the locals appreciated the humor, and nobody would snitch them off.

"Heh heh heh, that's a pretty good one," Dick says scooping out more ice cream.

"Hey, did I ever tell you about the great Webber Air robbery those guys got accused of?" I ask.

"Nope, I heard about the robbery, but never did hear who did it," he answers.

"Well, the same bunch were partying at the Arctic one night, and when the bar closed at two AM, the bartender just locked the door and they continued drinking. When it started to get daylight, about four, somebody decided that the thing to do was to go water skiing. Don's boat was tied to the dock down behind the bar, so the whole bunch went out to watch the fun. Gus Peterson was going to ski first and was sitting on the airplane float wearing a wetsuit with the skis on his feet and the tow handle in his hand. Don was idling in neutral a few feet off the dock and they were about to take off, when all of a sudden this loud, amplified voice bellowed out.

"**'FREEZE, NOBODY MOVE OR WE'LL SHOOT. WE KNOW YOU STOLE THE SAFE FROM WEBER AIR!'**

"There was a moment of frozen silence as everybody looked around. There were cops everywhere. Over on Paul Hanson's dock, on the fireboat behind the civic center—everywhere—and armed to the teeth.

"Suddenly, cool as a cucumber, ole Gus says in a deep voice, '**Yeah, and we're escapin' on water skis.'**

"The whole gang from the bar busted out laughing, and before long the cops stood up and left, without saying another word."

"Ha ha ha, that's a good one, I bet those cops didn't come around there for a while," Dick said, scooping the last of the ice cream out of his bowl.

"Well, Dick I 'm beat, I think I'll hit the rack," I say, rinsing my bowl in the sink and throwing the empty ice cream box in the trash.

"Yeah, me too, it's been a long day."

The racket of town, sirens, horns honking, cars with loud exhaust, and loose nuts behind the wheel wake me several times, but eventually morning comes. I coffee up with

Dick and head for the skiff store about 9:30.

As I push open the door of Timber and Marine Supply store, the smell of new machinery hits my nostrils, and I feel the growing excitement at the prospects of a new skiff. I stop at the rack filled with new Evenrude outboards and look at price tags. They aren't cheap and I realize that I will have to settle for a small one.

As I stand looking them over, a voice behind me says, "Can I help you find something?"

"Yeah. I'm interested in a small, aluminum skiff and an outboard for it," I answer.

"Okay. What did you have in mind?"

"Well, I want something I can tow behind my boat. Maybe a twelve-foot Lund, or something similar," I answer.

"Let's go out to the warehouse and you can look at what we have in stock," he says.

I follow him through the shop and into a big building that has many boats of different sizes and types. There are fiberglass runabouts and Boston Whalers on trailers, and along one wall there several different sizes of aluminum skiffs standing on their transoms and leaning against the wall.

"How much is a twelve-foot Lund with an eight-horse motor?" I ask, running my hand over the smooth bottom of the first boat in the stack.

"The skiff is a little over twelve hundred, and the motor would be about a thousand. With tax and everything it would be about twenty-five hundred for the package."

"That's a little more than I can spend; I have about two thousand dollars." We dicker back and forth for a while. He gets down a cheaper skiff for me to look at, but it's not what I want. I finally accept his offer for the Lund with a four and a half horse motor at twenty-two hundred, including oars tie-up lines, and a gas tank. The motor is a little smaller than I wanted, but it will do. We go back to the front desk and I peel twenty-two crisp, new, hundred-dollar bills off my roll and lay them on the counter. After the paper work is finished, he tells me that it will take a couple of hours to get the boat in the water and the motor installed. He says he will have the mechanic run the motor on a test stand for a few minutes to see that everything is working properly, and that I can pick it up at the dock behind the store about one o'clock.

Boy oh boy! I can hardly wait. This is something I have dreamed about for years. I have been getting by with old, worn-out skiffs ever since I came to Alaska, and it's about time I had a good one.

I go back to the boat and have lunch while I'm waiting, then about twelve-thirty I see them lower my new rig out the back door of the warehouse and into the water. I take off for Timber and Marine, trying to look nonchalant, but have a hard time maintaining. When I walk in the store, I'm grinning like an idiot. But what the heck, it's not every day you get to buy a new car!

The salesman leads me through the shop and warehouse and we climb down the ladder to a narrow float where the new, red skiff is tied. He hands me a plastic bag with the manual and warranty card in it and wishes me good luck.

"If you have any trouble, send it in; as long as the warranty is good we'll pay the freight," he says.

"Okay thanks," I say and turn to start the motor. I lift the tank and it is full of gas. It was nice of them to fill it for me. I pull out the choke and open the throttle to the start position. When I pull on the starting rope she fires right up, and after I push in the choke the motor settles into a quiet purr. The salesman unties the lines and shoves me off. I pull the shift lever into forward and wave at the man on the dock as I open the throttle and pull away.

I point the bow toward Tongass Narrows and open the throttle all the way. The bow raises, then when the stern starts to plane, the bow drops level and I'm skimming along the surface at eight or nine miles an hour.

I run up the Narrows, then down the Narrows, then up the Narrows, then down the Narrows. Like a kid with a new bike. Grinning from ear to ear. All right! This is why I got out of bed at three AM all those mornings, whether I felt like it or not.

I finally tire of going nowhere and idle into Bar Harbor. Dick is standing on the dock as I pull up, trying to keep the grin off my face. I toss him a line, then kill the motor.

"Did it, huh?" he asks.

"Yup. What do you think of her?" I ask back.

"Looks pretty nice. You'll get a lot of use out of it. What did it cost?" Dick asks.

"Little over two grand. They threw in the oars and tie up lines and filled the gas tank. I would have rather had a little bigger motor, but this one will do. The difference in price will buy a lot of gas," I answer, climbing up onto the float.

We go aboard the Spray and have a cup of coffee.

"I think I'm going to do my shopping this afternoon, then fuel up in the morning and head for home before the weather changes. What are you going to do?" I ask

"Oh…I guess I'll hang out a few days and take Boots out when she's done. I've got some business to take care of and some shopping to do. We'll be there in a couple of days."

"Okay, sounds good," I say, rinsing out my cup and climbing out on the dock.

"See you later," Dick says. "Better come over for supper when you get done." I wave affirmatively and head for the grocery store.

The next day I gas up the boat and buy a barrel of outboard mix at the Union Oil dock. When I'm done at the fuel dock, I pick up Henry's propane tanks at Petrolane, then head out of town. The run home is boring and uneventful, but the little red Lund, bobbing contentedly along behind, seems to exude a subtle excitement. I can hardly wait to settle in at home and do some beach combing!

22

I pull into Happy Harbor in the middle of the afternoon and go straight to Hank's float to unload his Propane bottles. He comes down as I'm tying up and we admire my new skiff for a while. I help him wrestle his propane up to the woodshed and Mrs. Hamer comes out to say hi. Their place is beautiful; it looks like a postcard with its emerald green lawn, and Arlie has flower beds everywhere. We chat for a while and I decline a cup of coffee, but promise to come over soon to tell them about Port Alexander.

I idle back across the harbor and tie in front of my tiny floathouse. It has weathered the summer well and I soon have a fire crackling in the stove.

The house is tiny, eight by ten, with a lean-to porch on one end for firewood and storage. There is a bunk built across the back end, with a storage shelf above. A counter runs down the north side, with a large window over it. The end of the counter near the bed is a desk, and the other end has an apartment-sized, propane stove built into it. A stack of shelves fills the corner behind the door, between the cookstove and the wall. The shelves are for food storage and there is a woodbin under the bottom shelf. The south wall has an easy chair near the end of the bunk, and a small wood-burning heater by the door. This wall also has a large window, and there is a smaller one over the bed. I horse-traded Elden Heib a thirty-thirty rifle and several other items for the float-house and it has been a small but cozy home for the last couple of years.

I heat water on the propane stove, then stir up a cup of coffee. When the coffee is ready, I turn on the short-wave radio and tune in CBC out of Prince Rupert, BC, and sit down in the big chair with my feet on a toolbox. The lord of the manner is home!

I sit sipping my coffee, listening to the radio and enjoying the comfort of my castle, be it ever so humble. I think of the new skiff and decide that if the weather is nice tomorrow I'll go down south of Daisy Island and explore a small cove that I've wanted to check out. It's about five miles away and should take less than an hour to get there.

I rustle up some dinner, then unload the boat. It will be nice to have a little more room to spread out, and not have the pressure of fishing every day. I turn in about dark and read myself to sleep, satisfied with the accomplishments of the summer, and anticipating the freedom that the new skiff will bring.

Morning comes moments after I fall asleep, and the Ravens wake me out of a sound sleep. One of them is kind of a pet that comes every morning around daylight for a handout. Obviously he has already figured out that I'm home, and is walking up and down the dock making croaking noises, demanding his breakfast.

"Quiet down out there or I'll get the shotgun and have you for breakfast," I yell at him, which only makes him squawk louder. I get up and throw him a couple of bread heels and that shuts him up for a while. He takes them one at a time and disappears into the trees ashore. I think he stashes them to keep the other birds from finding them.

After breakfast, I splice an eye in one end of a hundred-foot hank of 3/8 Nylon rope and backsplice the other end. This will be an anchor line for the skiff and a towline for bringing in driftwood logs for firewood. When the line is finished, I get a fifteen-pound trolling lead off the Nomad for an anchor, and put it in the skiff along with the line. I siphon ten gallons of outboard gas out of the barrel into Jerry jugs and fill the outboard tank. I load the fuel aboard, then go in the shack for my rifle and backpack of survival gear. It contains a small hand ax, matches, candles, extra cartridges, binoculars, an army poncho, compass, sweater, food, etc.

When everything is loaded, I fire up the little motor and head for the south entrance of the harbor. Kasaan Bay is flat calm and I'm soon heading SW toward the cove south of Daisy Island. The new motor purrs smoothly along, and I sit with one hand on the tiller enjoying the warm morning and the freedom that my little skiff has brought.

I cruise past Daisy Island, then follow the steep, rocky shore to the tiny, sandy cove that is about halfway between Daisy and Skowl Point. The tide is pretty well out, and as I pass close along the cliffs, I see many different types of sea life clinging to the rocks. There are blue mussels in colonies and many barnacles, limpets, sea urchins, snails, and starfish. The starfish lend brilliant colors—orange, pink, blue and green—to the other wise drab, gray rocks.

In one place, I see a mink crawling in and out of hidden grottos among kelp-covered boulders. He looks up as I motor past, his pink nose searching the air, trying to figure out what the sound of my motor is. Suddenly he vanishes among the rocks as a shadow crosses the beach. I look up and see a huge bald eagle soaring above the cove, his snowy, white head and tail brilliant in the morning sun.

Before long, I turn into the tiny cove I have come to explore. It goes farther in than I realized it's entrance partially hidden behind a point. There is a crescent sand and gravel beach that is only partially visible from out in the bay. It is a beautiful spot with a large boulder in the middle of the beach and a small stream gurgling over the gravel and into the salt water.

I idle slowly toward the beach. The seawater is crystal clear and I can see bottom about twenty feet down. I ease in and kill the motor just before the bow touches the sand. When the motor stops, I tilt it up till the catch clicks into place, then step quickly ashore and pull the bow up as far as I can. .

I look around the pristine little paradise. The morning sun twinkles in the creek as it tumbles over the stones in its bed, and its gurgling chuckle fills the tiny cove with music. Cool moist air flows down the small valley that the creek drains, and the air has the combined smell of clean seawater and the cool, dark forest.

I unload my pack and rifle, then take the anchor line out and lay it on the sand in front of the skiff. I tie the end of the line to the eye on the stem of the skiff, then get out the trolling lead. I pass a bight of the line through the eye of the lead, about fifteen feet from the boat, then set the lead ball on the bow. I check the coil of line to make sure it will run freely, then give the boat a hard shove out into the cove. I quickly pick up the line as it streams past me, and guide it off the coil till the skiff is about twenty feet from the beach. When I 'm satisfied that the boat is out far enough, I yank the cannon ball off the bow, and it sinks out of sight with a satisfying thunk. I pick up what's left of the coil and carry it up the beach, paying out line till I reach the Alder trees that line the shore. I tie the end of the line to a stout branch, then go back down for the pack and rifle. The boat is safe and no matter what the tide is doing when I come back to the beach, I can pull the skiff in.

I take off my wool coat and stash it in the pack and lever a cartridge into the Marlin's chamber. I set the hammer to half cock, then shove another cartridge into the magazine. When the rifle is ready, I settle the pack on my shoulders and push through the bushes into the forest. The woods here are open, without much underbrush. The ground is covered with moss and the creek tumbles down a long, gentle slope among the giant Hemlocks. There are several, old logs lying on the floor of the small valley in various stages of decay, and there are hundreds of saplings growing out of the moss on their rotting trunks. Foresters call these nurse logs, and they nourish the small trees that thrive on the sunlight shinning through the hole in the canopy, left by the dead tree when it fell. In time, the ones that get the most light will grow up through the canopy, and shade the smaller ones till they die.

As usual, I am filled with a sense of other-worldliness that haunts these places. I feel welcome here, but also feel the awsomeness of the life force at work. I walk around the end of the first nurse log and start up the small valley. To my right is a low cliff, covered with moss. Upon this hill is a grove of huge Hemlock trees that go on to infinity up the side of the mountain to the north. I am drawn to this grove, but the mystery of the valley is stronger. The mossy ground cascades down out of the distance in a series of green terraces. The small stream pools on each level, then burbles over tiny falls down to the next level. Wet areas are lush with Skunk Cabbage, whose giant leaves look like tobacco plants, and I see pits where a bear has been digging up the roots. The creek banks are covered with Devil's Club with it's thorn-covered stalks supporting twelve-inch wide leaves that reach out into small patches of sunlight. Each leaf has several rows of stickers on its under-side, and some of these plants are taller than me. I have to ease carefully through the patch to avoid the stickery trunks. There is a faint path up the valley floor, worn by deer and bears using this route to travel from the alpine meadows above, down to the cove.

As I gradually gain altitude, the giant trees near the beach, thriving in the deep, rich soil carried down by the stream, give way to smaller trees. The species also become more diverse as the valley opens up and more light is available. Western Red Cedar, Alaska Yellow Cedar, and a few Red Alder trees begin to appear. The underbrush also changes and thickens because of the more-abundant light.

Several hundred feet above sea level, I clamber up a bank and push through thick berry bushes into a small muskeg meadow. There is a deep pool of water stained rich brown, and lilly pads dot its surface. I walk around the pond and out into the sunlit opening. Now I'm in a place of dry Cedar ridges, with open muskeg bogs winding in between. There are deer tracks everywhere, and at the base of one small hill I see the scar on a small Hemlock where a buck has rubbed the velvet off his antlers. The air smells like Heather, Juniper, and sunshine; a more pleasant place I cannot imagine.

I round a small ridge and find a large muskeg that is on a shelf of the mountain. There is a spectacular view to the east and south, where I can see the timber-clad slopes of the Kasaan Peninsula to the NE. The silver-blue water of Clarence Strait sparkles in the noon sun to the south.

In the middle of the meadow is a single Bull Pine standing on a dry mound. Its trunk is knarled with age and the harsh winter storms that roar across these hills. It looks like a giant Bonsai tree from some ancient, Japanese garden. I shrug the pack off my shoulders and lean the Marlin against the tree trunk. On the SE side, the roots of the tree form a chair, and I sit down in the sun-dappled shade to rest and eat the peanut butter sandwich that I brought for lunch. Ravens call in the distance and overhead I hear the rumble of a jet-heading south, leaving a white trail through the sky.

The jet is an intrusion into my mood and leaves me thinking for a while of the encroaching civilization that is eating at the forest like a cancer. It seems, sometimes, all that humans see when they look at this country is the dollar value of the trees and animals. Everything must be co-modified, rendered into merchantable products. I think it most valuable just as it is. I believe we are privileged to live on the Earth, responsible for the damage we do here, and will be held accountable, eventually, for our misuse of it. We may not suffer the vengeance of the gods, but we will certainly get to enjoy the results of our actions. "Pave paradise and put up a parking lot."

I shake off these thoughts and get back into the moment and the wonder that surrounds me. There is a pool a few feet away and several large, iridescent-blue dragonflies hover over the surface, feeding on the mosquito larva as they surface for air. I doze for a while, lulled to sleep by the peace of the place, but I'm eventually reminded of the passage of time by the humm of a floatplane heading for Craig or Klawock, across the island. Its annoying racket sours my mood again and this time I can't shake it off. I soon find myself heading back toward the beach, lost in thought about machines and pulpmills, tourists, etc. Even I wear rubber boots, made in a factory, from petroleum. I came here in a skiff made of aluminum, processed with electricity generated by damming one of the largest salmon-producing rivers in the world. How can we live on this beautiful planet without ruining it? This question always plagues me but I can never figure out a solution.

I soon climb out through the Alders onto the beach. I have been so lost in my thoughts that I have no memory of the walk back down the valley. The little Lund is floating serenely in the cove, and as I pull it in, I mentally kick myself for not staying in the moment and just enjoying the day.

When I get to the lead ball, I set it carefully in the skiff and lay the coil of line on the front seat. I pick the rifle up, being careful not to touch the metal parts with my hand, which is wet with salt water. I climb in the boat, giving it a shove as I step aboard. I lay the gun across two seats, where it will stay dry, and start the motor. When the engine is running smoothly, I shift into forward and head out into the main bay. As I throttle up, the motor starts to misfire and almost dies. I manipulate the choke and throttle to keep it going, but soon it is only running on one cylinder, so I shut it down to see if I can find the problem. I take the fuel filter apart, but it's clean and fuel is flowing. I pull the spark plugs to check them for spark and discover that one is wet with seawater. I dry off the plug and try to start the motor again, but it will only sputter for a moment, then die. Damn! Can't even trust a new motor. I pull the plugs again and the lower one is covered with drops of water again. The head gasket must be blown, and I don't have a wrench that fits the head bolts.

I look toward Kasaan Island, several miles to the north, dreading the row home. I put the oars in the oarlocks and start rowing. The skiff is designed for power and the bottom is shaped wrong for rowing, so I stop and take the motor off the transom. Carrying it forward, I put it in the bow of the boat, along with the gas tank and Jerry jug of spare fuel. This raises the stern to the surface, so the water can flow past without causing a vacuum behind the boat.

I try rowing again. It's better but the skiff feels too light and does not carry well between strokes. There is a rocky beach nearby, so I row over to the shore and put several stones in the boat to give her a bit more mass. It's harder to get it up to speed now, but once it is moving it doesn't stop between pulls on the oars. I look over my shoulder and point the bow at Kasaan Island, then look back and pick a landmark directly astern to steer by.

Pull, pause, pull, pause, pull, pause. I soon pick up a rhythm, and the clack of the oars soothes me into a kind of trance. I pull both oars for a while, then alternate right, left, right, left, to allow my muscles to rest by changing the stroke pattern. It seems like I'm getting nowhere, and as I angle off the beach, the moving visual reference of watching the shore go by is lessened. It seems like I'm going slower and slower.

Gradually, foot by foot, the miles inch by. My hands are blistering and an old injury in my lower back is aching. The tide is pulling me out into the bay and my steering reference point behind will no longer work. I remember the pocket compass in my pack, so I get it out and put it on the back seat, where I can see it clearly. It's one with a rotating bezel, so I line the case up with the center line of the boat, and with the skiff on course I turn the ring till the arrow on the lens lines up with the needle. Now all I have to do is keep the two arrows lined up to stay on course for home. It works but I have to keep looking down at it and can't enjoy the scenery as much.

It's clouding up to the SW and soon the late-afternoon sun disappears behind the clouds. I look over my shoulder again and realize that I'm well beyond the halfway point. This knowledge energizes me and I pull harder in anticipation of home and supper. Thank God there's no wind. I don't relish the idea of spending a couple of days on the beach in the rain.

The water is oily-calm and the green fluid seems to thicken as I get closer to Kasaan Island. The clouds have moved in to cover most of the sky now and the only blue left is a narrow band in the north. It's amazing how fast the weather can change in this country. Only about an hour and a half ago there were just a few mares' tails in the sky, and now it is almost completely covered with lowering clouds.

Finally the island is near and in another half-hour I am rowing through the entrance of the harbor. The tide is still ebbing, so I have to buck a current going in. I have rowed in and out this gut many times over the years, and by using the eddies along the shore and angling across a couple of times, I eventually make it through and soon tie up to the float. I grab my gear and climb stiffly out of the skiff. When I'm on the dock, I stretch the kinks out of my tired muscles and sore back, then go in the cabin and fall into my easy chair, glad to be home.

I get up in a few minutes and stir up a cup of coffee, then sit back down to wonder what's wrong with my new motor. My mind sorts through the possibilities as I drink my coffee, and I finally decide it must be a blown head gasket. After I have rested for a while, I take the tool box out and take off the head. Sure enough, the part of the gasket between the water jacket and the combustion chamber on the lower cylinder is blown. I consider my options, and decide to make a new one out of a piece of thick gasket paper I have been hoarding for years. If it will work for a while, until I can get a new one out from town, I'll at least have use of the skiff. I use the old gasket for a pattern, and carefully cut out two new ones with an X-Acto knife. The second is a spare that I will carry in the skiff, along with the tools necessary to change it.

I coat the new gasket with Permatex and bolt the head back on the motor.

When it's all back together, the motor starts up and runs like new. I let it run for a while, to warm up so the permatex will set, then shut down and tighten the head bolts again. I'll send the blown gasket in on the mail-plane and hope they will send me a new one to install myself. I don't want to have to send the motor to town and have to wait two or three weeks for it to come back. After all, it's brand new and I want to use it now!

As I pick up my tools and head in to fix dinner, the first few drops of rain are starting to fall out of the leaden sky and cats' paws of wind are starting to disturb the smooth surface of the harbor. I'm thankful again that I'm not crouched under a tree south of Daisy Island, waiting for the water to get calm enough to row home. Sometimes these late summer blows can last several days. Next time I will take a piece of plastic for shelter and more food. I was lucky this time.

I enjoy a simple dinner, then listen to the radio for a while before reading myself to sleep. Great gusts of wind roar through the trees that protect the harbor and rain hammers on my roof. I'm warm, dry, my belly is full, and occasionally I hear a reassuring pop as a steam pocket bursts in the heart of the fire.

23

In the morning, the weather is wind and intermittent rain, so I spend the day puttering around the cabin. In the early afternoon the wind shifts to the SW and the rain lets up. I tidy up the Nomad and put the fishing gear away. I will troll up some canning fish in a few days, but for now I plan to take it easy for a while. The afternoon forecast says that tomorrow will be nice, so I decide to tow the Lund up to the salt chuck at the north end of Kasaan Bay and poke around in the old mine for a day. I fix a simple one-pot bachelor's dinner and hit the hay early.

The next morning is nice. There is a hint of fall in the air and the possibility of a shower or two later, but the bay is calm so I tie the skiff behind the Nomad and head out. It's about an hour and a half run to Salt Chuck from Happy Harbor. The trip up is uneventful, and I'm soon approaching the string of small islands that form the south side of Brown's Bay.

This is a beautiful place; the small, tree-clad islands have white sand-bars at their north ends, made up of clam shells. The brilliant white is a nice contrast to the deep green of the trees and the blue sky reflected in the water. There is a long, timbered point that sticks out into the bay from the north, and after you clear the pass between the islands you keep this point to port and head for the end of the bay.

In the NW corner of the cove there is a narrow entrance that is barely wide and deep enough to pass through. As you turn left and start in there is no indication of the surprise to come. The channel makes a ninety-degree turn to the right and a large salt lagoon opens before you. A long, low island divides the lagoon into two parts. As you approach the south end of it, you hang a hard left and enter a big open bay that is about a quarter mile wide and a couple of miles long. The water to the west of the island is deep and a good anchorage. It can be windy during a strong south wind, but is safe if you snug up at the south end. The east side of the island is a tide flat that goes dry at low tide. The tidelands extend around the north end of the island and part way down the west side.

There are strong tidal currents in the entrance and down the east side of the island. You need to know the right lineups to get in without running aground, but once you're in the deep part of the lagoon, you find yourself in a unique and beautiful place.

East of the south end of the island, just inside the entrance, is a clearing with an old, shingled cabin in the middle of it. The place was built by a Chinese fellow named Charlie Wong, who was a cook at a local mine back in the forties. Charlie liked the place so well, he built a home and stayed after the mine closed. He grew an extensive vegetable garden, and sold produce to the residents of Kasaan Bay for many years. When I first came to the area in the early-seventies the place was abandoned and I lived there for a couple of years. Various people have used the place over the years. Two good friends of mine, Steve Cord and his wife Nina, lived there for a couple of years while they built a float house. The house was made of lumber that they milled with a chainsaw and was built on a log raft.

The old Chinaman's place has been abandoned for a couple of years now and the garden have grown up to weeds. It looks kind of lonely and forlorn as I anchor in the bay. I have a lot of good memories of the place, and this is the first time in ten years that there hasn't been smoke coming out the chimney and someone in the yard, waving me over for a visit.

It's about two hours before high tide and perfect for exploring the lagoon with the skiff. When the hook is down and set, I load my day-pack and rifle in the skiff and head for the north end of the island. The bay narrows as I cruise up the west side of the island, and as I approach the north end, it widens to the east then falls away to the south, form-ing the channel that separates the island from the east shore of the bay.

The first thing that catches the eye is the huge, multi-story, corrugated iron building at the head of the lagoon. It is the old mill at the Salt Chuck Mine. It is an enormous structure, full of giant machinery and various mining equipment. I've passed many a pleasant hour poking around in the place, examining the old machines and trying to figure out what each one did. Basically, this artifact turned large chunks of rock into powder that was barged to smelters in Terrace, British Columbia.

The place was first prospected in the late-eighteen hundreds, as the Klondike gold rush was winding down. The first metal mined here was copper, which was in demand during WWI. At that time the ore was hauled by mule wagons to Hadley, on the east side of Kasaan Peninsula, south of where Kasaan Village is today. There was a mill at Hadley and a deep-water harbor, suitable for barging the ore south. If you know where to look you can still find the old haul road, and I have walked most of it over the years. Kasaan village was located down in Skowl Arm in those days, and because of a smallpox epidemic, the village was later moved to its present site.

The mine closed after the war because of lower copper prices and the expense of transporting the ore to the smelters in Canada. In the late-thirties however, the metal palladium started to be used in industry, and the ore at Salt Chuck Mine is rich in it. The mine was reopened and the mill was constructed to crush the ore, which was shipped by barge to Terrace.

I nose the skiff up to the old, wooden barge that is imbedded in the sand in front of the mill building. The barge was a machine shop when the mine was in operation, and there are piles of bolts, pipefittings, and machine parts rusting in heaps where the shelves and bins that held them have rotted away. This place must have been a treasure house before the roof started to leak and dry rot set in.

I pick my way carefully through the junk piles, watching for rotten decking on the old barge, then stop to stare in awe at the building rising in a series of layers up the side of the mountain. From the ground where I stand, the roof of the highest part is over a hundred feet high. The first time I stood here in 1970, the building was pretty much intact. Then during the mid-seventies, some turkey set a charge of dynamite in the building and knocked the whole SW corner off it. It was an act of brainless vandalism and completely uncalled for. So many of the old artifacts in this country have been destroyed by people, bent on nothing more than wanton destructiveness; it really is a shame.

I climb up the hill along the north side of the building until I'm above the wreckage from the dynamite blast. I squeeze through the broken door and step in on a concrete slab running across the building. Mounted on this slab are three giant, Fairbanks Morse, diesel engines. They are so big that they have ladders up onto a catwalk eight feet above the floor, so the mechanics could work on the heads. There are some spare pistons in a storage loft above the engines that are bigger than five-gallon buckets, and the connecting rods are five feet long.

As I stand on the concrete, the flywheels are higher than my head. Great flat belts lead from the flywheels to a six-inch diameter jackshaft that runs across the building. Other belts run from pulleys on the jack shaft to pieces of machinery all over the building. In a concrete bunker on the next level below the diesels is a water motor in an eight-foot square iron box. The output shaft on this thing is eight inches in diameter, and it is also belted to the shaft that the diesels are hooked to.

Looking east up through the building, there are three bulldog crushers. These are great iron cylinders standing upright on concrete slabs. Inside each one is a mechanism like the auger in a meat grinder that rotates, smashing pieces of ore between enormous iron plates. The top of each crusher is funnel-shaped, and at the bottom crushed rock spills onto a conveyor belt. The ore was dumped from small railway cars down a wooden shute into the upper crusher, then passed through onto a conveyor belt into the second one, then onto another belt and into a third. Each crusher was set to grind finer than the one before it.

The pebbles that came out of the lowest bulldog were transported by another belt to a ball mill that looks like a giant cement mixer. This monster is twenty feet from base to mouth and is fifteen feet in diameter. It is partly full of cast iron balls, and as the machine spins, the balls grind the ore into a fine dust. Imagine the racket these machines made, grinding boulders two feet in diameter into powder! It must have been excruciating for the men working in the mill, and you could probably hear the thing running for miles.

I climb up through the mill past the bulldog crushers, then out of the upper end of the building. I clamber up the pile of spilled ore along the dump shute and come out on a narrow road. I stand for a while, panting after the steep climb from sea level.

There are two iron rails fastened to crossties on the road and the tracks disappear around a curve to the north. To the right is a small shed made of poles and Cedar shakes. The roof has long since rotted away and fallen onto the tiny locomotive that is parked inside. The engine is a rectangular, iron frame, eight feet long and four feet wide, with a metal box filled with batteries mounted on it. There are eight wheels in four sets of two, and each set of wheels has its own electric motor for power. On one end of the frame is a small platform with the controls and a bench seat for the operator. There are the remains of a heavy-duty, electrical panel screwed to the wall and there are still large cables plugged into the side of the machine.

I follow the rails north through the Alder saplings that have almost made the railway impassable. Around the curve there are several small ore cars and another tumbledown building. This shed housed the shop where the air drills were repaired, and drill steel was re-forged when the bit ends wore out. Above this building was another filled with several giant air compressors that fed air into the mine to run the rock drills. These compressors were powered by big electric motors, and I'm sure must have contributed to the horrible din of racket that this place must have produced.

A few yards farther on, is the entrance to the mine. It is a dark, wet, foreboding hole in the side of the mountain, with a cold draft of dank air wafting out into the warm fall sunshine. I am reminded of Mordor, in Tolkine's "Lord of the Rings." With a little imagination, you can hear the sound of Elves' hammers in the pits beneath the mountain. I have considered exploring the mine several times, but have always managed to come up with a reasonable excuse of some kind.

I head on up the hill on a well-worn deer trail. The mountain here is thickly timbered with second growth Spruce, Hemlock, and a few patches of Western Red Cedar. This hillside was logged off when the mine was in operation for timber to use in the mine. Typical of these pole patches, it is dark under the upper canopy and there is little underbrush.

After climbing about three hundred feet, I see a clearing ahead and when I climb the last pitch, I suddenly find myself on the brink of an enormous hole in the top of the mountain. It is three or four hundred feet across and narrows like a funnel as it descends three hundred feet to the level of the entrance tunnel below. The miners have tunneled in under the ore body, and hollowed out the mountain until they broke through to the surface. As the ore was blasted loose, it fell down into the tunnel and was shoveled by hand into the ore cars. Then it was hauled by the tiny locomotive to the shute where it was dumped into the bulldog crushers at the mill.

The magnitude of the labor necessary to dig out this volume of rock, crush it, and haul it away is staggering. It boggles the mind to realize that most of the rock was loaded by hand by Chinese laborers who were paid as little as ten cents a day. The mine probably ran twenty-four hours a day, seven days a week and the shifts were probably twelve hours or more for the laborers. It's incredible what humans will do for money.

Across from where I stand there is a hole in the side of the wall with rails hanging out. This probably leads to the beginnings of another "Glory Hole" that didn't break through the surface before the mine closed. I have no idea as to the actual extent of the mine but I suspect I'm only looking at a small part of it.

I sit eating my lunch in the warm, fall sun with my feet dangling into the awesome pit, and wonder at the brutal labor it represents. The backbreaking drudgery of working shift after shift in this dark, dangerous pit. Clinging to the dream of home and loved ones far away across the sea. Hoarding every penny you were paid against the day when you could finally book passage aboard some steamer for home with your meager savings. Over the years I have found several tiny opium bottles in the garbage pits around the old bunkhouses, a clue as to how the time here was made more bearable for some.

I also wonder what happened to the men who were injured. Was there a company doctor, and if so, how were the injured Chinese laborers treated compared to the whites that worked here? The stories that have trickled into the present from these days imply that they were basically looked upon as draft animals and treated accordingly.

I finish my lunch and head on back down the mountain. It will be high tide soon and I have to get the skiff off the tide flats before the tide goes out, or spend the next twelve hours here waiting for the it to float again. I enjoy poking around in the ruins for a while, but there are a lot of ghosts in these old workings, echoes of the misery suffered here, and the agony of the land torn apart in the ruthless search for profit. It's always a relief to leave after a few hours, and I've had my quota for today.

Back on the water it's hot in the afternoon sun, and the breeze on my face from the passage of the skiff is welcome after the sweaty exertion in the woods. The tide is just now high, so I run down the east side of the island toward the Chinaman's Cabin. I beach the skiff on the gravel beach in front of the clearing, then walk up to the shack. The big windows that my friend Dave and I put in the west side of the cabin some years ago have several bullet holes in them. I enter the porch on the south end. The door is hanging open and books, magazines, and other stuff are strewn all over the floor and out the door. The place is a wreck.

It really bums me out—the contemptuous, destructive behavior displayed by some people when they find an abandoned place like this. My friends and I have always loved this place and maintained it over the years. We've always tried to leave it in better condition than we found it, keeping tools and other things here so if someone was in trouble, or needed a place to live for a while, the basic necessities were available. The country is filling up with rude, selfish, destructive people, who come here looking for wilderness but seem compelled to ruin it.

I have met the man who owns the place, and he has left it unlocked and welcomed our use of it in return for keeping the place clean and in good repair. One time when I was living here, he and his son came to spend a few days. Steve and I offered to take off for a while, so they could enjoy their cabin, but they insisted we should stay and they camped out in one of the buildings at the mine. That kind of neighborliness is not often encountered anymore. Before me is the thanks this man has received for his generosity.

I tidy the place up as best I can, but the task seems pointless and my heart isn't in it. My mind turns to Port Alexander and I think some more about staying there next winter. Between the clear-cut logging that is stripping Kasaan Bay of its forest, and the increase of vandalism in the area I figure it's time to move on. I'm fortunate to have lived here between the boom years when the few people who used the area had come for the wilderness lifestyle. "All things pass."

I go launch the skiff and head back to the boat. If I leave right now, I can get out of the chuck before the tide is too low. This place is too full of memories that I don't want ruined. When I am back aboard the Nomad, I start the engine and go forward to pull the anchor while it warms up. When the anchor is aboard, I head for the chuck and pass through quickly with the ebb tide and out into Brown's Bay.

The trip back to Happy Harbor passes uneventfully and in a while I'm chugging up the harbor toward the dock. The old Spray is tied to the float, and Hank, Boots and Dick are gossiping in the afternoon sun. Hank is sitting in his Lund skiff and Dick and Boots are standing on the float beside a pile of grocery boxes that they have unloaded off the Spray. I swing the stern in and step off with the centerline.

"You guys must have had a good crossing; been pretty calm here in the bay today," I say, throwing a couple of turns on the cleat bolted to the deck on the float.

"Yeah, it was calm as a lake out in the strait, just the way I like it," Boots answers.

"Where you been?" Dick asks, after he finishes tying up my bowline and rubbing the crick out of his back.

"I took a spin up to the Salt Chuck at the north end of the bay; haven't poked around in the old mine up there for a while. Boy somebody sure trashed the Chinaman's cabin; shot out the window Dave and I put in, and the inside looks like a whirlwind ripped through it. Garbage everywhere, rotten food, the books thrown all over the floor and the door ripped off its hinges. The Swede saw is gone along with the ax and splitting maul, we used that place for ten years and left it better than we found it. These people come along and trash the place in a couple of days," I answer disgustedly.

"Awghh, that's too bad, In the old days people appreciated a cabin like that. Even the outlaw element appreciated the value of a good shack off someplace where a man could go to get away for a while. What's the world coming to anyway?" Hank says with a growl.

"I started cleaning it up, but it would have taken a couple of days, and what's the point? Somebody would just trash it again," I say.

"Well since you guys didn't bring any whisky, I'm going home," Hank says, giving the starting rope on his outboard a yank, and waving at us as he shifts into forward and roars off.

"Let's load those boxes in my skiff and haul them over to the beach in front of the house. It's low tide, but it'll be easier than packing it all up the stiff-leg," I say, untying the skiff from the stern cleat and pulling it over to the dock.

"I thought you'd never ask," Dick says, grabbing the stern line and tying it to a big staple in the deck of the float.

We soon have the skiff loaded, and Boots and Dick walk up the ramp while I idle the skiff over to the beach. After a sweaty half-hour, the groceries are piled in the middle of the living room floor, and Boots has a fire crackling in the kitchen stove.

"You guys better stay for supper," she says, putting a big, cast iron, frying pan on the stove.

"Sounds like a deal to me, it's that or Alpo at Dick's," I say.

"See if I ever invite you for supper again, ya hurt my feelings now," Dick says, firing up a smoke.

In a while, Boots serves up smoked salmon patties and fried potatoes, with a lettuce salad out of the garden. It is delicious, and most of it came for the garden or the ocean. We visit for a while after dinner, and I tell them of my decision to stay in P.A. next year.

"We'll miss you around here, but I know what you mean. I hope I can move further out somewhere, too," Boots says, lighting up a Lucky Strike.

"I hate to go, but all my old haunts are about gone now, and I can't stand to stay around here and watch it die. I want to remember it the way it was a few years ago. Can't understand why everybody only sees this country in terms of how much money they can sell it for. I think it's most valuable left just like it is," I say sadly.

"Well, I'm headin for the bunk. It's been a long day and I'm beat," Dick says, getting up.

"Yeah, me too. Thanks for dinner Boots, we'll se you tomorrow," I say, standing up and following Dick out onto the porch.

"Okay, come on up for coffee in the morning. I get up early. If there's smoke coming out the chimney there's coffee on the stove," Boots says, following us out the door. The sun has set and the stars are brilliant overhead.

"Burrr, feels like fall tonight. God I hate to see winter come. It seems like just the other day it was spring. Seems like time goes by faster every year," Boots says, holding herself in the chill night air.

"That's for sure," Dick says, as we crunch down the gravel path to the stiff-leg and down to the boats.

"See you in the morning, Partner," I say, opening the door of my shack and going in.

"Yeah, good night," he says, heading for his boat.

24

August changes to September, the days are getting shorter, and the feeling of fall in the air is becoming more profound every day. The weather is a mixture of warm, Indian summer days and wet, windy spells as the first of the fall storms roll in off the North Pacific. By the end of the month the cool, crisp mornings, when the sky is clear between weather systems, stir my hunter's blood. One especially fine autumn morning, I get up at first light and take my coffee outside. As I stand on the deck of the float, reveling in the special morning light and the cool, clean, fall air, there is a peculiar itch in the back of my brain. Some half-formed notion trying to push its way into consciousness. Suddenly it pops through, and I am overwhelmed with an over-powering urge to be sneaking along some Cedar ridge with the old Marlin in my hand.

I toss the dregs of my coffee in the bay, and go in to consult the tide book. It's a couple of hours before low tide, perfect for anchoring the skiff out for the day. I throw together some breakfast and a sandwich for lunch. When the food is finished, I take my pack and rifle and head for the skiff.

As I motor out the harbor entrance, I decide to hunt the south side of Baker Point, a peninsula that sticks out of the west side of Kasaan Bay. It is only a couple of miles from Happy Harbor, and there is a small cove with a gravel beach where I can anchor the skiff. Up the valley from the cove is a ridge with clumps of Cedar and small meadows that are perfect deer habitat. The ridge rises to the west in a series of terraces to a summit of about eighteen hundred feet. The south side gets sun all day in winter, and provides shelter from the frigid, arctic wind that howls out of the north.

During heavy snow years the deer come down into the heavily timbered, old growth areas along the beach to nibble Alder buds and
browse on Huckleberry twigs. These heavily timbered areas are crucial
to their survival when the snow lays several feet thick on the hills. One
of the detrimental effects of clear-cut logging is that it destroys these
wintering grounds. The second growth timber that grows after an area
has been logged is so thick that the berry bushes and other browse that
grew in the old growth are choked out for many years. Under the canopy in these pole patches little grows but moss, and these dead zones
offer little food or shelter for many years.

I motor around the south end of Kasaan Island, then point the skiff
north toward Baker Point. The sun is just coming up over Kasaan Peninsula to the east and the first rays paint the hills on Baker Point a
beautiful, yellow green. As I motor up the west side of the island the
tops of the trees on the small islands scattered along my route are also
beginning to glow in that special morning light.

As I pass the clear-cut on the north end of Kasaan Island, I remember my friend Tom Dalquist, who was killed in a logging accident on
that hill a few years ago. Tom was working for Dave Salee, who had an
A-frame on a log float, with a yarder for pulling logs off the hill. They
had cut a small patch on the hillside and were skidding the logs down
to the water and bundling them for shipment to Ketchikan. Tom was
setting chokers on the hill and Dave was running the yarder down on
the float. Tom had hooked up a couple of big, Cedar logs and signaled
Dave that the turn was ready. He was standing on a stump in what he
thought was a safe place, but when Dave took up on the main line one
of the logs hung up. He slacked the haulback and then gave the log a
yank. The log came loose all of a sudden, and when it broke free there
was too much slack in the mainline. The end of the log swung over and
knocked Tom off his perch, then landed on top of him.

Dave saw the log hit him, so he set the brake on the winch and took
off up the hill to see how bad Tom was hurt. It was about three hundred feet up through a terrible tangle of limbs and tree trunks to where

Tom lay. When Dave got there he found Tom pinned under the end of the four-foot diameter log, but he seemed to be alive. There was no way to move the log off Tom except with the machine, so Dave ran back down the hill and took up a few feet on the haulback to raise the log. This was very dangerous, because if the log moved any direction but straight up, it would crush Tom into the hillside. Dave was very good with the giant winch, and the log lifted just enough so he could pull Tom out from under the log. He set the brakes to hold the log up and ran back up the hill.

Tom was conscious but hurting very badly. Dave moved him out from under the log to a safer spot and made him as comfortable as possible. It was September and pouring down rain and Tom was soaking wet and shivering. Dave took off his raincoat, covered Tom with it, and ran back down to the float to go get help. The A-frame was about two miles from Happy Harbor, so Dave fired up the plywood, cabin cruiser that they were using to get back and fourth to work in, and took off for the harbor at full speed.

It took him about fifteen minutes to get to the dock at Henry's place. Hank came out and Dave told him what had happened. Henry had the State radio in his house, so he hurried back in to call the Coast Guard and have them send the helicopter out to get Tom. While Hank was on the radio, Dave came over to Boot's dock and rounded up several of us to come help get Tom off the hill. We grabbed a stretcher and some blankets and headed for the work site as fast as the boat would go. There were four of us: Dave, Boots, Bob Bennett, and myself.

The weather was deteriorating rapidly, and by the time we got to the A-frame it was blowing about forty SE and still flogging-down rain. We tied the boat up and scrambled up the hill as fast as we could, with the stretcher and blankets. We found Tom sitting on a small log, hunched under Dave's raincoat, trying not to shiver. He was a bedraggled looking wreck. He hurt too bad to lay on the stretcher, and we were afraid to move him till the medic got there. We wrapped the blankets around him and in a few minutes we could hear the helo coming. As the aircraft roared by, Dave fired a flare to show them where we were. They made a couple of passes to get a feel for the wind, then tried to hover over us to lower the medic and a stretcher. The wind was very gusty, and williwawing off the hill above us. It soon became obvious that there was no hope of hoisting Tom up; we would have to come up with another plan.

The hello fluttered down to a rocky point just north of the A-frame. Two men climbed out and started up the hill. It took them about fifteen minutes to work their way up through the slash and across the hill to us. They were wearing street shoes and no rain gear, and by the time they got to us they looked almost as bad as Tom did.

The medic checked Tom over and asked him a few questions. We told him we had tried to lay Tom on the stretcher when we first got there, but that he was in too much pain. I suggested a shot of something to help Tom bear the pain, while we carried him off the hill. The medic refused, saying that if Tom had a concussion the Morphine might kill him. They dithered around trying to make up their minds what to do until Tom finally said through clenched teeth, "Give me the goddamn Morphine."

"Look, if we don't get him out of this rain and into the hospital soon he's going to die anyway. Give him the shot so we can move him down to the water. The helo can land in the water and we can haul him out in the boat," Bob said.

The medic finally reluctantly agreed and gave Tom a shot. Even with the Morphine he couldn't lay down on the stretcher, so we put him on it in a sitting position, then started down the steep hill, through the tangle of logging debris. Four of us carried the stretcher with the other two holding Tom upright and keeping him from falling off.

It was a nightmare and took over an hour to get him down to the beach. The hill was so steep that the two carriers in front had to hold the handles of the stretcher over their heads, while the two on the uphill side had to carry it stooped over with the handles below their knees. Poor Tom would moan every time we slipped or lowered our corner of the stretcher. He looked terrible, with rainwater running down his face and under the blankets in a steady stream.

While we were struggling down the hill, the helicopter had landed in the choppy water and the pilot was having a difficult time trying to keep it in position in the gusty wind. When we finally got Tom down to the end of the stiff leg, a crewman from the helo launched a small, rubber raft out the side door and paddled in to us, trailing a line that was tied to the aircraft. We tied the line to the stiff leg and loaded Tom in the raft.

He must have gone through hell while we lowered him into the pitching rubber boat, but we eventually got him in a kneeling position, hanging onto the side of the raft with his good hand. The medic pulled Tom and himself out to the chopper, and when they finally had Tom in the door, we pulled the raft back to us. The other two crewmen got in, and a man in the door of the machine pulled them out to the helo. When they were aboard and the rubber raft was inside, the helicopter took off with a roar and disappeared toward Ketchikan.

After the helo was gone we discovered that the boat had pounded on the float so hard in the chop that it was full of water, and the tie up lines were the only thing keeping it from sinking. What a day. There was a huge hole in the boat and the motor was under water. Our only option was to walk home through the woods, which we did. We got home totally exhausted just before dark, and I fell into bed immediately. In the morning Tom's daughter called Henry on the radio, and told him that Tom had died during the night when a blood clot stopped his heart. It was a sad fall for us that year. Dave blamed himself for Tom's death, and the trees they had cut stayed on the ground for several years. Dave eventually sold his equipment and moved into Ketchikan.

I shake off the memory of that sad day as I approach the sandy beach where I'm going to leave the skiff. The morning sun is shining warmly on the shore, and the excitement of the first hunt of the fall soon drives away the past. When the bow crunches gently on the gravel, I tilt the motor out of the water and lock it in the "up" position. I climb out over the bow and pull the boat up as far as I can, then throw the anchor up the beach as far as the bowline will allow. I will let the skiff go dry this morning because the tide is about low and it will be coming in all day. When I get out of the woods this afternoon it should be floating again, and all I will have to do is pull it in and take off. I string the rest of the line up the beach and tie it to an Alder branch. It feels like it will be a warm day, so I hang my coat on the Alder where the skiff is tied. I shrug on the small daypack, load the rifle, and go into the woods.

A small stream trickles down between cliffs on both sides of the tiny valley. As I work my way up the game trail along the stream, I find my way blocked by several trees that have been sawn down across the creek. I push through the branches and climb up on the first log. There is a hundred-foot wide slash going as far as the eye can see in both directions. In a row down the middle of the slash is a row of steel fence posts, each with a yellow sign proclaiming; **"Boundary, Tongass National Forest."**

I stand there for a few minutes gawking at the mess. The idiots have cut a one hundred foot wide swath around the Alaska Native Land Claim Selection Area. Much of the land in Kasaan Bay has been given to the Natives by the Federal government. I don't have a problem with that, but to wantonly cut thousands of trees to mark the boundary is totally unnecessary. It must have cost the taxpayers tens of thousands of dollars, and for what? This is the kind of forest management stunts that are destroying the Tongass National Forest.

I am beside myself with fury! What a stupid, wasteful, and unnecessary thing to do. I have hunted here many times over the years, and words can't express the anger and frustration I feel to find this ugly wound on this beautiful mountainside. I decide at that moment to leave in the spring, and never come back. There is nothing here for me any more. The Native Corporation is already logging some of their land down in Skowl Arm, and I know it will only be a matter of time till they cut this area too.

I cross the slash and continue on up the mountain, but my heart isn't in it any more. On top of the ridge I stand for a while looking out over the beautiful bay that I have called home for so many years, and feel a sadness for my species. We have such opportunity to study the natural world here, to try and find some way we can fit ourselves into it. Unfortunately we are so driven by our lust for personal gain, that we must commodity everything, and anything that gets in the way of progress is trampled under our feet. In our arrogance, we believe that we must modify ecosystems that have been functioning on their own for millions of years without our meddling.

I turn to head up the ridge, and standing across the muskeg is a nice, forked-horn buck. I freeze and we stand looking at each other for a few moments, then he bounds away in a series of stiff-legged bounces, with his tail up and his ears erect. He stops about a hundred yards off and looks at me again, then disappears like a wraith into the timber. Somehow the notion of shooting him never crosses my mind. I shake my head and grin at myself, then head back down to the boat.

The skiff is still high and dry, but the tide is flooding, so I poke around in the piles of driftwood for a while, then eat my lunch sitting in the gravel with my back against a log. The fall sun hangs in the southern sky and I doze for a while, trying to stay in the moment and not think about the future.

After a while, the sound of the gentle surge lapping at the stern of the skiff awakens me. I get up and carry my gear down to the boat. By the time the anchor is aboard with the line coiled on top of it, the water is halfway up the bottom of the boat. I put the pack and rifle in the boat, lift the bow, and shove off. After the motor is running I follow the west shore of the bay, enjoying the warm sun and the freedom of my skiff.

After a while I come to a small island that is one of my favorite places in the bay. This island is only about two hundred feet in diameter and is covered with trees. The trees are special though because most of them are Pacific Yew, a tree that is rare this far north. There are several hundred on the island, ranging in size from tiny saplings to several that are a couple of feet in diameter and fifty feet tall. The Yews produce a red berry that the crows love, and when the trees are fruiting the crows hang out on the island, feeding on the berries and spreading the seeds.

Along the shore of this island there are many Serviceberry bushes. The fruit of this tree looks like a large Blueberry and is delicious. Serviceberry jelly is probably one of the best jellies in the world, and this time of year the bushes are loaded with them.

I pull up on the gravel at the south side of the island and go ashore. The trees are full of cackling crows and the Serviceberry bushes are full of fruit. I wander around on the island for a while and then pick a plastic bag full of berries to take home. The racket from the crows soon gets overwhelming, so I shove off and head on down the bay.

A little farther on there is a tiny, round island that is attached to the main shore by a narrow sandbar, which is only covered with water at high tide. This is a special place also. On the main shore there is a creek that runs out onto the beach, and if you follow the stream for a couple of hundred yards into the woods, you will find an open meadow with a series of small Beaver dams in it.

I follow the stream into the meadow and walk through the tall, sedge grass along the small ponds. I find one narrow pool with a gravel bottom, and decide to take a bath. The water is clear and warm and about three feet deep. I strip down and settle in for a refreshing soak. After the water settles, several tiny trout come out from under the overhanging bank and nibble at my skin. It is a strange sensation; I guess they think I'm some giant, white grub that has fallen in their pool, a gift from the trout Gods, perhaps.

The chill water soon drives me back out on the bank and the bugs drive me into my clothes. I follow the stream around a bend and find myself in front of a large dam. My eyes are about level with the water behind it, and as I stand there looking at the reflection of the sky and trees, a beaver swims across the lake toward me trailing a vee shaped wake. He stops a few yards away and looks at me for a moment. Then with a great SMAKK, he slaps the water with his tail and disappears. The noise startles me half to death. My heart pounds with adrenaline and it takes me a moment to understand what has happened. I see the Beaver surface across the pond and disappear into the grass. I chuckle to myself and head back toward the beach. It's getting on into the afternoon and the peanut butter sandwich I ate for lunch is wearing off.

Back down at the beach, while I'm pulling the skiff in to the gravel bar that separates the island from the shore, I remember an incident that happened here a couple of years ago. It was February, and bitter cold. There had been an arctic, high-pressure area stalled over the coast for days, and until that day it had been very windy. I was suffering from cabin fever, and since it was finally calm I decided to take a tour in the skiff. All I had for a boat at the time was a raft made out of small, Cedar logs. The raft had a tiny outboard for power and a wooden box for a seat. It wasn't much of a boat, but in calm weather it would get me around. I had stopped here and anchored out while I took a walk up to the ponds. When I came back to the beach, the tide was almost high and the raft was quite a ways out. When I tried to pull in the anchor it hung up on something, and when I pulled harder, the rope broke.

So there I was, late afternoon, the temperature was in the low-twenties, and seventy-five feet of very, cold water between me and the raft. I stood there for a while, weighing my options, and decided to try for the raft. It would be dark soon, and it was six hours till low tide. I didn't relish the idea of crouching by a fire all night in freezing weather. I knew I could do it if I had to, but I was afraid the north wind would come back up, and even if I had the raft, I wouldn't be able to get back over to Kasaan Island.

The piece of rope I had was quite long, and I figured it might reach out to the raft. I found an oblong rock and tied it to the end of the rope. Holding the coil of line in one hand and the rock in the other, I flung the rock out across the top of the raft. I started pulling gently on the line, but after hanging on briefly, it slipped off and I pulled it back in. It took about ten tries before I finally got it tangled in the line from the raft to the anchor and managed to pull the raft in to the beach. I was dang glad to get home that night, and the next day I found a stronger rope to use for an anchor line.

This time the anchor came in without a hitch, and I was soon motoring toward home. It had been a pleasant day, in spite of the memories of Tom and discovering the boundary slash. My little float-house was a welcome sight, with a trickle of smoke coming out the chimney and the last of the afternoon sun shining on the deck. After I shut the motor down I could hear Hank singing across the bay, and the ring of the splitting maul on a wedge as Boots broke up another round of Hemlock to stash in her woodshed for winter.

For the moment everything was right with the world, at least our little corner of it.

25

The weeks seem to fly by; September is gone and October arrives with a fury of great storms off the Pacific. Vee-shaped flocks of Canada Geese migrating south decorate the sky during the brief spells of nice weather. Their honking cries are present day and night, and an occasional small flock drops into the harbor for a day or so to shelter from the storms and rest before they resume their journey. The sedge grass along the beaches is turning brown and the leaves on the Alders and Crabapple trees are beginning to fall. By the middle of the month there is a light frost on the dock on clear mornings.

The hunting itch really stirs in me now. By the last week in October the weather has cooled off enough to hang a deer, and there has been enough frost to kill off the flies. The rut, or mating season, is just starting. The old bucks are sorting out their territories and driving the younger bucks away. These two and three year olds that are for the most part unable to participate in the mating rituals are the best eating, and they are extras in the gene pool. Very few bucks actually mate with the does, and to kill these dominant males just because they have big horns doesn't make much sense to me. If you had a herd of goats that you maintained for food, you would cull out the extra young males to eat. You wouldn't eat your breeding stock. I believe in minimizing my impact on their natural selection by leaving the breeding bucks and does alone, and not concentrating my hunting in a single area.

The deer live in herds that are separated by natural boundaries such as drainages, bays and inlets. There is enough intermingling to keep the gene pool from becoming stagnant, and the dominant bucks also steal does from their neighbors' territories. The non-breeding males spend most of their lives within a few miles of where they were born, unless they are disturbed by things like clear-cut logging or over-population. Sometimes, due to mild winters or lack of predation, an area will become over-populated, and some bucks will wander out of their home range looking for food. The young bucks do some wandering during the rut also, looking for does, but woe to the little forked-horn that trespasses on the territory of some prime buck.

I like to hunt Kasaan Peninsula; it is home range to several herds, and I have become familiar enough with this area over the years to know where some of the breeding areas are. By hunting the fringes between them, it is easy to find a tasty, tender young buck, and now's the time.

I'm up early this morning; it's clear and calm outside and a light frost sparkles on the dock as the first streaks of dawn light the eastern sky. It's the first nice day after a series of SE storms and conditions are perfect for a hunt. I treat myself to a high carbohydrate breakfast of eggs, fried potatoes and toast, and while the spuds cook I pack a lunch and get my other gear ready. Before the sun is over the mountains to the east, I'm on my way across the bay to Andrews Mountain, a sixteen hundred-foot hill on Kasaan Peninsula. There is an old copper mine on top of this small mountain, and several of the buildings are still usable. Tom Dalquist showed me the place a few years ago, and we used to climb up there occasionally. We would camp overnight in one of the cabins that still had a serviceable oil stove in it. Tom had found a couple of barrels that still had stove oil in them, and so with the stove going it was a comfortable place to camp in the middle of superb hunting grounds.

It's not far across the bay to the trailhead, maybe a mile and a half, so I 'm soon idling in toward the small, gravel beach where I will leave the skiff. The beach is steep and the gravel is coarse. It's not an ideal place to leave the boat, but the tide will be out most of the day, so I'll let the boat go dry and drag it to the water when I come back down the mountain. There is lots of driftwood here, and it will be easy to make a skid-way to the water. I soon have the skiff secure and enter the woods.

It's very open in the forest here; the ground is mossy and there is very little underbrush. A creek tumbles along a bed of coarse, red and green stones and the old trail follow it up a gentle grade to the foot of the mountain.

When the mine was in operation there was an aerial tramway to the top of the hill, and the remains of the landing are still visible among the large, Spruce trees that cover the area. This was all cleared off when the mine was in operation, but because of the flat area and the buildup of soil from the mine tailings, the forest has grown back rapidly.

Scattered among the trees are the remains of several iron boilers and two enormous steam engines that were used to pull the tram buckets up and down the mountain. I don't know the history of the mine, but I suspect it was operating just after the turn of the century while the mill was in operation at Hadley, which is on the east side of the mountain. The haul road from Salt Chuck Mine goes through a low pass on the north side of Mount Andrews, and we have found the remains of a road that goes from the foot of the tram to the other road.

The old trail up the mountain is made of short sections of small logs and split boards. Some of it is still in good shape, but in other places there is nothing left but a few rotten boards. At the base of the hill the trail zigzags up a steep slope in a series of switchbacks, and as you gain altitude the Spruce woods give way to giant Cedars. Although the trail is steep, the beauty of the open forest is worth the climb.

After about twelve hundred feet of switchbacks, the trail passes between two low hills and then comes out into an open muskeg. The muskeg is in a small basin on the south side of the mountain, and when you come out into the open, the trail crosses a small pond on a rickety, wooden bridge that has seen better days. Across the meadow you climb another small hill through thick Alder brush to a bench just below the summit. You come out of a thick patch of stunted Alders into another open place—and there is the mine.

There are several small, plywood buildings in the clearing that were built in the early-seventies to house a drilling crew that was doing exploratory drilling at the old mine site. The original buildings are nothing but piles of rotten boards with pieces of rusty machines scattered about here and there. On the north side of the clearing there is a cliff with a tunnel disappearing into the mountain, and on the very top of the hill is a glory hole similar to the one at Salt Chuck but much smaller.

I work my way up past the old workings, then out into an area of muskegs and small hills covered with stunted Cedars and Bull Pines. There are deer tracks everywhere, so I sit down under a tree and take out my deer call. The call is made of two pieces of Red Cedar with a reed made of plastic electrician's tape sandwiched between them. When you blow on the call it makes a high-pitched bleating sound that is similar to a fawn's distress call. During the rut the bucks will come to investigate this sound, hoping to find a doe.

I give a series of three long bleats and sit motionless for about ten minutes, then repeat the call. The echoes have barely faded away from the second series of calls when I hear a thump and a stick crack in the brush, about forty yards off to my left. I ease back the hammer on the Marlin and call again. MAAAAAA. There is a high, whistling snort and the sound of trotting hooves behind the bushes. I can hear the deer moving from left to right, so I sit as still as I can, and in a moment a big doe trots boldly out into the opening. She stops and looks me right in the eye.

As we look at each other, frozen in the moment, there is a new sound on a low ridge off to my right. The doe looks that direction, and in a moment two nice, forked-horn bucks trot out into the clearing. I bring the rifle up till my left elbow is resting on my knee, and look through the peep sight at the smaller of the two bucks. The deer are very nervous, so as soon as I have a good sight-picture on the head, I squeeze off the shot. KABOOMMMMMM. The gun kicks and the sound echoes off into the distance. The doe and other buck stand frozen, looking right at me for a couple of heartbeats then bound off in different directions.

The buck I shot at is lying in the frosty grass with one leg moving slightly. I dread walking over to it; I don't like killing them, but it is part of the lifestyle I have chosen, and I have the same right to food as any other predator. I never take more than I need, and I try to kill them cleanly and as instantaneously as possible. A three hundred-grain bullet through the brain is an instantaneous transition from life to death, and is probably preferable to being run down by wolves and torn apart before you are completely dead.

I reload the rifle and walk over to the deer. He's quite dead; the big slug passed through the brain and out the other side. He is in prime condition, with a thick winter coat and small, forked antlers. The horns are a reddish-brown color and polished, ivory- white on the tips. As I stand looking down at him, I hear hoof beats coming up the trail behind me. I turn, and standing a few yards off is a magnificent three-point with a swollen neck and a wild look in his eye. He's so close I can see the pupil in his eye and individual hairs on his neck. We look at each other for a couple of seconds, and suddenly he snorts out a high-pitched, whistling sound and bounces away. At the edge of the meadow he stops and looks back for a few seconds, then disappears into the trees. My heart pounds with adrenaline and I stand there for a moment looking at the spot where he disappeared. What a privilege to encounter such a beautiful creature in this wild place.

Meanwhile I have work to do. I lean the rifle against a tree and open my pocket knifes to field dress the young buck I have shot. I open his paunch and roll the guts out onto the ground. When the cavity is empty and the organs cut free, I separate the heart and liver from the other parts and put them in a plastic bag in my pack. I lay the carcass belly down on a hump so the remaining blood will drain out while I wash my hands in a muskeg pond. When I'm done cleaning up, I take the rifle in one hand and a horn in the other and begin the long journey back down the mountain to the boat. It's hot work, and even though it's downhill, I'm pretty worn out when I finally drag him the last few yards to the beach.

The skiff is high and dry, so I gather up as many old boards and other pieces of flat wood I can find, and lay them in a row down the beach toward the water. When the skidway is ready, I grab the bow of the boat and spin it around onto the first pieces of wood. It's a bit of a struggle to get it turned around, but when it's finally up off the gravel and onto the wood it slides down the hill quite easily. When it reaches the last of the wood the water is still a few yards away, so I take some of the boards from behind the skiff and complete the skidway. This time she goes all the way into the water, and I turn it around and throw out the anchor. In a few minutes the deer and my gear are loaded into the skiff and I'm on my way home.

When I get back to the harbor I pull up in front of Boots' place and pull the deer out of the skiff onto the beach. As I start dragging it up toward the woodshed, Boots and Dick come down and give me a hand.

"All right, heart and liver tonight," Boots says with a grin. "Where did you get him?"

"Over in Tom's secret spot," I answer as we drop the carcass in front of the wood- shed.

I cut off the hind legs and slit the skin at the hock. Dick hooks each hind leg over the ends of a short stick that has a rope tied to its middle. The line passes over a pulley that hangs in the rafters of the shed, and when he's finished Boots and I haul on the other end of the rope hoisting the animal off the ground. When the deer is hanging at the right height I tie the rope off on a post, and we step back to inspect our handiwork.

"You're probably pooped. Why don't you go in and wash up while we skin him out. There's hot water in the teakettle and coffee on the stove, help yourself," Boots says.

"Yeah, it was a long drag, all right. The heart and liver are in the skiff; I'll put them in a pan of salt water to soak," I say, heading for the skiff as they start working on the hide.

I look forward to sharing the meat with them. Boots feeds me quite often and I eat with Dick regularly. Hunting is something I'm good at and the meat is better with friends to share it with.

I put the heart and liver in a bucket and cover it with water with a bit of salt mixed in. I've heard that this takes the blood out. I don't know but everybody does it and who am I to break with tradition. When I'm finished, I wash up with hot water from the big teakettle that is simmering on the back of stove, then pour myself a cup of coffee. I take my coffee and wander back out to see how the skinning crew is doing. They are almost finished; the skin is off and Boots is wiping out the body cavity with a damp cloth. The meat looks good hanging there in the evening light, with the smell of split Cedar kindling in the crisp, fall air. I feel a sense of well being and satisfaction. I'm in the company of true friends and tonight we will dine like kings on the bounty of the Earth, and the fruits of our labor.

"I'm going to go put the skiff away before it floats off," I say, heading down the beach.

"Okay, I'll get dinner started. Come on back up when you get done," Boots says.

I paddle the boat over to the dock, and when she's tied up I bail the bloody water out of her. After the skiff has been taken care of I take my pack and rifle into the shack. I run a brush through the bore of the rifle and wipe the outside down with WD-40. After those chores are done, I stoke up the wood stove, put on my deck-slippers, and go back up to Boot's place. The sun has set in the west and the first stars are beginning to show. The temperature has dropped and the chill air is invigorating. I stand on the gravel walk for a while and savor the evening, but the warm glow of the lamps shining out the windows and the delicious odor of frying venison soon draw me into the house. Dinner is ready and we pig out on heart steaks, tenderloin tidbits, and liver smothered in onions. There are new potatoes from the garden and various fresh salad makings. We are soon so stuffed we can hardly move, and we pass the rest of the evening relaxing around the table with coffee and tobacco.

"Wonder what the rich folks had for dinner tonight," Dick says as he lights a Marlboro and sighs contentedly.

"I don't know, but it can't compare with that," I say sipping coffee.

"Couple more feeds like that and I'll be able to crawl under a stump and hibernate for the rest of the winter," Dick says.

"How the heck am I going to get my venison ration if you're not around here in the fall?" Boots asks.

"Well, I guess you'll have to go into town and lasso some young stud and bring him back out here for the winter," I reply.

"That's all I need, the last one didn't last a month. Soon as they sober up, all they can think of is getting back to town so they can soak in the bar," she says.

We visit for a while longer, but the food and the days exertion soon exact their toll, and I say good night and head for home. I stoke the stove and fall into the bunk. As I drift off, I hear Dick climb aboard the Spray. The next thing I know, it's morning.

I awaken to the sound of the tame Raven raising a ruckus on the float outside my window. We exchange insults and threats for a while, and I finally get up and throw him a stale biscuit. That shuts him up for a few minutes, but he's back before I get the coffee on, walking up and down on the bunk log and demanding more food. I throw him another biscuit and he flies off with it.

It's a frosty morning outside and the fire crackling in the stove feels good. I sit for a while listening to the radio and enjoying my coffee. The news is mostly rape and murder, war and destruction. I finally get disgusted and turn it off. After breakfast, I go over to chat with Dick for a while. When we run out of anything to say, I go home and saw up a firewood log and split the rounds into stove-size pieces. By noon I have the wood all stacked on the porch and the wood box in the shack filled. The day passes from one little chore to another and before I know it it's evening again.

The days pass one into another. Boots is canning her garden and Dick goes back into town. He says he will be back in a few days, but I suspect it will be a while. He can get TV on the boat in town, and once you get plugged in it's hard to cut loose.

November rolls around and we get a couple of big storms around Thanksgiving. The first of December brings a big dump of snow, but as Christmas approaches the weather warms up and rains it all off. We are looking forward to Christmas because the music and the adds on the radio are driving us nuts. We're all avid, radio addicts and the Christmas hype gets pretty sickening after a whole month of it. We are also tired of visiting with each other and everyone sticks pretty much to themselves.

The next ten weeks or so are the worst part of the year. It's dark from three-thirty in the afternoon till eight-thirty in the morning, and the weather is too rotten to do much of anything outside. I read a lot and whittle some. I'm also customizing an old, Mauser rifle, so that occupies some of my time. On the few, nice days I go out in the skiff and beachcomb for firewood logs to bring home. The stove has a tremendous appetite this time of year.

Winter is a time for rest and reflection and I'll be damn glad when it's over.

26

The weeks pass slowly in mid-winter, but gradually December becomes January, and January fades into February, then March arrives. By the middle of the month the weather has warmed up into the forties, and the first hints of spring stir restlessness in me. I'm tired of the long nights and loafing around the cabin. As the days lengthen and the moist, south wind blows in off the ocean, I begin to think of warm, summer mornings and the excitement of putting the gear out in the golden, dawn light. There are many chores to be done on the boat and I spend some time each day working on her.

One day late in the month I run the motor for a while to give the batteries a good charge, then remove the head to clean the carbon off the pistons and from around the valves. The engine runs at a slow idle while trolling and during a season quite a lot of carbon builds up. While the head is off I lap the valves and adjust them carefully. The little engine has many months of work ahead and all the energy I put in now will pay off later. When the fishing is hot a breakdown can cost hundreds, even thousands of dollars.

Over the next several days I also rebuild the carburetor and the ignition system, replace a worn impeller in the water pump, check all the hoses and lines, service the fuel filters, and change the oil. I also give the outside of the engine a good cleaning and dab some paint on areas where it has flaked off.

After the engine work is done I take up all the floorboards and clean out the bilges. This is a dirty, miserable job, but if it isn't done every year dirt and other crud accumulates in all the nooks and crannies and starts to stink.

Next I fix up some of the wiring. During the season any changes, such as adding a new Fathometer, tend to get done in a hurry. I redo the new circuits and solder all the connections.

The oil stove also gets a thorough cleaning. This is also a dirty job. Oily, black soot accumulates in the stove and chimney, and it's impossible to do this chore without getting it all over yourself and anything else you touch. A friend of mine was cleaning out his stove one spring with a vacuum cleaner. As he was merrily sucking the soot out of the stove, he noticed that the lights in the foc'sle were getting dimmer and dimmer. When he looked around to see what was happening, he discovered that the air was full of soot. He had forgotten to put the bag on the vacuum cleaner, and all the soot he was sucking out of the stove was blowing straight through into the air. He spent the next few hours scrubbing every surface inside the cabin with soap and water.

After the stove is cleaned up the whole galley gets a good scrubbing, and I even paint the inside of the trunk cabin and wheelhouse. I had just built the cabin the year before and the season rolled around before I got the inside painted. A coat of white paint really lightens up the galley area, and I'm glad I take the time to do it.

By the time I'm finished inside the boat it's well into April and the weather has improved enough to paint the outside of the boat. This is also an annual task that really helps keep the boat in good condition. I start by beaching the boat early one morning and letting her go dry as the tide goes out. As the water drops I wade along the boat with a long-handled scrub brush and clean off the algae and other stuff that has accumulated over the year. The growth slows the boat and so increases the fuel consumption, also any bare spots are an invitation to wood-eating organisms that can destroy a plank. They start life as a tiny speck that eats into the wood, leaving a hole so small it's hard to see. As they eat into the wood, they grow until they can become half an inch in diameter and several inches long. They will eventually eat most of the board from the inside out, without ever showing on the surface. Every year the underwater parts of the boat get a good, thick coat of paint that contains a high percentage of copper. This metal is poisonous to these animals, and as long as there are no bare spots, the hull is protected. Because the boat is lying on her side, this job has to be done over two tides. After the first side is painted I wait until the tide refloats the boat, then turn her around and let it go dry with the other side exposed.

After the bottom is painted the rest of the hull gets scraped, sanded, and repainted dark green. Next, the cabin sides get a coat of medium gray. On the wheelhouse I paint a two-foot wide strip of white to break up the gray, then all the trim is painted black, and finally the decks and cabin top get a coat of Silver Seal.

I luck out on the weather; there is almost two weeks of hot, sunny days in the middle of the month, and it takes all of them to get the paint on every surface of the boat. I'm pretty pooped by the time the last brush is cleaned, but the little Nomad looks pretty perky, with her new paint and everything inside and out all tidied up.

After the painting is finished the weather turns wet for a few days, and I spend the time sorting what I want out of the shack and trying to fit it all into the boat. I have to make some brutal cuts in my junk collection. I don't know how long I'll be living on the boat, so only the main treasures get to come along. I never have been very sentimental about things, and it actually feels good to get rid of a bunch of the stuff that has accumulated over the years. The world is full of stuff and I never have trouble getting something if I really need it. I give the propane stove to Boots, along with the tank and regulator. My chain saw, I keep; it has a lot of life left in it and I manage to find a place to fit it in.

The weather clears on the twenty-fifth and I'm itching to take off. I visit with the Hamars in the afternoon, then have dinner with Boots. The next morning I head for Ketchikan, to fuel up and collect Dick for the trip to P.A.. I haven't seen him for a couple of months, but I suspect he's starting to get the urge to move, too. The King season opens in less than three weeks!

There is a leftover southerly swell in the strait and the boat rolls like a pig all the way across. The trip takes longer than usual because I'm towing the skiff, so it's past noon when I get to Guard Island, the entrance to Tongass Narrows. As I enter the Narrows, I meet a little, gray boat that I don't recognize. As it passes a couple of hundred yards off, two figures come out on deck and wave vigorously like they know me, but I don't recognize them. The tide is with me down the Narrows, and in a little over an hour and a half, I'm nosing into the stall between the Spray and the old, blue boat that belongs to Dick's friend George. The old skipper comes out to catch a line and we soon have her tied securely to the Spray.

"Hey, Partner, how ya been, you got this mud scow ready to go?" I ask, stepping aboard Dick's boat.

"Well I got a few things to do yet, but I should be ready in a couple of days. Did you see the Golden Eye on your way in"? He answers.

"I met a gray boat out at Guard Island; they waved at me but I didn't recognize them," I say.

"That was Marty and Jean Remund from Port Alexander. They've been here for a couple of weeks buying the boat. We were hoping you would show up before they left, but they wanted to get home and get the boat ready for Kings," Dick says.

"Huh, too bad I missed them; it would have been fun to run out with them. I used that spell of nice weather to paint the boat and move out of the shack. I figured you wouldn't be ready till about now either, and I didn't feel like laying around town for two weeks."

"Yeah, that's what I thought. So you're really going to make the big move and winter out there next year, huh?" he asks.

"Yup. I'm moved out; the boat is home. I'm not coming back."

"Well, I don't think I'll make it this year, but I think I'll sell the van next spring and stay out there next year. I have a lot of loose ends to clear up here, and there isn't time to do it all this year. How 'bout a cup of coffee?" Dick says, heading into the wheelhouse. I follow him in and we make up a plan of attack for the trip over a couple of cups of Taster's Choice.

The next few days are busy, getting Dick's affairs in order and buying groceries for the trip. I still have a few hundred bucks left from last year, so I stock up on things that will be hard to get in P.A., like canned goods, rifle shells, and hardware items. Finally on the second of May, we run down to the Union Oil Dock and fuel the boats up, and at dawn the next morning we point the bows north up Tongass Narrows.

We have an uneventful run and on the third afternoon we pass the red can into the harbor at P.A. But that's another story.

THE END

Afterword

Dick Upward passed away in 1996 in Ketchikan. The years of cigarette smoking and the resulting emphysema finally took their toll.

I have lost track of Bud and Celia Harwood; the last I heard of them they were living in Ketchikan and Bud's health was failing.

Dick Witham is still at large and every summer there is a rumor that he is on his way home. This year we heard he was in Craig Alaska and would be in PA any day.

Port Alexander is still a thriving fishing community and many of the same people are still there; others have moved on.

Glossary

BACK SPLICE: To braid the strands of a rope back into itself to keep the fibers from unraveling.

BINACLE: The surface where the compass is mounted, usually forward of the steering wheel in plain view of the helmsman.

BOOT STRIPE: A narrow stripe of paint applied at the waterline to accentuate the division between the bottom paint and the topside paint.

BRAILER: Large dip net used for scooping fish out of the purse seine into the hold of the seine boat. The net is a bag whose mouth is a metal ring several feet in diameter, and is suspended from the rigging of the boat. It can be lowered into the mass of fish trapped in the seine, then hoisted aboard and emptied into the hold.

CANNON BALL: A lead or iron ball with an eye molded in to it. The trolling wire is attached to the cannon ball and it acts as a sinker to hold the line at depth.

CLEAT: A device that is bolted to the deck of a boat or other surface used to tie a line to. It is usually made of metal and consists of a base with two horns opposite each other. The line is wrapped around the base several times, then half-hitched over one of the horns to secure it.

COCKPIT: A rectangular well about three and a half feet deep at the stern of a troller. The fisherman stands in this well to raise and lower the lines and land fish. The leaders are usually coiled behind the well when they are out of the water, and the gerdies that the lines are coiled on are in front of the cockpit well.

CLOSURE: A period of time during the fishing season when it is illegal to fish. A closure is implemented by the Dept. Fish and Game to allow fish to pass undisturbed through the area to the spawning streams.

COOKIE JAR: A slang term used to describe a productive fishing spot that the fish congregate in as they pass through an area. Certain bottom features and points of land cause disturbances in the tidal currents. These features will occasionally cause an eddy to form that traps plankton and algae. These tiny creatures provide food for Herring and Needlefish, which are the main food of Salmon and other species of predatory fish.

DEVIL'S CLUB: A plant that grows in the forest of SE Alaska. The leaves and stems are covered with thorns, and the plant usually grows in large patches that are very difficult to pass through without getting stickers in your skin.

DRAG: A trolling course past one or more good fishing spots. Usually the boats line up and take turns towing their gear past these hot spots. In the old days the boat with its right pole toward the beach had right of way on the drag, but after limited entry many aggressive people bought into the fishery. Many of these new people are unwilling to follow the unspoken rules that had developed over time, and will try to work the drag both directions.

FENDER: A rubber or plastic bag that is hung between the boat and a dock, or any other surface that the boat is tied against. The fender is used to prevent damage to the boat by any movement that might occur.

FLASHER: A metal or plastic rectangle bent in an S shape. When towed through the water, it rolls over every so often, making a flash in the water that resembles a feeding Salmon. Depending upon the clarity of the water, the flash can be seen by the fish for some distance. A hoochie or other lure is attached to the rear end of the flasher, so that when the fish approaches the flasher to investigate, he is presented with a bait.

FOUR BANGER: A four cylinder engine.

GURDY: The spool or reel that the trolling wire is wound on.

HANDTROLL: To use muscle power to crank up the lines rather than some form of power; i.e. hydraulic, mechanical or electric.

HOOCHIE: A plastic lure that looks like a squid. Hoochies come in various colors, and are usually run behind a flasher. Sometimes a piece of Herring is inserted inside the hoochie to add the smell of Herring to the lure.

ICE BLANKET: A piece of insulation cut to fit an ice bin in the hold of a fishing boat, usually made of closed-cell, plastic foam.

LEAD SPOON: A metal lure snapped to the trolling wire just above the lead cannon ball. This lure is usually run on a short leader, to give it a faster action than the lure above it. The turbulence behind the cannon ball also gives this lure an irregular action. This spread of gear is usually one of the most effective King Salmon lures.

NO-SEE-UMS: A tiny, biting insect common to the northern latitudes.

PACKER: A boat that is used to haul fish from the grounds to the cold storage plants in the larger towns. The packers also haul supplies such as groceries, fuel, and repair parts out to the remote, fish-buying stations.

PLUG: A hard plastic lure, cylindrical in shape, tapering to a point on the rear end with a flat front end molded at a slight angle to the body. When towed, the plug wiggles from side to side like a small, swimming fish. There is a towing ring in the head end and a hook hangs from the underside. Plugs come is several sizes and many different colors. In the old days they were made of wood, and sometimes the fishermen whittled their own.

POWERTROLL: A powertroll license permits the holder of the permit to use some type of power to crank the lines up and down. In the early days of powertrolling the gerdys were powered by a shaft that was driven by a vee-belt of the engine. The shaft came out the back of the wheelhouse and passed across the deck to the gurdys. In more modern times hydraulic motors are used. Occasionally a set of electric gurdys can be found on a boat, however due to the difficulty of maintain in the corrosive salt atmosphere they have never found much popularity in the fleet.

PORT SIDE: The left side of a boat if you are facing forward. In early times, boats were steered with a large oar called a steer board. The steer board was attached to the right side of the boat at the stern. This oar made it hard to dock on the right side so the boat was usually tied with its left or 'port' side to the dock.

SALT CHUCK: A salt lake or bay that the tide runs in and out of through a narrow entrance, or chuck. The name probably has its origin in the Chinook Jargon, a trade language that was used on the NW coast of North America by the various native tribes and early traders. The currents in these narrow channels are very strong at times and large whirlpools sometimes make a "chukkk" sound, like the whirlpool in a bathtub.

SEINE SKIFF: A short, beamy, open boat with a large, powerful motor, used to pull the seine net from the stern on a seine boat around in a circle, to trap Salmon.

SHAKERS: King Salmon under the legal size limit of twenty-two inches. You pick the fish up with the gaff, by hooking the gaff hook in the throat of the fishhook outside the fish's head. When the fish is out of the water you give it a shake, and the fish falls off the hook to swim away.

SKUNK: When you have caught no fish you are "skunked." When the first fish of the day or season is aboard you have the "skunk off the deck."

SPOON: A metal lure with a spoon-shaped hollow in one end and a slight bend in the other. It wiggles when it is towed behind the boat, simulating the motion of a herring or other baitfish. Spoons are made of various metals such as brass, copper, and bronze. Some spoons are polished to a mirror-like shine and some are painted in bright colors. Most trollers have several hundred of these lures aboard of different sizes, shapes, and colors.

STABLIZERS: A triangular piece of galvanized steel or aluminum about 3/16 inch thick, with a fin welded on its upper side. A weight is welded on the bottom at one end, and a line is attached to the fin slightly back of the balance point, so it hangs slightly nose down. This device is towed from the middle of the trolling pole, and because of its design, it digs into the water, pulling down on the pole as the boat moves forward. This helps keep the boat from rolling in a swell, and makes the boat much more comfortable in a seaway.

STARBOARD: The right side of a boat as you look forward. In the old days, a steering board was hung on this side of the boat to act as a rudder. See also: PORT SIDE.

TAG LINE: A line fastened to the trolling pole, the other end of which is attached to the trolling wire when the line has been lowered to the desired depth. After the tag line is attached to the wire, the gerdy reel is slacked, and the trolling line swings out to tow aft of the attachment point, where the tag line is tied to the pole. This gives the lines separation, and allows the fisherman to bring up a line without tangling it with another.

TOTE: A plastic container used to transport fish or store ice. Some are insulated and some are not.

WEIR: A fish trap with doors at both ends that is placed in a spawning stream to capture hatchery fish for artificial spawning, or to keep hatchery fish from going up a stream where there is a wild run. The hatchery at Little Port Walter is an experimental hatchery, and they don't want the experimental fish contaminating the creek.

WILLIWAW: A burst of turbulent wind that tumbles down the side of a mountain without warning. Often there is a stream of swiftly moving air one or two thousand feet above the surface. If this wind is blowing across the tops of a mountain range, severe turbulence is produced. This turbulence sometimes races down the side of the mountain and dissipates its energy on the lower elevations or the water. If you are anchored in the lee of a mountain, or fishing near a range of hills, these gusts of wind can be dangerous.

YARDER ENGINEER: A yarder is a large winch loggers use to pull logs out of the woods. A yarder engineer is the person who operates the winch.

0-595-21426-6

Made in the USA
San Bernardino, CA
19 February 2015